P9-DXD-631

Anatomy of Big Business

OKANAGAN COLLEGE LIBRARY
BRITISH COLUMBIA

Anatomy of Big Business

Libbie and Frank Park

48285

James Lewis & Samuel
Toronto
1973

Copyright © 1962, 1973 by L. C. and F. W. Park

All rights reserved. No part of this book may be reproduced or transmitted in any form or by any means, electronic or mechanical, including photocopying, or by any information storage and retrieval system, without permission in writing from the publisher.

ISBN 0-88862-039-X (cloth)
0-88862-040-3 (paper)

Cover design by Christer Themptander

First edition published 1962
This reprint edition published by arrangement with
Progress Books, Toronto.

James Lewis & Samuel, Publishers

Egerton Ryerson Memorial Building
35 Britain Street
Toronto

Printed and bound in Canada

Foreword to the 1973 reprint

TO AGREE to the reprinting of a book first published eleven years ago obliges the authors to consider what they would add or modify or delete today.

In general we are unrepentant. Obviously a lot of material is dated, new relationships of power and influence have come into being, names, both corporate and individual, are different, the relative position of financial groups has changed, and the terminology of the book is that of the Fifties. But equally obviously, or so it seems to us, the same structure of power and control exists today as then, the examples given retain validity, and the main argument has only been reinforced by time and the work of later writers on the subject.

Our concern was with two related questions: Who owns Canada? and Can Canada survive? To us an affirmative answer to the second implied a change in the answer to the first. The dominant business interests in Canada had long since demonstrated their willingness to accept and even struggle for a junior partnership (the phrase of the Fifties) within the expansionist power structure of the mature imperialist power. Survival of Canadian sovereignty under the existing system of ownership and control of the economic and political structure was, in our view, completely unlikely, and we proposed nationalization of U.S.-controlled resources and industry in Canada (the key companies) to bring control back to this country, not as a final solution but as a step towards the solution of the country's problems of development.

In some respects our approach may have been overly economic. Class was defined in economic terms without reference to the role of class consciousness; nationalization was discussed with only a passing reference to Canada as a bi-national state. (Interestingly enough, the most enthusiastic comments on the original edition came from articles in *Cité Libre*.) And while we saw economic growth as something more than an increase in per capita gross national product, the problems of development in Canada as in the Third World were seen mainly as turning on the growth of manufacturing industry and not in their wider social-political context.

What was not sufficiently emphasized was that capital is more than a collection of useful things and techniques, more than the amount of money needed to set in motion certain productive forces. As Marx was fond of emphasizing, it is a "definite social relationship" and thus it is the total social relationships involved in control of the economy by foreign capital that need analysis.

When in 1956 we began the project that eventually took shape in this book the relationship between monopoly control and foreign capital was a field largely unoccupied. Earlier critiques of the nature of capitalism in Canada, whether from liberal or socialist (Marxian or otherwise) points of view, had been based on the extent of monopoly control and the concentration of economic power and political influence in the hands of the few. The traditional western farmer anti-monopoly position expressed in the *Grain Growers Guide* had been carried on by the Saskatchewan CCF in *Who Owns Canada?* (1934/5).[1] The facts were illustrated by a diagram of Canada as a milking machine operated for the benefit of the men of Bay and St. James Streets, the "50 Big Shots".

The *Report of the Royal Commission on Price Spreads* (1935)[2] (secretary, Lester B. Pearson) offered an analysis of the relationship of ownership and control in the modern corporation in Canada based on the study by Berle and Means in the United States, and making no distinction between corporations controlled by domestic and foreign capital.

The substantial collective volume issued later the same

year by the League for Social Reconstruction, *Social Planning for Canada*,[3] using the Price Spreads material, gave
an illuminating run-down of the extent of non-Canadian
ownership in Canadian industry, startling even at that time,
but the author of that section drew the classical conclusion:
"That foreigners control this or that particular industry will
trouble none but those earnest patriots who, in defiance of
all the evidence, persist in believing that the Canadian capitalist is a different kind of being from the foreign, that the
one is a philanthropist, the other a robber and cheat."[4] The
real problem was seen as the outflow of interest and dividends and its effect on the balance of payments.

At this time the Carnegie Endowment for International
Peace undertook a full dress multi-volume study of the
relations of Canada and the United States. In *Canadian-
American Industry* (1936),[5] hailed by the editor of the
series as "a pioneering enterprise", the authors argued that
U.S. industrial investment in Canada and "certainly Canadian industrial investment in the United States, are not to
be thought of in terms of 'economic imperialism' " (the
authors at once added: "except in a very few cases") "but
rather as a normal result of geographical propinquity."[6]

Public opinion, in the view of the authors, "will tend to
be less suspicious of, or hostile to, foreign investment in
Canada", and they considered it probable that capital imports by Canada on a large scale were "entirely a thing of
the past."[7]

The major document of the Communist left at this time
was the submission of the Communist Party of Canada to
the Rowell-Sirois Commission (1938).[8] The distribution of
the national income and the effects of monopoly control
were examined but the only references to foreign capital
came under the head of taxation of exported profits. Canada during the depression years was an exporter of capital
and there was no reference to a possible change in that
situation.

The anti-monopoly approach of the *Price Spreads Report* was continued by F. A. McGregor in an official report, *Canada and International Cartels* (1945).[9] It included a section on the international affiliations of Canadian companies. The Carnegie Endowment study was quoted and the question raised but not answered as to whether the branch-plant situation meant early access to technical processes developed in other countries (a good thing) or too little research in Canada (a bad thing).[10]

In 1947 the up-dated edition of *Who Owns Canada?*[11] noted the international connections of companies operating in Canada and contrasted the rate of profit on capital of 12 monopoly corporations including eight "international monopoly corporations" with the profits of industry as a whole. But the 50 Big Shots approach was accompanied by a warning against those who draw "artificial distinctions between 'national capitalists' who are good, and 'international capitalists' who are presumably bad." [12] Profits are profits, and consumers and workers should "be on guard when Capital wraps itself in a flag and exploits patriotism."[13]

This whole discussion was soon to turn to the neglected question, the effect on Canadian development of outside control of key sectors of the economy and the erosion of sovereignty that accompanied it. As the expansionist drive of U.S. capital took form and the first of a series of post-war dollar crises for Canada occurred in 1947, attention was necessarily drawn to the effects of U.S. policy on Canada. The Communist left was raising the problem by the end of 1947[14] but criticism of the results of U.S. investment in Canada came from a whole spectrum of opinion that included George Drew, Walter Gordon and James Coyne.

A special study, *Canada-U.S. Economic Relations* by Brecher and Reisman (1957)[15] was commissioned by the Gordon Commission on Canada's Economic Prospects but the authors approached the problem with caution. There had been benefits from U.S. investment, and there were disadvantages; the benefits were "clear-cut and well-established", the "adverse consequences" were "possible".[16] The

Report itself followed the same two-handed approach; its main recommendation was criticized in our final chapter.

Our own point of departure was the existence of an identity of interest between the largest financial institutions and the largest industrial corporations, the visible expression of which was the directorships in each held by key figures. The evidence indicated the existence of powerful financial groups, working alliances of members of an active and energetic capitalist class, who see the path of profit and class stability in collaboration with foreign capital, not in opposition to it. The power of these groups and of the class forces behind them was and remains the problem.

February 1973 L.C.P.
F.W.P.

1. Watt Hugh McCollum, Who Owns Canada?, Regina, 1935
2. Report of the Royal Commission on Price Spreads, King's Printer, Ottawa, 1937
3. Research Committee, League for Social Reconstruction, Social Planning for Canada, Toronto, 1935
4. Ibid., p. 55
5. H. Marshall, F. A. Southard Jr., K. W. Tayor, Canadian-American Industry, A study in international investment, New Haven & Toronto, 1936
6. Ibid., p. 3
7. Ibid., p. 295
8. "Submission of the Central Committee of the Communist Party to the Royal Commission on Dominion-Provincial Relations," 1938
9. Report of Commissioner, Combines Investigation Act, Canada and International Cartels, An Inquiry into the Nature and Effects of International Cartels and other Trade Combinations, King's Printer, Ottawa, 1945
10. Ibid., p. 42
11. Watt Hugh McCollum, Who Owns Canada?, An examination of the facts concerning the concentration of ownership and control of the means of production, distribution and exchange in Canada, Ottawa, 1947
12. Ibid., p. 8
13. Ibid., p. 9
14. T. Buck, Canada, The Communist Viewpoint, Toronto, 1948
15. I. Brecher, S. S. Reisman, Canada-United States Economic Relations, Royal Commission on Canada's Economic Prospects, Queen's Printer, Ottawa, 1967
16. Ibid., p. 158

Foreword

THIS BOOK discusses the structure of Canadian monopoly and the alliance of Canadian and U.S. capital that is bringing about U.S. domination of Canada.

It deals with the time-honored and meaningful question—Who Owns Canada?—and argues that control by U.S. finance capital of an important and growing part of the country's means of production is accentuating Canada's problem of growth, and contributing to the tendency to stagnation in the economy.

Financial groups in Canada are parting with control of Canadian resources and industry in order to share in the profits of U.S.-controlled monopoly enterprises.

These enterprises operate as part of the system familiarly and accurately described outside the United States and Canada as U.S. imperialism, a phenomenon that is still very much a reality and a threat to Canada in spite of the distaste shown for the phrase by many editorial writers.

We argue that the answer to the effects of U.S. domination of Canada is to nationalize the main U.S.-controlled enterprises operating in Canada, and bring control over policy back to Canada.

Such an action would open the way to the independent growth of the Canadian economy, strengthen Canadian independence, and help place relations between Canada and the United States on a solid basis of mutual respect.

We have written with a sense of urgency on a large and important problem, conscious that many aspects remain to be examined in greater depth. But the outline of the problem is clear and so is the need for action if Canada is to progress.

Sections of this book represent an extension of ideas expressed in The Power and the Money (1958) and in fact the present book was originally undertaken as a second edition of the earlier booklet. But as new material was added and new points of view developed and as the manuscript grew to more than double the size of the first, it became clear that this was a new book.

We have retained in a considerably expanded form two case histories from The Power and the Money, those of the Argus Corporation and of the Iron Ore Company of Canada, since they illustrate so clearly the closely related aspects of Canadian finance capital—the aggressive drive for profit and the eager search for a basis of alliance with U.S. capital.

The information we have used is in the main derived from financial manuals published during 1959, brought up to the end of 1961 where later developments were important.

Statements that a given U.S. corporation belongs to this or that monopoly group are in general based on The Empire of High Finance by Victor Perlo (International Publishers, N.Y. 1957).

The book has benefitted greatly from discussions with friends while the manuscript was being prepared for publication although no one but ourselves can be held responsible for what is said.

1962   L. C. P.
                                                        F. W. P.

TABLE OF CONTENTS

ABBREVIATIONS OF COMPANY NAMES

BRINCO   BRITISH NEWFOUNDLAND CORPORATION LTD.

CIP   CANADIAN INTERNATIONAL PAPER CO.

COMINCO   CONSOLIDATED MINING & SMELTING CO. OF CANADA LTD.

CPR   CANADIAN PACIFIC RAILWAY CO.

DOFASCO   DOMINION FOUNDRIES & STEEL LTD.

DOSCO   DOMINION STEEL & COAL CORP. LTD.

IMPERIAL-COMMERCE   CANADIAN IMPERIAL BANK OF COMMERCE, THE

INCO   INTERNATIONAL NICKEL CO. OF CANADA LTD., THE

IOCO   IRON ORE COMPANY OF CANADA

MEXLIGHT   MEXICAN LIGHT & POWER CO. LTD.

STELCO   STEEL COMPANY OF CANADA LTD., THE

CHAPTER I

The Soaring Sixties

A CANADIAN BANK PRESIDENT complained a year ago that the Soaring Sixties had so far failed to get off the ground as far as Canada was concerned; at the same time one of his colleagues was heatedly denouncing the "twaddle-talk" of those who criticized the growth of foreign (U.S.) investment in Canada.

Both of them would no doubt have denied any connection between the failure to soar and the growth of U.S. control in Canada, but it is the existence of this connection and the growing awareness of it among Canadians that sparks an intensifying debate over the direction of Canada's national policies.

For some years newspapers have been reflecting the popular concern over Canada's relations with the United States. They have asked such questions as: "Is Canada a sovereign nation or is it a humble satellite of the U.S.?" (Globe & Mail: 23 Jan. 59); "After 92 years is Canada a nation?" (Toronto Daily Star: 30 June 59); "Is Canada Now A Lost Cause?" "Has Canadian independence already been lost? Is Canada now only a captive satellite of the United States? Is our national independence now merely a polite fiction and our labor in self-government an empty charade?" (Financial Post: 3 Sept. 60). Many others could be cited.

Another aspect of the problem is raised, ironically enough by the U.S.-born head of a U.S. subsidiary operating in Canada: Canadians, he says, are fooling themselves if they go along with the popular idea that Canada is fast becoming an industrial giant. (Financial Post: 7 May 60).

9

And in a series of addresses during 1960 and 1961, James
E. Coyne, then governor of the Bank of Canada, argued
that foreign investment in Canada contributed more to un-
employment than to employment, that no developed country was one-quarter as much dominated by foreign capital
as Canada, and that it was very doubtful if Canada has
benefitted at all from foreign investment.

"If," says Coyne, "our population and our employment
are to continue to grow, we must concentrate on producing
a great part of all the capital goods, the productive machinery, and other raw materials that we are going to use, in
this country." (Financial Post: 8 Oct. 60).

Coyne put his finger on the most sensitive side of the
question when he emphasized the connection between Canada's economic difficulties and the growth of foreign
(U.S.) investment in Canada. But he and the newspaper
editorial writers have not stopped to ask another question,
the answer to which might shed more light on the kind of
remedies called for. Is there also a connection between the
growing U.S. control of Canada, to which they object, and
the growing concentration of production and power in
Canada in the hands of a few tycoons, a situation on which
they have not commented?

There is a double problem to be discussed: the relationship between the control of Canada by a small group of
big shots — the top layer of Canada's ruling class — and
their alliance with U.S. financial groups that results in
the growth of U.S. domination in Canada.

All these concepts need clarification.

By "class" is meant a section of the population that
differs from other groupings by virtue of the place its
members occupy in relation to the means of production.
Our concern is with the top layer of the class that owns and
controls the mines and mills and factories of Canada. We
are dealing therefore with an economic and not a cultural
concept.

The concept is also a political one. We treat this owning
class as the ruling class, a phrase repugnant to some critics

who see in it an improper linking of economic and political concepts. But it is surely a fact beyond dispute that ownership and control of the most important means of production by a small group gives that group a predominant influence on the policies of government. Our argument assumes that those who govern represent the interests of the owners of the principal means of production.

We spoke of ownership *and* control. The power of the upper layer of the ruling class is based on their control of capital and the means of production, the control in turn resting upon direct ownership of only a fraction of the total capital controlled. But there should be no doubt that the total control is based on ownership and that without ownership control vanishes.

To speak of an "elite" and not deal with their power as a class power based on ownership, or with their relationships with government does not fully come to grips with the problem. Here we shall use such terms as "tycoons," "big shots," "financial oligarchy" and "elite" more or less interchangeably and always in reference to the most influential sector of the class owning the means of production and exercising predominant influence on government policy.

To speak of "monopoly" or "monopoly capital" in Canada is to invite the sarcasm of those economists who argue that in the strict sense of the word, monopoly (control of a branch of industry by one firm) can never, or only very rarely, exist. Imperfect competition, yes; oligopoly, perhaps; monopoly, no. This ingenious verbal play does not affect the reality of the economic scene.

Not all economists have been afraid of the word monopoly. The Price Spreads Report of 1937 spoke of "the tendency towards monopoly . . . evidenced in the record of consolidations in Canadian industry" and of the "headway" made by "monopoly," the latter being considered to be "any form of industrial organization with sufficient power over the supply of a commodity to enable the organization to modify the price to its own advantage." The

Report added that "in industries where there is monopo-
listic domination, a large measure of control may rest with
a single concern in spite of the fact that it is not alone in
the field."

As the Gordon Commission economists, Messrs. Brecher
and Reisman, put it, twenty years later, "it is widely known
that in many Canadian industries a small number of large
firms account for a high proportion of output; and that
many of these companies are owned and controlled by non-
residents." (Canada-United States Economic Relations:
1957, page 278).

These guarded admissions of the existence of a phenomenon in Canada that we shall briefly describe as monopoly,
deal with limited aspects of a complex and many-sided
concept.

They refer to the ability of monopoly to influence prices,
to the concentration of production in a few firms, and to
U.S. control of big firms.

They do not refer to the concentration of control of
capital in the hands of financial groups and the interlocking relationships of these groups, centred on the banks,
with the big industrial enterprises.

They do not refer to the influence of the financial groups
on governments and the intimate relations that exist between the apparatus of monopoly capital and the apparatus of government.

They do not refer to the world-wide connections of the
monopolies, or to the export of capital that forms part of
an international struggle for markets and profits.

But all these aspects must be considered if we are to
discuss monopoly capital in Canada and the effects of U.S.
domination in any meaningful way, and the failure to
consider them has weakened several recent discussions of
Canadian monopoly.

We speak here of "U.S. domination" of Canada as the
sum total of U.S. influence (the influence of the dominant
U.S. financial groups) over the Canadian economy and the

Canadian government, an influence that is partially indicated by the huge volume of U.S. investment in Canada
and by the interlocking of U.S. and Canadian financial
groups. It is expressed in political "me-too-ism," in the
steady erosion of Canadian independence, in the one-sided
development of the economy, in the export of jobs, in over-
dependence on U.S. markets, in U.S.-imposed restrictions
on trade, in the dependence of Canadian subsidiaries on
their U.S. parents for research and for parts, it is, in short,
expressed in a structural dependence of the Canadian economy on that of the United States.

We do not imply that the domination is absolute or that
the Canadian government and Canadian tycoons have no
freedom of action. They have; but they have chosen to
exercise it in a way that puts the national interests of Canada a poor second to their own chance to share as junior
partners in enterprises controlled by U.S. monopoly capital; they have accepted as inevitable and more or less
desirable the concept of a kind of economic and political
integration of Canada and the United States that in reality,
as Coyne has said, represents the absorption of Canada by
the United States and, if continued, is bound to end in
loss of independence.

In speaking of the national interests of Canada (and in
advocating, as we shall, changed national policies for Canada in the interests of the Canadian people) we use a
terminology familiar to Canadians and for which, in spite
of its incorrectness, there is no simple alternative; what we
are dealing with is the interests of the country as a whole,
of Canada as a bi-national federal state, and the interests
of its people—those of both Canadian nations.

Not every U.S. influence on Canada has been bad; an
imposing list of benefits to Canada resulting from prox-
imity to the United States could easily be compiled. But
the point is that in the world of today with the U.S.
government seeking by every means possible to maintain
its short-lived period of world leadership, the expansion
of U.S. influence in Canada in the forms referred to is

preventing Canadian governments, themselves linked to big business, from taking effective steps to preserve the national identity of Canada and develop Canada on the basis of Canadian needs.

The analysis of monopoly and large-scale enterprises will not be based on an assumption that what is big is bad. What is at issue is not bigness but how and in whose inter- ests bigness is to be controlled and operated.

The argument is that what is big and affects the nation- al interests should not be operated by a small group in their own interest. The Canadian tycoons, very closely identified with U.S. capital, exercise great economic and political power for their own profit. They have used it to encourage the integration of the Canadian and U.S. economies to the point where U.S. domination is taken for granted, and the Canadian economy, after a period of distorted growth, is failing to develop in line with Canada's possibilities and the needs of its people. The power of the tycoons over the economy, over government, over the cultural life of the country, is increasing as the enterprises they control become bigger, more closely interlocked, more profitable, and come more and more under U.S. control or influence.

The policies of these people have come under increasing fire from Canadians in all walks of life; as the criticism of the policy grows, the basis of their power will itself come increasingly under challenge.

Much more is involved than the enrichment of the few at the expense of the many. The danger resulting from concentration of power in the hands of the few is accen- tuated by the close relationships established between fin- ance capital groups in Canada and those in the United States, a relationship in which Canadian development is distorted and Canadian national interests are subordinated to a share in immediate profits.

No financial group operating in Canada can be analyzed solely in terms of its Canadian operations. In our view the most influential financial groups in the country are those centred around the Bank of Montreal and a group of financial and producing companies closely associated with the bank. These include the Canadian Pacific Railway and its subsidiary, Consolidated Mining & Smelting, the Steel Company of Canada, Dominion Textile Company, to take examples from companies considered truly Canadian. But to stop there would be to ignore the influence within the bank of the big U.S. financial groups, the Morgan, Mellon, Rockefeller, and other interests controlling Aluminium Ltd., International Nickel, Canadian General Electric, British American Oil, Bell Telephone of Canada and Northern Electric, all U.S.-controlled companies in close relationship with the groups working through the bank.

And there is as well a substantial but much weaker degree of U.K. influence through the Standard Life, Canadian Industries Ltd., British Newfoundland Corporation, etc.

But the point is that Canadian financial groups must be discussed on the basis of their relationships with U.S.-based groups; in these relationships and the consequences that flow from them is involved the question of national policy and national survival, the "Can Canada Survive" question of the editorial writers.

Must Canada accept a state of affairs in which the development of this country's fabulous natural wealth is based on and subordinated to the interests of the big U.S. financial groups?

Or is it possible for Canadians to give priority to the development of Canadian resources and the growth of Canadian manufacturing on the basis of what is good for the Canadian people, and so guarantee for Canadians the golden future that the financial pages used to speak of?

If the latter choice is to be made then it follows that the control of U.S. financial groups and their Canadian partners over the great mines and factories of Canada will have to be limited, and the relationship of these enterprises with U.S. industry placed on a basis of equality, so that independent growth is possible.

We shall argue that this will mean a degree of nationalization of U.S.-controlled enterprises in Canada as a step essential to the national growth of Canada. Not nationalization in the limited sense of forcing these enterprises to take on Canadian boards of directors while control still rests in the United States, but nationalization in the sense of vesting ownership of a controlling interest in the hands of Canadian agencies and enabling the enterprises, freed from the limitations imposed by U.S. ownership, to be operated on the basis of providing the highest possible level of industrial development and the greatest possible number of jobs.

This is the course of action that opens the way to the all-round industrial development of Canada, that would enable Canada to solve the problem the bankers refer to as "the absence of a high growth rate."

It is control that is at issue. Control of highly organized, carefully planned enterprises by U.S. groups and their Canadian allies for their own profit, or control in the national interest so that the potential of our country's growth can be realized.

CHAPTER II

We Are Being Robbed

THE INFLUENCE OF U.S. financial groups and of U.S. government policy is felt, directly and indirectly, by every company and every financial group operating in Canada. Even the "purest," most Canadian firms, with no U.S. capital in them, no interlocks with U.S.-controlled firms, and all-Canadian boards of directors, are affected by fluctuations in the U.S. economy and by the pervasive influence of U.S. capital through the boards of directors of companies with which they are associated.

We shall consider here some of the effects of the tremendous U.S. influence on the Canadian economy, based on the very large U.S. investment in Canada and the resulting partnership (a very unequal one) of U.S. and Canadian capital as shown in the interlocking corporate relationships between Canadian tycoons and the dominant financial groups in the United States.

This analysis will not show by any means the full picture of U.S. influence in Canada. Our approach is based on formal, obvious, published connections expressed in interlocking directorates and figures of total investment, whereas the unseen, informal, unpublicized ties that link tycoons of both countries and their governments are stronger and of greater importance. Not all decisions are taken at meetings of boards of directors nor by directors. And the formal relationships do not express such important aspects of U.S. control as the technological dependence of many U.S.-owned subsidiaries in Canada on their U.S. parent, the influence exercised through control of patents and licencing, the way in which Canadian subsidiaries are restricted in export markets, etc.

The reality of U.S. control is primarily reflected in the volume of U.S. investment in Canada and we shall deal with some neglected aspects of this much discussed question.

There are times and circumstances in which the import of capital is of benefit to the importing country. Generally speaking, these circumstances arise in the case of economically under-developed countries where large-scale sources of capital accumulation do not exist and where the national surplus is relatively small and difficult to mobilize. Even in such circumstances the possible benefit to be realized from capital imports has to be measured against the cost.

To be helpful, foreign capital must enable the people of a country to do something they did not have the physical or technical resources to do themselves. It can enable them, by bringing in skills and machinery from abroad, to build something that could not otherwise be built at that time. The result is a new producing asset, from the profits of which the capital imported can be repaid.

In these circumstances the foreign capital is most helpful if it takes the form of a loan or credit to enable the borrowing country to buy what it needs, from any source it likes, retaining control of the asset to be developed.

But groups of monopoly capitalists are not thinking in terms of development. They export capital for quite different reasons. Their whole purpose is to get control of sources of raw materials or energy sources, and, in the case of U.S. capital entering Canada, to get control of industry within the Canadian tariff system to reach Canadian and Commonwealth markets with made-in-Canada goods (based on lower wage rates and to a greater or lesser extent on imported parts). And with the export of capital, the monopoly groups expect to export their own system of social relationships by virtue of which the exporter of capital will remain for ever in control of the asset that is being developed.

The aim in the investment they make is control in order to maximize the world profit position of their group; any development that takes place in the country where the investment is made is subsidiary to this.

The essential points to be considered in assessing the benefits of foreign investment are, first, whether it enables a new asset to be created in the receiving country, and second, whether this investment is part of an orderly development of resources and industry, or is an invasion by foreign capital to get control of resources in its own interest. And finally, who is going to own the asset to be developed? Will its future earning power be used to extend a one-sided development in the interest of the controlling group, or will future profits be available to contribute to the all-round growth of the economy?

It is misleading to speak of foreign investment in general; whether or not a given investment helps the country in which it is made can be seen only after an analysis of the circumstances.

The usual classification of foreign investment is as direct investment or portfolio investment. Direct investment is that which controls the enterprise in which the capital is invested. Portfolio investment is non-controlling; it may take the form (in Canada) of investment in Canadian bonds (federal, provincial, municipal, corporate), in Canadian mortgages, in Canadian stocks.

The distinction between the two classes of foreign investment is important, as we shall see, but there are cases in which the distinction is unreal, notably in the case of portfolio investment in stocks.

Investments not in themselves controlling (hence classed as portfolio) may actually be an essential element in the control exercised by financial groups allied to those who own the portfolio investment. Thus the value of shares held by U.S. investment trusts in Canadian corporations is shown by the Dominion Bureau of Statistics as U.S. portfolio investment in Canada, although there can be no doubt that in many cases these shareholdings form part

of the apparatus of control by which U.S. groups maintain
their hold over the Canadian corporate structure.

In other cases the difference is clear. The U.S. portfolio
investment in Canada includes $2.8 billion in Canadian
government or municipal bonds. The existence of this large
U.S.-held investment has an adverse effect on Canada's
balance of payments since interest and repayment of principal have to be provided for in U.S. funds, but U.S. investment in this form is not directly related to U.S. control
of Canadian industry. So, the sale of $500 million of
Canadian municipal bonds in New York in a given year,
considered by itself, has effects on the Canadian economy
quite different from the taking over by U.S. interests of
Canadian enterprises with a book value of $500 million.

At the same time, the effects of U.S. portfolio investment
in Canada cannot be completely separated from the whole
penetration of Canada by U.S. capital since it is no doubt
true that Canadian bonds could not be sold as easily in
New York were it not for the fact that U.S. direct investment in Canada had already reached such a high level.

Investments, domestic or foreign, direct or portfolio,
may turn out to be based on capital that is fictitious. Instead of representing the development of a new productive
asset, the investment may represent nothing more than the
purchase on the market of stocks and bonds in existing
enterprises. The money invested goes to the seller of the
securities, not into the enterprise.

Let us suppose that U.S. financial interests are buying
Massey-Ferguson shares, either with a view to getting
control of the company or simply as a portfolio investment.
In either case the total U.S. investment in Canada rises,
but the actual investment in Massey-Ferguson is unchanged. The same number of workers continue to be employed with the same amount of machinery. Titles to
ownership, claims on future profits, control of the company,
may pass from one financial group to another, but nothing
has been added to the means of production already in

existence. The capital is fictitious. There is no real investment.

Thus in 1959 according to the Dominion Bureau of
Statistics, "most, if not all" of the increased movement of
foreign capital to Canada for direct investment was related
to the purchase of already existing Canadian assets, and
not to new capital formation. Investment of this kind adds
nothing to a country's real wealth.

Once a country has achieved a reasonably high level of
industrial production and is producing a substantial surplus, then any need for the import of foreign capital dis-
appears. But the drive of foreign capitalist groups to get
control of assets does not, and continues as intensely as
before.

If foreign monopoly interests are allowed to penetrate
a given national economy freely, then a number of consequences follow: the growth of national industry suffers,
the development of the country is distorted to suit the
profit position of the foreign monopolies, the content and
direction of the country's trade will be affected by non-
national considerations, and profits are in part taken out
of the country (a drain on balance of payments) and in
part re-invested and used to extend the control of the
outside group. The sovereignty of the country, the power
to take decisions in the national interest, will be under-
mined, and political independence threatened.

We shall see to what extent this is true of Canada.

The total long-term foreign investment in Canada
amounted at the end of 1959 to $20.7 billion. (See Table I,
page 234)

Of this total, 76%, or $15.7 billion, is U.S. long-term
investment in Canada, 16%, or $3.2 billion, is U.K. invest-
ment, and 8%, or $1.7 billion, from other countries.

If we go back to the end of 1945, the total foreign long-
term investment in Canada was $7.1 billion, of which the
U.S. share was $4.9 billion (70%), the U.K. share $1.7
billion (25%) and other foreign investment was under
$400 million, or 5%.

The foreign investment problem that we are about to examine is then, as far as Canada is concerned, a problem of U.S. investment. We do not intend to lose sight of the important enterprises controlled by British capital or the increasing investments of other European, mainly West German and Belgian, capital. But without minimizing the role played by outside capital from other than U.S. sources, it is nevertheless true that British and other non-U.S. investments in Canada do not today involve domination of the Canadian economy as the huge volume of U.S. investment does.

An alternative measure of the expanding U.S. influence in Canada is in the rapid increase in Canada's gross liabilities abroad (mainly to the U.S.). This figure is larger than the foreign investment figure but is growing more or less in proportion with it. It includes, in addition to the total foreign investment, other Canadian indebtedness to outside interests: short-term commercial payables, and the holdings of non-Canadians in Canadian corporations operating abroad. Canadian gross liabilities abroad totalled $24.1 billion at the end of 1959. The increase has been from $8 billion at the end of 1945 to $24.1 billion at the end of 1959.

To what extent does foreign investment (mainly U.S.) dominate the Canadian economy, and what have been the effects of this domination? It is at once apparent that the problem is not based on emotionalism or narrow nationalism but is severely practical.

The extent of foreign domination has been expressed by the former governor of the Bank of Canada, James Coyne, in the following terms:

> No country in the world with anything like our relative state of development has ever had such a degree of foreign domination, or even half or one-quarter the degree of foreign domination...
> By 1956, the whole of our manufacturing industry was 48% foreign-owned and 52% foreign-controlled, and in many important types of manufacturing the foreign predomination runs from 75% to 100%. In petroleum and natural gas the

percentages for the industry as a whole were 65% foreign-owned and 80% foreign-controlled . . . By far the lion's share of the foreign control rests with American (U.S.: Ed.) companies, the growing predominance of which has been a marked feature of our postwar history.

Coyne: Calgary speech, Financial Post: 8 Oct. 60

The kind of one-sided development that has taken place as a result of parting with control of resources and enterprises to U.S. monopoly groups was described in the Monthly Review of the Bank of Nova Scotia (March, 1958). In a discussion of "External Capital and Canada's Growth," the Review spoke of "the apparent tendency for foreign capital to increase the orientation of the economy towards the export of basic commodities." And added:

by far the biggest part of the postwar inflow of funds for direct U.S. investment in Canada (and a substantial volume of reinvested earnings as well) must be attributed to . . . the large-scale development of raw-material resources, mainly for export to the U.S. parent company or other foreign users . . .

Coyne carried this argument a step farther. He says that as a result of the structural dependence of Canada on foreign capital

the entire economy was put under strain and the structure of employment and production was distorted in a way which was inimical to steady growth and stability. The result, in my opinion, was to create not more employment but less, when averaged out over the cycle of boom and recession, and to create many difficult problems for the future, which are at the bottom of our present troubles.

Coyne: Calgary speech.

It is the flow of U.S. capital into oil and mining and the large-scale development of raw materials for export that led the Globe & Mail to argue in an editorial (9 Jan. 57) that the Canadian export of raw materials was at the same time an export of jobs, and had created two million jobs in manufacturing plants abroad based on the manufacture of Canadian natural resources.

The increase in foreign investment (including the re-investment of profits) has given additional impetus to the concentration of production and power in U.S. hands. The same issue of the Bank of Nova Scotia Monthly Review referred to "the concentration of (U.S. direct investment) in a small number of large firms." In 1953, "twenty-five large U.S. firms (each having an investment of $25 million or more in this country) accounted for no less than 60% of the total amount of capital invested in all U.S.-controlled manufacturing companies in Canada."

The effects of U.S. domination of the Canadian economy are strongly felt in the so-called balance of payments problem.

In its dollar form the problem can be quickly stated: in 1959 Canada sold abroad less than she bought (a deficit on merchandise trade of $380 million), paid out more in dividends and interest than was received from abroad by Canadian investors (deficit of $473 million), and had a deficit on other non-merchandise items of $576 million, to make a total deficit on current account dealings with all countries of $1,429 million, 85% of which was incurred in dealings with the United States.

The existence of a Canadian deficit on current account is nothing new. In the ten years 1950-9, total deficits reached the enormous total of $7.6 billion; since 1956 the deficit has been running at over one billion dollars a year, almost entirely, as we have said, arising from dealings with the United States.

The statistical approach to this deficit is to speak of it as offset by a credit balance on capital account resulting from the large inflows of foreign (mainly U.S.) capital for direct and portfolio investment in Canada.

Thus, speaking in these terms, Canada's 1959 deficit on current account with all countries was covered by capital inflows during that year of $500 million for direct investment, $661 million for portfolio investment, and $268 million in short-term transactions.

But this book-keeping method of considering the problem hides the fact that the deficit and the inflow do not in any real sense cancel each other out. Both the deficit and the inflow are functions of the growing U.S. domination of the economy, both are indicators of increasing U.S. control.

The origin of the balance of payments problem is to be found largely in the effects of the past inflow of capital from the United States, and further inflows that add to U.S. influence only make the problem more difficult of solution.

The share of the deficit directly attributable to the payment of interest and dividends has a direct relation to foreign (mainly U.S.) investment. These payments to outside interests are rising sharply and will soon reach $1 billion' a year. And the non-merchandise deficit of $576 million included an item of $198 million representing payments made by foreign subsidiaries in Canada to their head offices "for services rendered," another form of the export of profits.

Canada's deficit on merchandise trade also had its roots in U.S. exploitation of the Canadian economy. In fact, in 1959, Canada had a trade surplus of $137 million with all countries except the United States. A total deficit on trade with the United States of $517 million resulted in an over-all trade deficit of $380 million.

The deficit (and the over-emphasis on Canadian-U.S. trade) is linked to the heavy U.S. investment in Canada.

To the extent that U.S. capital has developed large export industries in Canada, mainly of raw and semi-processed materials, it has diverted resources from the development of manufacturing and has maintained conditions requiring the import of manufactured goods — from the United States.

And to the extent that U.S. branch plants in Canada rely on parts imported from the United States, there is a further increase in imports.

Thus, according to the Bank of Canada Annual Report for 1960, Canada's net imports in 1959 of trucks, farm machinery, electrical machinery, and other kinds of machinery and equipment and parts amounted to $1,020 million at wholesale or manufacturer's prices (before addition of customs duties and excise or sales taxes). The part of the total representing imports from the United States was $890 million. These tremendous totals were net amounts, that is, after the value of Canadian exports in those categories had been deducted from imports.

And on top of these forces influencing the content of Canadian trade and turning it towards the United States (as if other trading countries did not exist) there is political pressure from the United States urging the Canadian government to accept the politically restrictive U.S. trade policies and thus distort the direction of Canadian trade.

A change in the pattern of Canada's trade is urgently needed but any suggestion of change runs into powerful opposition. Spokesmen for Canadian banks for whom the continued import of U.S. capital is highly profitable and whose boards are linked to U.S.-based or U.S-controlled export industries argue strongly against any interference with existing trade patterns; they profess to fear that any Canadian tariff increase to encourage new industries in Canada would provoke reprisals against Canadian exports of raw materials. They repeat that Canada should concentrate on what she can do well and profitably. The president of the Bank of Nova Scotia argued that Canada should stick to "the particular lines in which we have some reasonable chance of being efficient, and therefore competitive, producers." (Financial Post: 10 Dec. 60).

Who should decide what these lines might be, why Canada can only compete in raw materials, and the effects on national development of the policy suggested — these things are not discussed.

The same defence of existing policy was expressed a few years ago by an economist who is also an assistant general manager of the Royal Bank of Canada. His statements, expressed facetiously, were apparently intended as a serious comment:

I think there's a future in that (the sale of primary materials by Canada. Ed.). With so many countries trying to industrialize and cutting down on the things that we have, I think that the "hewers of wood and drawers of water" are going to have a good time. We are going to be able to sell that stuff.

D. B. Marsh, as quoted in The Telegram: 8 Mar. 56

Five years later, without regard for the passage of time or the lessons of events, we find an academic economist, one of the leaders of the anti-Coyne group, repeating the same argument:

Hewers of wood and drawers of water can be very wealthy—provided they are efficient hewers and drawers and that they charge enough for their wood and water.

H. S. Gordon: Social Purpose for Canada (1961), page 268.

No one has argued that pulp and paper companies are badly off, but that is not the point. By 1961 the results of the policy of concentrating on selling "that stuff" (the elegant words of the Royal Bank economist) had piled up a total deficit of $7.5 billion, conservative financial papers were asking if Canada will survive, and the further inflow of U.S. capital is only preparing a worse problem for the future.

Nothing of this has impressed itself on Professor Gordon. In fact the "good time" so blithely foreseen by his colleague in 1956 was over before it started; over, that is, as far as the people of Canada and the future of the country were concerned, but not for the actual sellers, many of them U.S.-controlled. Professor Gordon wants us to believe that Canada will benefit if the hewers and drawers get high prices, but the hewers and drawers have long since been incorporated and have no thought of distributing their profits to the people. And he has not stopped to consider, let alone answer, a very complete reply given by Coyne to this whole line of argument:

It is conceivable that the average standard of living per head of population would be greater in Canada if we had never produced anything but fish, or furs, or wheat, or lumber, or metals, but the population would only have been a small fraction of what it is today, and from generation to generation there would be increasing discontent at the lack of

variety of outlets for the talents and tastes of young men and
women coming to maturity.

Coyne: Calgary speech.

It is clear from these points that the value of the development of Canadian resources that has taken place as a
result of foreign investment has to be considered in relation to the disabilities imposed on the economy by the high
degree of U.S. control.

Apologists for U.S. capital and its contribution to Canadian growth, a numerous and vocal group, insist on
looking at only one side of the balance sheet and at only
one or two items on that side. Before dealing with their
arguments and the question whether loss of control by
Canadians of the main resources of the country was
inevitable, it is time to look more closely at the elements
making up the enormous total of $15.7 billion of U.S.
investment in Canada (direct and portfolio) upon which
U.S. control rests.

We have spoken of the increase in foreign investment in
Canada over the past fifteen years as a measure of the
increase in foreign (essentially U.S.) control of the Canadian economy. And read as a warning of the rapid growth
in U.S. influence, the figures of total foreign investment
are useful and valuable. They do not however, give a
complete picture of the extent of that control.

The official figures for total foreign investment measure
the book value of the foreign investment in Canada, and
not the assets controlled by the investment.

The distinction can be substantial. The book value of
investment is derived from company balance sheet figures
and represents the net value of the investment after payment of company obligations. (Balance sheet figures are
notoriously unreliable as far as the valuation of assets is
concerned, but that is another point). The official figures
also show the book value of assets controlled, but in both
cases—book value of investment, book value of assets controlled—the figures are net, after payment of outstanding
claims. In fact a gross figure, the total assets controlled at

any given point, gives a more realistic picture of the influence of the controlling group.

An example will illustrate the point. Massey-Ferguson (end of 1958) showed assets of $312.3 million. The net worth of the company (after allowance for obligations) was $153.3 million. Effective control was exercised by the holding of Argus Corporation owning 15.6% of the outstanding shares with a market value of $15.9 million.

The book value of the Argus investment in Massey-Ferguson was $15.9 million. It controlled a net worth of $153.3 million and total assets of $312.3 million. These figures illustrate the difference between the concepts, even though they must be regarded as hypothetical in spite of being derived from balance sheets. The market value of a large block of shares involving control of the company is not necessarily equivalent to the day-to-day price of smaller lots of shares.

Investment then is the basis of control, but the figures for total investment based on book values will considerably understate the total assets controlled by the investing group.

The total foreign investment in Canada of $20.7 billion is divided into $11.8 billion direct investment and $8.9 billion portfolio.

U.S. direct investment in Canada, close to $10 billion ($9,850 million) makes up 83% of the total direct investment; U.S. portfolio investment, just under $6 billion ($5,875 million) makes up 66% of all foreign portfolio investment in Canada. The figures are for the end of 1959.

The U.S. control of key sectors of the economy is therefore built on the $10 billion direct investment with support from U.S. portfolio investment in stocks of Canadian companies, amounting to $2.6 billion. This gives an outside figure of $12.6 billion in U.S. investment as the basis of U.S. control.

The $12.6 billion is itself made up of two elements: capital inflow from the United States over the years, and

OKANAGAN COLLEGE LIBRARY
BRITISH COLUMBIA

profits made in Canada and re-invested in, or ploughed
back into, the business concerned.

The inflow came from the United States; the re-invested
profits were made in Canada by Canadian workers employed in factories in Canada using Canadian machinery and
Canadian materials. These profits (the part that is re-
invested) are labelled as U.S. investment only because
U.S. interests own the factory or enterprise in which they
were made; in no way do they represent anything added
to the Canadian economy from the outside. The profit
would have been available to whoever made the original
investment.

The relatively minor role actually played by foreign
capital in the formation of new capital in Canada has
been noted by several commentators. Thus, in 1959, Dr.
O. J. Firestone, one-time economic adviser to C. D. Howe,
explained the distinction between inflow of capital and
re-invested profits:

> A comparatively small amount of capital will suffice to estab-
> lish control of an enterprise in its early stages. Then, through
> good management, the retaining of earnings and borrowings,
> the enterprise is expanded. Canadians contribute to the ex-
> pansion . . .

Toronto Daily Star: 10 June 59

Donald Gordon, president of the Canadian National
Railway, in a speech in New York discussed the use by
U.S.-controlled firms of depreciation reserves, depletion allowances, and re-invested profits, all made in Canada, in
order to expand their operations:

> Only 31% of the capital required by U.S. subsidiaries opera-
> ting in Canada came from the U.S. in 1957. The remainder
> of the capital invested represented retained profits, depre-
> ciation and depletion allowances and capital funds obtained
> from Canadian institutions and individual investors. The situ-
> ation is even more emphasized in some of Canada's key indus-
> tries. In mining and smelting, more than half of which is
> controlled by U.S. interests, only 2% of all the capital re-
> quired by the U.S.-controlled part of the industry came from
> the U.S. in 1957.

Financial Post: 19 Nov. 60

The point is clear; the actual contribution of outside capital (U.S. capital) to the process of new capital formation in Canada is small, very much smaller than the defenders of foreign capital like to admit, and in some important branches of industry is now almost nil.

Thus in considering the effects of foreign investment in Canada one must distinguish between the growing domination exercised by foreign (U.S.) capital (the rate of increase in the domination being expressed fairly accurately in the rapidly increasing total of U.S. direct investment in Canada) on the one hand, and, on the other hand, the total inflow of capital on which control is based. The total inflow is one thing; the extent of control to which it has given rise is another.

Official Canadian estimates exist for the amount of U.S.-controlled re-invested profits on direct investment in Canada. These estimates cover the postwar period during which the largest increase in U.S. investment in Canada took place.

U.S. direct investment in Canada rose from $2,304 million at the end of 1945 to $9,850 million at the end of 1959. The Dominion Bureau of Statistics estimates that the increase can be divided into $4,399 million capital inflow and $3,147 million (40%) re-invested profits. A substantial part of the $2,304 million with which the period began must also represent re-invested profits.

If we assume that the 40% figure applied throughout the period of U.S. investment, then we conclude that the total inflow from the United States for direct investment in Canada has been over the years in the neighborhood of $6 billion. To this we should add, to be conservative, between $1.5 billion and $2 billion of portfolio investment in stocks of Canadian companies ($2.6 billion minus re-invested profits) to arrive at an outside total of $8 billion as the part of the $12.6 billion that represents capital inflow from the United States, by the investment of which U.S. monopoly groups have been able to get a stranglehold on the Canadian economy.

And it must be re-emphasized that the main role of this inflow was to secure control over sources of capital accumulation, of immediate and future profit, in Canada. What was added to the Canadian economy was outside control. As a result of the inflow, already existing Canadian labor power was put to work under control of U.S. capital.

The stranglehold is that of the major U.S. financial groups (Rockefeller, Morgan, Mellon, duPont, Cleveland, Chicago) and other smaller groups and some big companies (Ford, Chrysler) not directly linked to the major U.S. groups. All these interests have extended their operations to Canada on the basis of a certain capital invested and the re-investment of profits, and have formed alliances with Canadian banks and Canadian financial groups.

Their influence is exercised in a variety of ways: in some cases through Canadian subsidiaries controlled by U.S. parent firms and wholly or largely owned by the parent, generally with a number of Canadian tycoons on their board of directors; in other cases through U.S.-controlled firms like Inco that have no U.S. parent; in still other cases through the formation of parallel companies, one in the United States, the other in Canada, not legally connected as companies but with the same financial group in control of both, as in the case of the Aluminum Company of America and Aluminium Ltd. Other firms are alliances of U.S. and other capital in varying proportions in which the influence of U.S. capital is felt with increasing force. An increasingly important part in the growth of U.S. influence is played by the investment trusts, Canadian in form but U.S. in control.

The ability of clever corporation lawyers to mask and almost conceal the reality of U.S. control was illustrated in the successful application of Shoreacres Broadcasting Co. to take over radio station CKEY in Toronto. (Globe & Mail: 25 Feb. 61).

The public and the Board of Broadcast Governors are assured that the company "would be controlled in Canada by Canadians" even though Westinghouse Broadcasting

Co. of the United States and Canadian Westinghouse (U.S.-controlled) were putting up $4,101,000 out of a total capital of $4,404,000. But the Globe & Mail interests, the unequal Canadian partner in the transaction, were to own 50% of the voting stock, based on a subscription of $202,000 for common and first preferred shares. Four individual Canadians: W. P. Wilder, a vice-president of the Wood, Gundy investment firm, J. S. D. Tory, a leading corporation lawyer, and two partners in another Toronto law firm, were to have a 25% voting interest, based on a subscription by them of $101,000.

Leaving aside the interesting question of what forces these four represented (Wood, Gundy and J. S. D. Tory, as we shall see, have both had a lot of experience in representing non-Canadian interests), on the face of the matter the Canadian interests hold 75% of the voting stock—control in Canada by Canadians.

In the application the U.S. Westinghouse Company was pleasantly described "as really the banker of this organization." (There was a slight hitch at this point in that the non-voting debentures for which the U.S. interests were subscribing could, under certain conditions, be turned into voting shares, but there is more to the story than that.)

In fact the "banker" called the tune. An arrangement existed "according to which 80% of the voting stock would be required to control the board of directors." The Canadians, be they ever so bold, and ever so united, mustered only 75%; the Westinghouse interests not only put up the money; they also held a veto over all decisions since nothing could be done without their consent. The Globe & Mail planned to present news "in depth" via CKEY; subject of course to Westinghouse approval.

The most important factor in the extension of the influence of U.S. financial groups in Canada is the role played by the substantial number of Canadian tycoons who act as directors of U.S.-controlled corporations, who accept to one degree or another the need to integrate the two economies, who subordinate capital generated in Canada to the

control of U.S. capital and for whom this is the way to
participate in large and profitable undertakings.

Through these men and as a result of the policies they
follow, the influence of the U.S. financial groups is felt in
the Canadian banks, where the percentage of U.S. capital
invested is small but the number of bank directors linked
to U.S. interests is high, in the Canadian Pacific Railway,
and in other enterprises advertised as Canadian. (In an
appendix at page 236 we have listed U.S.-controlled companies with one director or more in common (usually Canadians) with the three largest Canadian banks).

Thus it is with the eager co-operation of the Canadian
tycoons that the major U.S. groups operate in Canada.

All these U.S. groups enjoy intimate relationships with
the Canadian financial groups expressed in an intricate
series of corporate interlocks, based on influence flowing
from investment. The U.S. groups dominate the relationship, and their economic power is also expressed in political
and cultural matters.

Our argument was that the controlling position of the
U.S. groups is based on an actual capital inflow of some
$8 billion. The point at issue is not primarily the accuracy
of the calculation by which we arrived at that total. The
point is in the light shed on the arguments of the apologists for U.S. investment by the distinctions between direct
and portfolio investment, and between inflow and re-invested profits.

The apologists are distinguished in general by the vague-
ness with which they approach the discussion and by their
reluctance to examine the visible effects on Canada of foreign investment.

They repeat propositions they regard as needing no
proof: that Canada could not have grown without large-
scale foreign investment, that future large-scale development will not be possible without large-scale capital imports, that this is the way the United States grew, that
without foreign investment Canadian development would
be ten years behind its level of today, that Canadians are

too conservative by nature to put up money as risk capital, that money simply was not available in Canada to support the growth that has taken place, that the import of foreign capital has also meant the import of skills and technology not available at home, and has provided an assured market for Canadian exports.

These arguments are all presented as if Canadians had borrowed abroad in order to develop Canadian resources on their own account, a perfectly sensible policy if it had been adopted.

Investment is treated as if all foreign investment were portfolio investment; there is no mention of control and there is great emphasis on development, as if all investment had gone into the development of new assets and not to a considerable extent into the taking over of existing assets. But the problem arises because control has been lost, and it is precisely the kind of development to which the investment gave rise that is at issue.

A perverse presentation of the investment question has been put forward by the Carleton University economics professor from whom we have already quoted:

> If the funds we borrow abroad lead to such an expansion in our ability to produce that we can pay the foreign lenders their interest and dividends and still have a substantial part of this new production left over for ourselves, are Canadians the losers by the transaction?
>
> The Economists versus the Bank of Canada. H. Scott Gordon, 1961, page 43.

Professor Gordon protected himself with an "if" and took further refuge in an undefined "we" but the lack of clarity goes deeper. We, whoever we are, are not borrowing; the tycoons are selling. It is not we for whom "a substantial part of the production is left over", it is "they", the new U.S. owners, who get it. They are the winners; Canadians are the losers. In the same paragraph of this ambitiously titled booklet, Professor Gordon feels able to describe Coyne's ideas on foreign investment in Canada as "muddle-headed".

There is very little substance to the summarized arguments of those who defend Canada's wide open policy towards foreign investment. It might be said that if in the past capital was not available in Canada, then loss of control while regrettable was inevitable.

But the fact that loss of control took place does not prove that it was inevitable. Governments determined to maintain Canadian sovereignty and develop Canadian industry and resources in the interests of the Canadian people could have done so, and can in fact still do so. What has always been involved is policy.

And in considering the magnitude of the sums involved, we must bear in mind that Canadian control over the resources now controlled by U.S. monopoly interests could have been maintained by matching the $8 billion inflow from the United States upon which U.S. control of the key sectors rests.

But even if Canada did not have capital available in the past (we shall return to this point) today there can be no doubt that the only limiting factor on Canadian growth (aside from the restrictions imposed by U.S. domination of the economy) is the physical capacity and skills of the Canadian people.

The great lesson of World War II financing was that what was physically possible was fiscally possible, that capital by itself could add nothing to the productive capacity of the country unless there were men and machines available to do the work. Today the resources needed to develop industry in Canada exist in Canada; if experts or certain types of machinery are needed, they can be obtained on the basis of resources now available.

Canada is not an underdeveloped country. What has been lacking is not capital nor capital prepared to take risks; what has been and still is lacking is capital prepared to play an independent role, a role based on national development, prepared, if need be, to run counter to the line of U.S. capital. And this capital is lacking only in the sense that the line of maximum profit continually draws

Canadian capital into the orbit of U.S. capital as a junior partner, away from national development.

The capital needed to develop Canada is available in Canada but it will have to be made available in a national form, under public control. What is really lacking is not capital but decisions on what to do.

The $8 billion on which U.S. control in Canada rests is no small sum, but at the same time it is not at all large in relation to the billions spent by Canada in a much shorter period to implement a defence policy that has begun to achieve fairly wide recognition as a total waste.

During the seven year period, 1951-8, the Canadian government spent $12.4 billion on arms. And in the same period Canadian financial groups expanded their holdings abroad by $1.7 billion. (Research Bulletin, United Electrical Workers, August, 1959).

Here was a total of $14.1 billion available over a seven year period for the development of Canada, minus such proportion of the total as a defence policy based on Canadian needs would have required.

In the same period U.S. direct investment in Canada increased by $4.9 billion, of which we can estimate that $2.9 billion was inflow and $2 billion re-invested profits.

Thus, in that period, Canadian spending on arms was more than four times greater than the capital inflow from the United States for direct investment in Canada, and arms spending plus capital exports was greater by $6 billion (in a seven year period) than the total inflow for direct investment from the United States since such investment began.

The decision to spend on arms and allow U.S. penetration of the economy expresses a policy that is both the result of U.S. economic and political influence, and the cause of growth in that influence.

The reality is that U.S. policy has imposed on its ally Canada a U.S.-oriented military program, worthless in terms of Canadian defence, for which Canada has to pay. And at the same time U.S. monopoly capital unselfishly takes over control of the most profitable sectors of the Canadian economy.

For the fiscal year 1956/7, according to the Research Bulletin of the United Electrical Workers (September, 1959), 49% of all Canadian military expenditures on goods and services went to fifteen big contractors.

Six of the fifteen are U.S.-controlled: General Motors of Canada (duPont interests), Imperial Oil (Rockefeller interests), Canadair (subsidiary of General Dynamics, linked to Lehman Brothers financial house), Canadian Pratt & Whitney Aircraft (subsidiary of United Aircraft Corporation, linked to First National City Bank of New York), Bell Telephone Company (Morgan-Rockefeller interests), Canadian Westinghouse (Morgan-Mellon interests). It will be seen that the most powerful U.S. groups are involved.

In other words, a substantial part of the military spending imposed on Canada by U.S. policy goes directly to benefit the Canadian representatives of U.S. monopoly, making a further contribution, at the expense of the Canadian taxpayer, to the ability of U.S. monopoly groups to extend their influence over the Canadian economy.

Both sides of the picture, the military spending and the increased U.S. investment in Canada, are part of the efforts of U.S. capital to expand its deteriorating world position. The process has extraordinarily little to do with the national interests of Canada.

We, Canadians in general, are being robbed, and the robbery can and must be stopped. How long are Canadians expected to tolerate the distortion, imbalance and lack of jobs imposed on Canada by the growing U.S. domination of the economy, all consequences of the line of action followed by the financial oligarchy and their allies in government?

CHAPTER III

The Sellers of Canada

THE FACT THAT IN CANADA a few giant monopolies dominate the field in every branch of industry and that these giants are themselves controlled by small interlocked groups of financiers (largely English-speaking) has been a commonplace of Canadian politics for years. In spite of the reality of this fact apologists have always been available to deny the existence of monopoly, or to prove that it is really a good thing, or to argue that control over the structure of monopoly is now exercised by a multitude of small investors.

We shall therefore deal briefly with the realities of the corporate scene.

In Chapter IV we shall describe the structure through which the oligarchy maintain control; here we are concerned to show the fact of concentration of production and of control by the few, those who are busy selling Canada to the U.S. financial groups.

The Gordon Commission study, Canada-United States Economic Relations (1957), effectively sets out the degree of concentration in production and shows to what extent non-residents controlled the most important enterprises operating in Canada.

The study is based on data of 1954 but its conclusions would be strengthened by developments since that date. It examines most branches of industry in terms of the role played in each branch by the six most important firms. Several criteria were taken into account in establishing the order of importance: book value of assets, output, plant capacity, employment. In fact, to choose six firms in each branch of industry was misleading, since in the majority of cases the leading role was played by two, three or four firms. And the method adopted fails to show interconnections among the six largest and between the largest and the smaller enterprises.

The results of the study were as follows: (we have added information on control where there have been recent changes, and inserted assets for companies that do not appear on the list of companie in Table III at page 239).

PETROLEUM

In *crude production,* the six largest firms accounted for 68% of the net value added in production. All six were controlled outside Canada, five of them in the United States. In *refining,* the six largest (four controlled in the United States) accounted for 93% of net value added. (In both branches of the industry the Rockefeller-controlled Imperial Oil Ltd. was the most important single factor.)

MINING

In *nickel-copper* mining, the six largest firms accounted for 100% of the net value added. International Nickel Co. of Canada Ltd. is far in the lead, followed by Falconbridge Nickel Mines Ltd. (assets $77.2 million, end '58) and Sherritt Gordon Mines Ltd. (assets $65.9 million). Inco and Sherritt Gordon are both U.S.-controlled; Falconbridge is part of the Ventures-McIntyre Porcupine set-up. In *lead-zinc* mining, six firms accounted for 86% of the value added in production, with Consolidated Mining & Smelting Co. of Canada controlled by the CPR, far ahead. In *copper-gold* mining, the six leading firms accounted for 88% of the net value added, with Hudson Bay Mining & Smelting Co. Ltd. (U.S.-controlled, assets $70.3 million, end '57) and Noranda Mines Ltd. much the more important. In *iron-ore* production, six firms accounted for 100% of value added. This field is dominated by the Iron Ore Company of Canada and now, since the Gordon Commission study, other U.S.-dominated firms in the Labrador area are coming into production. In *aluminum,* only one firm is shown, the U.S.-controlled Aluminium Ltd., with its world-wide string of subsidiaries. The Canadian British Aluminium Co. Ltd. (assets $98.9 million), U.S.-U.K. control, is now producing. In *asbestos,* the six largest account for 94% of the net value added, and two are controlled in the United States. Canadian Johns-Manville Co. Ltd. (U.S.-controlled) and Asbestos Corp. Ltd., are the most important. In *gypsum,* the six largest account for 97% of net value added and three of them are U.S.-controlled.

MANUFACTURING

In *pulp and paper,* the six largest account for 46% of the net value added and only two are shown as controlled outside Canada. But an intricate system of alliances and interlocks prevails throughout this industry and Canadian control is not nearly as solid as the Gordon Commission study suggests. A further step towards concentration of control in the industry was taken by the merger of Mac-Millan & Bloedel Ltd. and the Powell River Co. Ltd. on December 31st, 1959. *Chemicals* is broken down into *fertilizers,* and *acids, alkalis and salts.* In the former, the six largest account for 92% of net value added, in the latter 63%. Of the former, two are controlled in Canada, of the latter, one. In *electrical apparatus and supplies,* the six largest account for 52% of net value added. Here Canadian General Electric Co. Ltd., Canadian Westinghouse Co. Ltd., and Northern Electric Co. Ltd., dominate the field, all three U.S.-controlled, although the Gordon Commission study considers Northern Electric as Canadian. In *primary iron and steel,* the six largest account for 84% of value added. There have been important changes in control in this field in the past few years. Dominion Steel & Coal Corp. Ltd. is now controlled by the Hawker Siddeley interests of the United Kingdom; Algoma Steel Corporation Ltd. is controlled by a Canadian-West German-U.K. consortium. In *automobiles,* the six largest, all U.S.-controlled, account for 97% of net value added; the three giants are General Motors of Canada Ltd., Ford Motor Co. of Canada Ltd., and Chrysler Corporation of Canada Ltd. In *rubber goods*, the six largest account for 77% of net value added and the first four are U.S.-controlled. In *railway rolling stock*, the six largest account for 84% of net value added, and three of the six are U.S.-controlled. *Primary textiles* is subdivided into *synthetic fibres* and a category that includes *all other varieties;* in the former there were only four firms in 1954 and they accounted for 100% of net value added; all are controlled outside Canada. In the latter the six largest accounted for 90% of net value added, and all are Canadian-controlled. In *agricultural implements* the six largest accounted for 91% of net value added, two being controlled in the United States. Massey-Ferguson Ltd. and International Harvester Co. of Canada Ltd. are the unquestioned leaders.

The Gordon Commission study did not include transportation companies, companies producing aircraft, or beverage companies; by definition utilities were excluded, as was merchandising. The same concentration at the top and a substantial U.S. influence exist in these branches.

The Income Tax returns are a further confirmation of the situation. Out of 78,789 companies fully tabulated for income tax purposes in 1958 (there were in all 80,770 active taxable corporations) only 86 had assets of $100 million and up. Thirty-seven of this group were manufacturing companies. Seventy-seven companies had incomes of $5 million and up in that year, and the total assets of the companies in this income group amounted to $15.6 billion out of total assets for all fully tabulated companies of $53.1 billion. Less than one one-thousandth of all companies held almost 30% of all corporate assets.

· · ·

Control over the small group of big companies that dominate the economy and their billions in corporate assets rests in the hands of a small group of tycoons and it is with them and their actions that we are concerned.

We propose to consider them under several related points: the basis of their power; their relations with U.S. groups; their connections with government; their wealth and their integrity.

We have already stated our point: that the power of the tycoons is a class power, that this group, the most important sector of the ruling class, own the principal means of production in Canada and their power is based on this ownership.

Now the means of production are in fact owned by corporations, the handful of giant corporations that we have referred to. Corporations also have owners, and in the last analysis, after stripping away the holding companies that complicate the picture, the financial groups in control of the corporations control them on the basis of owning a controlling interest. They own enough to give them control. How much is enough for this purpose depends on the distribution of shares and shareholdings in the particular corporation under consideration.

Those who own the controlling interest generally do not manage the corporations they control. Managers can be hired—and fired. And the ablest managers have not yet found a way to take control from the owners although from time to time a certain number of managers are brought into the controlling circle. The fact that the controlling group may play a smaller role in active management does not mean that their power over the corporations and their managers is any less. The power remains and is exercised whenever big decisions have to be made. Not all big decisions are taken within boards of directors. Some boards include a high proportion of employees of the company, and in such cases effective decisions on major points are taken outside the board room by people other than the directors.

The tycoons then are themselves or are representing the owners of the means of production. They have developed to a high degree the ability to mobilize the capital generated from the savings of the people so as to extend their own control over the whole economic structure; they use other people's money to bolster and maintain their position which rests essentially on owning the right number of shares in the right corporations.

J. K. Galbraith, the economist recently named U.S. Ambassador to India, reviewing a book by fellow-Democrat A. A. Berle (New York Times: 6 Sept. 59) described the absolute power of the managers of the corporations who "meet with the shareholders in a gracious ritual, but appoint themselves and also their successors to office."

This is the theory that the managers of the corporations form the new ruling class. The owners have been displaced. On this theory no shareholder has any say (equal lack of rights for all), but the managers, according to Berle, (Galbraith has doubts) are "subject to the compelling force of public opinion" and hence, in a roundabout way, democracy does prevail.

That the ordinary shareholder has little or no chance to find out any material facts at a shareholders meeting, that such meetings in general are completely cut and dried—this is all true but the fact remains that the group who own the controlling interest call the tune. They are in control because they and their financial allies are able to bring together their own holdings and the holdings of others so as to combine the voting rights on all these shares in their own favor.

Their power rests on ownership, exercised in a complicated way. A few years ago, E. P. Taylor, who was and is chairman of Canadian Breweries Ltd., argued that he was only one of 18,000 shareholders in the company, and owned in his own name only 12,500 shares out of the 2,503,000 shares then outstanding.

This was all true, but he neglected to add other pertinent information: that Argus Corporation, the holding company of which he is president, and which is controlled by him and his allies, owned another 400,000 shares in Canadian Breweries, and through this holding he and his group were able to dominate Canadian Breweries.

It was a fact that Taylor owned only 12,500 shares. It
was also a fact that he did not "own" Argus Corporation,
but he did own enough shares in Argus to give him control
of Argus and of the investments owned by Argus.

The contributors to Social Purpose for Canada (1961)
have been unable to agree among themselves on the question of ownership and control.

Thus Professor Rosenbluth, after a careful argument
concludes:

> While it is true, therefore, that *most* owners cannot control
> and have no wish to do so, a few large owners *can* have ef-
> fective control and generally want to exercise it.
>
> Social Purpose for Canada, page 209.

But this approach is the reverse of that of Professor Wel-
don who criticizes the left for "having accepted (during
the Thirties) a fiction . . . equating ownership with control", (page 172), and of Professor Porter who states boldly
that "the concentration of economic power and the sepa-
ration of ownership from control are two of the most profound changes in twentieth-century capitalism." (page 44).

Professor Porter does not discuss the second of his two
profound changes but a few pages later we find him saying, more accurately, that the "technique of control is
simple . . . it is to buy up enough shares to outvote any
other combination of shareholders." (page 46).

The change is something less than "most profound".

Thus when it is said that a controlling group own very
few shares in the enterprise they control, the statement is
one that has to be examined with care. The point is, how
many shares are owned by groups or corporations allied to
the controlling group and what is the basis of the alliance.

If a large corporation has a great many shares outstanding (15 million would not be unusual) with a substantial
proportion held by smaller investors, then the controlling
group are probably safely in control if they and their allies
own, directly or indirectly, from 10% to 15% of the outstanding shares.

Then too, it is the group already in control who send out the notices to the annual meetings and urge shareholders either to come in person or to send in proxies in favor of the management.

This control over the organization can be very important in blocking opposition of dissident shareholders or directors. In 1957, two or three directors of Dominion Steel & Coal opposed the terms of the A. V. Roe Canada offer to take over the company. R. A. Jodrey, one of those opposed, a director of the Bank of Nova Scotia, denounced the Roe offer as a "simple, scientific steal." Jodrey at that time owned 100,000 Dosco shares but when he wished to get in touch with other Dosco shareholders to warn them against accepting the offer, he was refused access to the address lists. The only way he could reach his fellow shareholders was through newspaper advertisements that cost him thousands of dollars.

A company with 160,000 shareholders, like the Bell Telephone Co. of Canada, doesn't expect very many of them to attend the annual meeting, and would be horrified if they did. And someone who has saved a few hundred dollars and invested that amount in Bell shares is not going to travel to Montreal to a meeting that is a pure formality. In fact, at the 1959 Bell annual meeting, 100 shareholders were present in person, including, we may hope, all fifteen directors. But a total of 98,000 shareholders, representing in all two-thirds of the shares, had dutifully sent in proxies in favor of the directors. It would seem that 60,000 shareholders, owning one-third of the shares, took no interest at all in the meeting.

The American Telephone & Telegraph, with which Bell Telephone is affiliated, has gone to the other extreme. It has put a lot of effort into organizing monster annual meetings — it has millions of shareholders — and in 1961 held the world's largest annual meeting in Chicago, 18,420 shareholders present in person.

Annual meetings, large or small, are planned as formal affairs. The financial page of The Telegram (2 Mar. 57)

—the example is a random one—carried identically word-
ed announcements for the annual meetings of five fire insurance companies for the same day and same place, but
conveniently and efficiently spaced at 10 a.m., 10.30 a.m.,
11 a.m., 11.30 a.m., and 12.30 p.m., all "for the purpose of
receiving the annual statement, the election of directors,
and other general business." Clearly discussion in any form
was the last thing expected by the planners of the meetings.

But when discussion does come, the meeting becomes
"an annual agony" to use the words of the Globe & Mail
in describing the 1960 annual meeting of Canadian General Electric Co. Ltd. Why? Because a determined shareholder owning two shares turned up in 1959 and 1960 to
argue and ask questions about U.S. control of the company. In 1959 he was the only shareholder present who
was not also a member of the board of directors; without
him the meeting could have been a cosy affair. His questions enraged the U.S.-appointed president, J. H. Smith,
who burst out:

> this is a Canadian company, with a Canadian board of dir-
> ectors, doing business in Canada.
>
> Globe & Mail: 10 April 59

The reader is left to wonder about Mr. Smith and his
devotion to accuracy since the same news-story had referred to the well-known fact that U.S. General Electric owned 99.8% of the stock of Canadian General Electric.

At that Mr. Smith is no more inaccurate than the stock-
brokers who in 1961 heralded the action of General Electric "one of the first major American companies to give
Canadians the opportunity to participate as partners in the
affairs of a Canadian subsidiary company." (Advertise-
ment of Messrs Collier, Norris & Quinlan, Globe & Mail:
10 Oct. 61).

This "opportunity to participate as partners" arose because Canadian General Electric had taken over Dominion
Engineering Works, a Canadian company, on the basis of

an exchange of shares. As a result of the transaction former Dominion Engineering shareholders (mainly Canadians) would end up owning 8% of Canadian General Electric shares. (Globe & Mail: 28 Sept. 61). The 8% was the calculation of Mr. Smith who had perhaps forgotten his 1959 outburst. A real partnership as anyone could see.

The fact that the tycoons have a common class interest as owners of the means of production does not mean that they constitute one happy family. Over-all agreement on general objectives may and does exist alongside sharp disagreement over tactics and the division of profits. Personal differences can be important. The Canadian side of a U.S.-controlled set-up may develop differences of opinion over policy. Competition between rival groups can be ruthless and keen as alliances break down and shifts in control take place.

E. P. Taylor rose to fortune and power via a number of sharp encounters with financial rivals: to get control of St. Lawrence Corporation (1947-51), to defeat Norman Dawes and get control of National Breweries (1951-2), and the famous "ruthless surgery" employed in 1956 to remove J. S. Duncan from the presidency of Massey-Ferguson.

The differences, important though they may be, are minor in relation to the deeper unity, however subject to strain, achieved on fundamental issues. Thus the fact that tycoons who are bank directors may be calling for increased protection for their industries at the same time as the presidents of the same banks are denouncing any "interference" with trade, does not break up a financial alliance.

How many individuals should be included in the group of top Canadian tycoons has been a subject for discussion for years.

Fifty years ago, The Grain Growers Guide, organ of the progressive Western farmers, offered this opinion:

In Canada there is yet . . . only the beginning of the ruling plutocracy. But at the present rate, 25 years will see the wealth of Canada controlled by 100 men, and the most of it by a score. It is coming with tremendous speed.

> quoted in The Revolt in Canada, E. C. Porritt, London, 1911, page 110.

By 1913 the same paper undertook a listing of Canada's big shots in terms of the total assets of the companies in which each big shot held directorships.

This first attempt (25 June 1913) to identify the oligarchy by name and number listed 42 tycoons, ranging from Senator Robert McKay, holding directorships in companies with assets totalling $1.6 billion, down to D. Lorne McGibbon, with a pitiful $36.1 million. (It is interesting that twenty-five years later the daughter of Senator McKay was herself a senator, the first woman appointee).

Prominent in the list, as was inherent in the method of compiling it, are the names of the group who combined directorships in the Canadian Pacific Railway Company with directorships in the Bank of Montreal or Royal Bank, but there is no doubt that these mainly Montreal financiers represented the main centre of power in Canada at that time as they do, but not so decisively, today. Thus, in 1913, we find R. B. Angus, Sir William Van Horne, H. S. (later Sir Herbert) Holt, Sir Thomas (later Lord) Shaughnessy, Lord Strathcona, of the Montreal group, as well as such Toronto figures as W. D. Matthews, and Sir E. B. Osler, president of the Dominion Bank, all in the billion dollar class.

At least three more such lists have been prepared at different times. The big shots as of 1932 and 1943 are shown in the two editions of Who Owns Canada?; a comparable list for 1955-6 appeared in Maclean's Magazine. (12 Oct. 57).

The 1932 list is the best known of the series. It showed fifty tycoons holding directorships in companies whose assets totalled $1 billion and up; from this fact arose the phrase "Fifty Big Shots". The list began with Sir Herbert Holt at $4.8 billion and went down to Paul F. Sise at $1.0 billion. The CPR directors still predominated; eight of the first ten, ten of the first twelve, were CPR directors who were also directors of the Bank of Montreal or Royal Bank of Canada.

To keep the benefit of the catchy phrase, the 1943 list of Who Owns Canada? confined itself to the top fifty names, ranging from Morris Wilson of the Royal Bank and CPR at $5.8 billion to W. E. Phillips, later of Argus fame, at $1.6 billion.

The 1955-6 list took the hundred top names, starting with Charles Dunning (Bank of Montreal, Sun Life, CPR, etc., etc.,) at $10.8 billion, and ending with Norman Dawes at $2.2 billion. It will be seen that as the years pass corporate assets steadily mount.

Listings of this type have value in showing the fabulous assets over which a small group have control and in indicating changes in the financial hierarchy, but they suffer, especially in the 1943 and 1955-6 versions, from an air of unreality.

In fact they show neither wealth nor power. This is partly because of the purely mechanical approach: take all over one billion, take the first fifty, take the first one hundred—an approach that leaves out the reality of power: the group relationships and alliances.

The lists concentrate on the individual tycoon but the power of the big shots is a group power, a class power, much more than it is the power of individuals, even though some of the persons on the list are extremely powerful individuals. But any realistic analysis of the big shots must start with their group associations, bearing in mind that their power is based on their class position, and not on their personal qualities, important though those may be.

Another serious defect is that the listings do not show the connections of the big shots with U.S. capital. Thus in the 1955-6 list, the order of names would be thrown out if the assets of U.S. corporations were included. R. S. McLaughlin and Graham Towers would head the list if they were credited with the multi-billion dollar assets of General Motors Corporation (the parent company) of which they are

directors. And of course the power of the tycoons and their
wealth cannot be judged without taking their U.S. connections into account.

But while all the writers on the subject (there have not
been so many) have come up with different totals for the
Canadian elite, ranging from a high of 922 down to 200,
"ten dozen or so", and the traditional "fifty", the number
varying according to the criteria adopted by a particular
writer, there is no dispute over the essential fact, that a
very small group of people is involved.

The tycoons in the group are in the main Canadian citizens, although there are among them some important figures who are citizens of the United States, as well as a few
from other countries, but the nationality of tycoons is relatively unimportant. What is more important is the power of
the corporations they and their allies control and the policies those corporations follow. It is not in terms of their
birth or citizenship that the tycoons are un-Canadian but
in terms of their outlook.

They are concerned to achieve the greatest possible profit from the operations of the corporations they control.
The problem and source of danger to the future of Canada
lie in the fact that those who control the key sectors of the
economy have taken as their premise that U.S. capital is
and will be dominant, that Canadian development is necessarily subordinated to and dependent on ("integrated
with") the drive of U.S. groups for their own profit.

The Canadian tycoons have chosen to associate themselves as junior partners with U.S. capital, parting with
control to their dominant U.S. partners but sharing in their
profits.

Thus as U.S. capital increases control over the Canadian
economy, more and more Canadian tycoons become associated with U.S.-controlled companies, members of their
boards of directors, advising on Canadian operations,
sometimes rising to be directors of the U.S. parent
company.

It is not that these Canadian directors in U.S.-controlled corporations lose their capacity for independent thought and become mere agents for U.S. interests or that they are devoid of influence on the boards on which they sit.

They are not simple reflections of or mouthpieces for U.S. groups (even if the emphasis perhaps falls on the word simple). The relationships are often subtle and complicated. But the fact remains that the attitudes, policies and actions of Canadian financial groups cannot be understood without analyzing their ties with U.S. capital.

The Canadian tycoons have taken as their point of departure a relationship between capital, a relationship based on profit; national development is for them a secondary consideration. Their philosophy and their actions are naturally influenced by their close connections with U.S. monopoly groups. They could not retain directorships in U.S.-controlled companies if they were not in broad agreement with the policies of the groups in control of those companies.

Junior partnership, accepting a share in the profits of U.S.-controlled enterprises, pays off in short-term advantages to those associated with it from the inside, and the Canadian tycoons and groups sharing in the profits are anxious to see the relationship continue. They see advantages, not disadvantages, to a form of U.S. domination of their country that brings their group larger profits.

With the tycoons controlling the key sectors of the economy, the existence of the relationship they have established with U.S. capital is inevitable; what is not inevitable is that they should be in control.

Acting within this partnership they have achieved with U.S. capital, the Canadian groups have their own special interests, many of which depend on or are related to decisions taken by Canadian governments, federal, provincial, or even municipal.

This leads to the fascinating and complex subject of the relations between big business and government; we have already argued that the objectives of big business form the basis of vital government decisions that affect the future of Canada.

Wages policy, trade questions, arms spending, the rate of capital investment, the level of taxes on corporate profits, the attitude of the government on great questions, all these matters that affect everyone, are carefully and privately considered by tycoons and government figures.

Their opinions, colored by and reflecting class connections with U.S. monopoly groups, form the basis of government policy, subject always to the limitations imposed by popular action. The result is a policy national in name but very private in the way it is arrived at, and often anti-national in its consequences.

The power of the tycoons and their allies in government to achieve their aims is always limited by the existing degree of people's participation in public affairs. Their power is real and dominant, but it is neither absolute nor eternal; it can be ended by an organized, aroused people. Subject to these important qualifications, those who hold dominant economic power dictate the way in which the affairs of the country will be administered, and determine the policies of governments.

When the financial groups are not in agreement, then governments hesitate and stumble. When the financial groups are in agreement, then the decisions of government, no matter how attractively presented, reflect the interests of the oligarchy as directly as possible, having in mind the state of public opinion, itself subject to pressure through the mass media over which the tycoons also exercise strong influence.

The decisions taken have a Canadian form, and the power to influence the decisions gives the Canadian financial groups a chance to improve their positions in relation to their U.S. senior partners. But in exercising pressure along these lines, the Canadian groups as well as the Canadian government involved are acting within limits defined by their idea of what the traffic will bear. They want the junior partnership and the profits flowing from it to continue. Any struggle with their U.S. rivals and allies is over the division of profit within the framework of domination by U.S. capital; its range is limited.

In the past, Canadian politicians used to be franker in discussing the reality of the relationships of business and government. Of course, the question of the relationship with U.S. monopoly had not yet assumed the importance it has today.

When we go back to 1921, we find Mackenzie King, then leader of the opposition, with first-hand experience in the Laurier cabinet and later with the Rockefellers and Rockefeller-controlled companies, denouncing "the real though invisible government . . . the little oligarchy of interwoven financial, manufacturing, transportation and distributing interests." (Hansard: 19 May 1921, page 3603). And some years before, another Liberal ex-cabinet minister, H. R. Emmerson, had summed the matter up from his own experience in these words:

> . . . the great transportation interests, the great banking interests and the great industrial interests of this country have no party politics; they enter the door whether it is open or shut, and they care not whether that door is to your right, Mr. Speaker, or to your left.
>
> Hansard: 30 Jan. 1913, page 2419.

It can of course be argued that these are quotations from old, self-serving political speeches, that there was no basis in fact for the statements made, or that even if such things once were true, those bad old days have gone forever.

The arguments do not convince. They run into the political experience of Canadians with the way their country is being run. The case for the community of interest between the government and big business ultimately rests on an analysis of the actions of government and their effect on big business. In this chapter we take a short-cut; we propose to illustrate this community of interest through examples of the way in which prominent figures have moved from directorships in corporations to cabinet positions and vice versa, from high positions in the armed forces to directorships in aircraft manufacturers, from the civil service to industry and vice versa, from the banks and trust companies to the office of governor general and back, from the bench to the presidency of big corporations. And in all cases, the corporations are as likely as not to be U.S.-controlled.

The examples are personal examples; the relationship between big business and government is much more than a personal one; it rests on common class interest, on a community of understanding. The examples illustrate the relationship, but it exists and would exist even if cabinet ministers etc. never became company directors or vice versa.

The illustrative examples begin with prime ministers. Thus R. B. Bennett was a tycoon in his own right before he became leader of the government in 1930. He was, as Lord Beaverbrook has pointed out, a member of the notorious Canada Cement syndicate of 1909, a group that pulled off one of the most audacious and profitable financial coups in the history of Canada. Bennett put in $100,000 of borrowed money and his profit, notes Beaverbrook, was "considerable." The syndicate bought up the principal cement plants in Canada for $16.5 million and resold them to the new company they were promoting for $29 million. Beaverbrook's personal profit was said to have been $5 million. Bennett also participated in the Calgary Power enterprise, controlled by Beaverbrook, and later by I. W. Killam. It was Bennett who, as prime minister, was responsible in 1930 and 1931 for the two orders-in-council by which the Royal Bank of Canada and the Sun Life Assurance Co. were bailed out of their financial difficulties by being allowed to value the securities they then held at prices higher than the depressed market prices.

Bennett, after his defeat and retirement from politics, became a director of the Royal Bank of Canada.

Arthur Meighen, briefly prime minister in 1921 and 1926, achieved notoriety in 1917 as the cabinet minister responsible for the legislation by which the Canadian government took over the bankrupt Canadian Northern Railway. At the time the government and the Canadian Bank of Commerce held all or nearly all the common stock of the Canadian Northern belonging to Sir Wm. Mackenzie and Sir Donald Mann, as security for cash advances to the railway. The stock held by the bank had a face value of some $50 million; in fact it was worthless, and the Drayton-Acworth report of 1917 so described it.

To avoid embarrassing the Commerce and National Trust interests, the government included in the cost of taking over the railway an item of $10.8 million for the worthless common stock.

Cynics of the day pointed to the fact that Sir Thomas White, formerly of the National Trust, was then Minister of Finance and doubly interested in the transaction. Montreal financial circles (the Bank of Montreal-CPR alliance) opposed the Meighen policy, both because they opposed railway nationalization on principle, and because they would not have been displeased at the prospect of seeing their Toronto railway rivals take a knock. In a fit of anger, R. B. Bennett, then a Tory M.P., had denounced Meighen in the House of Commons during one of the earlier railway debates as "the gramaphone of Mackenzie and Mann." But as prime minister he later appointed "the gramaphone" to the Senate and to a post in the Bennett cabinet.

A latter day Conservative was also a well-known National Trust figure: J. M. Macdonnell, M.P., formerly minister without portfolio in the Diefenbaker government, was president of the National Trust Co. Ltd. from 1939 until 1944 when he entered the House of Commons.

When Meighen retired from politics for the first time, in 1927, after a series of defeats, he took on a number of directorates and later became Ontario Hydro Commissioner. An Ontario Royal Commission in 1934 investigated charges that companies in which he held directorates had benefitted from their dealings with Hydro, charges that were "born out" by the report, according to a Globe & Mail review of a history of Ontario Hydro (14 Dec. 60).

Meighen had close associations with the Massachusetts group of investment trusts and was chairman of three of these U.S.-controlled trusts: Canada General Fund, Canadian General Investments Ltd., and Third Canadian General Investment Trust Ltd., a director of Canadian Celanese Ltd., also U.S.-controlled, and a vice-president of Canada Trust Co. His son, Maxwell Meighen, holds a number of important directorships.

On the side of the Liberal party the links with big business in terms of the role played by individuals have been just as close. Mackenzie King remained a politician to the end but he had been in the confidence of the Rockefellers, and, according to a Rockefeller biographer, had been the "best friend" of Mr. John D. Rockefeller, Jr. Two other men close to Mr. King had Rockefeller connections. It was Mackenzie King who drew Louis St. Laurent into political life. St. Laurent was then a Bank of Montreal director and a director of the Rockefeller-controlled Metropolitan Life Insurance Co. Later Brooke Claxton, King's protege in politics, left the Liberal cabinet to become a director of the Metropolitan Life, head of its Canadian operations, and a director of the Montreal Trust Co.

Charles Dunning, Finance Minister under King, retired from politics to become a key figure in the financial hierarchy: chairman of Ogilvie Flour Mills Ltd., a director of the Bank of Montreal, Royal Trust, Sun Life, CPR, Cominco, Stelco, Hudson's Bay Co., etc. Dunning was the second former Minister of Finance to become a director of Stelco; the first was a Conservative, Sir Thomas White, on the Stelco board from 1919 to 1955.

In 1949, two Toronto dailies debated the fascinating question whether Tories or Liberals were most closely linked to big business. The Globe & Mail, irritated by a remark critical of big business made by Mr. St. Laurent, pointed accusingly at the then Prime Minister's former connections; later for good measure, it attacked the Minister of Justice, Stuart Garson, as a "creature of the Sifton interests." Mr. Garson had been so unkind as to refer to George Drew, the Tory leader of the day, as "the John Hampden of Bay Street."

The Toronto Daily Star was driven to argue in defence that there was nothing inconsistent in the position taken by Mr. St. Laurent criticizing big business. He had learned from his associations with it. "Why," complained the Star, "should anyone object to an attack upon control by high finance, whether it comes from Prime Minister St. Laurent or a Conservative leader?"

On his return to private life, Mr. St. Laurent also returned to participation in high finance, becoming a director of one of the largest U.S.-controlled investment trusts: Investors Syndicate of Canada Ltd. (assets $130.8 million), of the U.S.-controlled Famous Players Canadian Corporation Ltd., a director of Industrial Acceptance Corporation Ltd., and chairman of la Compagnie Miron ltee. (linked to Belgian capital), and of Rothmans of Pall Mall Canada Ltd.

Several Liberal cabinet ministers quickly found places in high finance after the defeat of their government in 1957. Most prominent among them was C. D. Howe, ex-Minister of Trade and Commerce, one of the executors of the multi-million dollar Dunn estate, who moved into a position comparable to that of Charles Dunning before him.

In 1961, at the time of his death, Howe was, like Dunning, chairman of Ogilvie Flour Mills Ltd. and a director of the Bank of Montreal. He also held directorships in National Trust Co. Ltd. and The Crown Life Insurance Co., was chairman of Price Brothers & Co. Ltd., a director of Dominion Tar & Chemical Co., Ltd., (the latter a Taylor-Argus company, and the Taylor interests having a substantial holding in Price Brothers), Atlas Steels Ltd., Rio Tinto Mining Co. of Canada Ltd., Hollinger Consolidated Gold Mines (the junior partner of the Hanna interests of

THE SELLERS OF CANADA

Cleveland in the Iron Ore Co. of Canada), and of two British Columbia enterprises, Evans, Coleman & Gilley Brothers Ltd., and Ocean Cement & Supplies Ltd., in which Bank of Montreal and Canadian Imperial Bank of Commerce interests take part.

Howe also held directorships in the following U.S.-controlled firms: Aluminium Ltd., (shades of the wartime Arvida strike!), RCA Victor Co. Ltd., and two New York-controlled investment trusts: Canadian Fund Inc. and Canadian Investment Fund Ltd.

Generally speaking the departments of government headed by Howe during the war were the ones whose activities impinged most closely on the activities of big business; for the tycoons it was imperative that these departments be operated by members of the oligarchy in a way that would raise the minimum number of problems for big business, interfere least with the pursuit of the largest possible profits, and leave the big companies in the best possible position after the war. As a by-product of their activities in those departments a number of young and promising junior tycoons established connections that served them well in the postwar. And it is instructive to note the way in which Howe maintained and developed his wartime connections in his post-government career.

Among the business figures associated with Howe during the war (or during such part of it as they gave to government service) were E. P. Taylor, W. E. Phillips, M. W. McCutcheon, H. J. Carmichael, Wilfrid Gagnon (all future members of the Argus board), Henry Borden (Brazilian Traction), J. D. Barrington (McIntyre Porcupine), W. J. Bennett (Iron Ore Co. of Canada), V. W. Scully (Steel Co. of Canada).

R. H. Winters, a cabinet associate of Howe, moved from the cabinet to the presidency of Rio Tinto of Canada at a salary reputed to be $60,000 a year. Rio Tinto's main interest is in uranium but it has a finger in the British Newfoundland Corporation and in the base-metal finds in

New Brunswick. Among Winters' other directorships are the Canadian Imperial Bank of Commerce, Toronto General Trusts and Bathurst Power & Paper.

Howe and Winters maintained their political association in the world of business. Howe joined Winters on the Rio Tinto board, and they both held directorships in the Crown Life Insurance Co. Howe and E. P. Taylor were both directors of the National Trust and of Dominion Tar & Chemical; Howe and Henry Borden were directors of the same two investment trusts.

Howe and Barrington and Bennett were connected in several operations.

Barrington, appointed by Howe to head Polymer Corporation, a Crown corporation, became a director of McIntyre Porcupine Mines Ltd. (he is now president) when that company was buying an interest in Algoma Steel from the Dunn estate.

Bennett, former private secretary to Howe, was head of Eldorado Mining & Refining Ltd., a Crown corporation, and of Atomic Energy of Canada. He later moved to the presidency of Canadian British Aluminium when it looked as if the Mellon interests would take over the Canadian company's U.K. parent. (Howe was a director of Aluminium Ltd.). When the take-over failed to go through, Bennett became a vice-president of the Iron Ore Company of Canada in which the Hollinger Consolidated Gold Mines (Howe a director) held a minority interest.

Other cases abound of civil servants and high-ranking officers of National Defence who have moved into important business positions: Graham Towers, former governor of the Bank of Canada, is now a director of the Royal Bank, General Motors Corporation, the Bell Telephone Co. of Canada, Hudson's Bay Company, and is in charge of two important U.S.-controlled investment trusts, to name only his most important directorships; Mitchell W. Sharp, former deputy Minister of Finance, has become a vice-president of Brazilian Traction; M. W. Mackenzie, another ex-deputy Minister, is president of the U.S.-controlled Canadian Chemical & Cellulose Co. Ltd.

Former Air Marshall Curtis is now a director of A. V. Roe Canada Ltd., two Air Vice Marshalls: F. S. McGill and Adelard Raymond, grace the board of Canadair Ltd. Lieutenant General Howard Graham, former chief of the general staff, has become president of the Toronto Stock Exchange. Major General Chris Vokes is president of the recently formed North America Arms Corporation, "wholly Canadian owned," "the only manufacturer of heavy calibre arms in Canada" (Globe & Mail: 16 Sept. 59), linked to the Toronto financial house of Gairdner & Co.

The trajectory of Lieutenant General Guy Simonds took a slightly different course. As president of Toronto Brick Co. Ltd. and Frontenac Floor & Wall Tile Ltd., he is in fact employed by the West German investment banking houses that control both firms, two of whose members, former Wehrmacht officers, he had once arrested. In the words of the Toronto Daily Star (23 Sept. 57): "the general is working for the Germans and he likes it."

In even higher echelons the picture is similar. Earl Alexander, former Governor General of Canada, has become a director of Aluminium Ltd.; his successor, Vincent Massey, has returned to the board of the National Trust, of which he had been a member before his term of office; the present Governor General, G. P. Vanier, was a director of the Bank of Montreal and Standard Life Assurance Company before his appointment. Lieutenant governors of the larger provinces show the same kind of connections.

Judges have been known to move from the bench back to the greener fields of corporate law practice and a place in the oligarchy. J. V. Clyne, former British Columbia judge, resigned from the bench to become head of Mac-Millan & Bloedel Ltd., now MacMillan, Bloedel & Powell River Co. Ltd., and a director in the Canadian Imperial Bank of Commerce; in Ontario, C. P. McTague left the bench to take on several directorships, among them John

Labatt Ltd. and a seat on the Toronto advisory committee
of the Royal Trust Company.

The point of this lengthy, though incomplete, listing of
individual cases is to show as directly as possible the existence of the community of interest between government and
big business. The same class interests are involved — the
interests of the monopoly groups that dominate the economy, that are coming into closer and closer relationship
with the U.S. groups and parting with control of Canada
in the search for profit. Government policy reflects these
class interests, directly or indirectly, depending on the
political climate in the country, and will continue to do
so, as long as power remains in the hands of the tycoons.

The tycoons at the top have great power and in most
cases great personal wealth as well. The wealthiest of
course is not necessarily the most powerful, nor the most
powerful the most wealthy, but in general control over
enormous corporate assets and great power go hand in
hand with the possession of great wealth.

Information on the size of the great fortunes is usually
only available from the wills of deceased millionaires. Thus
I. W. Killam (Royal Securities, public utilities) died in
1955 leaving an estate of $150 million; Sir James Dunn
(Algoma Steel) died in 1956 leaving an estate of $66
million.

Among living Canadians gossip points at John David
Eaton, head of the T. Eaton Co. Ltd. and Samuel Bronfman, head of Distillers Corporation-Seagrams Ltd., as
two of the richest.

As a private company the T. Eaton Co. Ltd. publishes
no balance sheet but supposedly all or nearly all of the
outstanding shares in the company are held by members
of the Eaton family.

More information (from U.S. sources) is available in
the case of the Bronfmans. The U.S. Security and Exchange Commission reports showed that in 1956 Samuel
Bronfman received a salary of $315,042, while Alan Bronf-
man, vice-president of the company, received $200,521.

But the Bronfman holding company, Seco Investments
Ltd., holds 38.5% of the outstanding shares in Distillers
Corporation-Seagrams Ltd. In terms of the 1958 net worth
of the company, this holding had a book value of some
$145 million; the dividend income of the holding com-
pany from those shares alone was close to $6 million a
year. Through another private holding company, Cemp
Investments Ltd., the Bronfmans control Royalite Oil Co.
Ltd. (assets $47.1 million). In spite of the great personal
and family wealth of the Bronfmans, the Bronfman interests are not linked, at least not in terms of interlocking
directorates, to the main centres of financial power. E. P.
Taylor, with a personal fortune (still growing) estimated
at a mere $35 million in the late 50's, exercises more power
and influence than the Bronfmans in the Canadian financial oligarchy.

The tycoons of today face a problem that an earlier
generation did not have to deal with, how to minimize tax
liability and receive from year to year the largest possible
sums of money in non-taxable form. It is a problem to
which a number of useful partial solutions have been
found.

When income tax figures tell us that in 1958 just under
3,000 Canadians (2,938 in all) had incomes of $50,000
and up, and that the total incomes of this group amounted
to $240.4 million, the emphasis must be put on the word
income. Large as it is, this sum of $240.4 million represents
only part, and perhaps the smaller part, of the total money
received by the rich in that year.

In Canada capital gains are not taxable. An increase in
capital is non-recurring, is not considered as income, and
hence is not subject to income tax. If tycoons can contrive
to receive large sums of money through the realization of
capital gains, these sums, generally speaking, are not taxable and do not show up anywhere in the tax statistics.

Even as regards taxable income the upper brackets do
not do too badly. It is they who benefit most from the
privilege of deducting an amount equal to 20% of what

they receive in dividends from Canadian companies from
the tax they would otherwise have to pay, and it is they
who benefit most from expense accounts and the ability
to charge it to the company. And looking only at the figures
of income, the top 3,000 average $82,000 a year before
taxes and still hold on to $48,000 a year after taxes.

A common practice in order to minimize tax liability is
for the controlling group to allow company directors and
insiders to buy large blocks of stock in the company at a
price well below the market value. This is justified as
giving the recipient "an interest" in the business. The real
point is that the interest is tax-free.

The Trans-Canada Pipe Line and Westcoast Transmission cases are notorious. When N. E. Tanner, former
Alberta Minister of Mines & Minerals etc., later president
of Trans-Canada Pipe Line Ltd. (TCPL), joined the company, he was given an option entitling him to buy 60,000
shares of TCPL at $8 a share and another 10,000 at $1 a
share. The first report of the Borden Commission on Energy
(October 1958) noted that by September, 1958, Tanner's
apparent gain was $1,457,000, without taking into account
the 10,000 shares bought at $1 (another $345,000 at 1958
prices) which he had transferred to his wife, or 5,000
shares on which he had still not exercised his option to
purchase (another potential $125,000 at 1958 prices).
Close to $2 million, tax-free, not shown in any income tax
statistics. And as president of TCPL Tanner was receiving
a salary, taxable, of $35,000 a year.

Charles S. Coates, the then vice-president and general
manager of TCPL, was given an option to buy 50,000
TCPL shares at $8 a share. From the Borden Commission
figures it can be calculated that his apparent capital gain,
tax-free, was at that time close to $1,300,000. His salary,
taxable, ranged from $45,000 to $50,000 a year.

Members of the U.S. financial syndicate and Canadian
financial experts shared in the bonanza. Francis Kernan,
a partner in the firm of White, Weld & Co., New York
investment dealers, subscribed to 40,000 shares at $8 a

share, half of this amount on behalf of his firm. He also received a fee of $20,000 and the right to subscribe to another 20,000 shares at $8, which works out to a capital gain of $1 million. T. H. Atkinson, retired general manager of the Royal Bank of Canada, a director of TCPL, got an option for 12,500 shares at $8 in return for his services "without remuneration" as chairman of the Finance Committee of TCPL. His capital gain, as of 1958, would have been $312,000. And it must be remembered that in these TCPL cases we are dealing not with the main figures and their profits but only with their employees and agents and the minor share received by them.

The Borden Commission made no attempt to calculate the gains of Mr. Frank McMahon, president of Westcoast Transmission. He had "bought" a total of 154,687 shares in the company at 5 cents a share and was given an option for which he paid half a cent a share to buy another 200,000 shares at a price that worked out to be $5.97 a share. At the end of 1958 his apparent gain was $6.4 million. Mr. McMahon later became a succesful backer of Broadway musical shows ("Pajama Game," "Damn Yankees") and made the news in 1960 during the provincial election campaign in British Columbia when he threatened to cancel $450,000,000 worth of development projects if B.C. voters did not elect a strong Social Credit government. (Globe & Mail: 12 Sept. 60).

Other techniques for realizing tax-free gains or gains at low tax liability exist. The Argus Corporation group, as we shall see in Chapter VII, have a highly developed technique, the Taylor touch, for making a killing by selling something to themselves. Tax experts and corporation lawyers are continually devising other methods by which the tycoons can minimize tax liability.

Whether through the organization of mergers and takeovers, through sales between controlled companies, or in stock options, the tycoons of today have been having a good run for their money and doing very well for themselves. They are following quite successfuly in the footsteps of the free-wheeling group who set up the big mergers in Canada some fifty years ago.

Large gains have also accrued to those with the foresight and the money to buy the right kind of shares and hang on to them. These are the direct gains of ownership, independent of any action on the part of the shareholder whose job was simply to keep the share certificates in a safe place.

Anyone who bought Stelco common shares in 1911 would find himself today approximately fifty times, 5,000%, better off by the simple passage of time.

To buy 100 shares of Stelco in 1911 would have cost between $3,600 (the high for the year) and $2,500 (the low). Let us assume $3,000 for ease in calculation.

The original shares were split 4 for 1 in 1928 and again 5 for 1 in 1950, and exchanged in 1953 for new shares on a one for one basis. At the end of 1960 the 100 original shares costing $3,000 had become 2,000 shares with a market value of $148,000.

And twice, in 1956 and 1961, shareholders were offered rights to subscribe to new shares at a discount, in proportion to the number they already owned. If our happy shareholder had been able to raise some $35,300 additional capital he would have ended up with 2,721 shares selling at a little over $200,000. Alternatively, he could have sold his rights and realized some $18,000, a tax-free gain. And 1960 dividend payments amounted to $2.40 a share, or $4,800 on 2,000 shares, 20% of which, or $960, was available as a deduction from his income taxes.

The number of Canadians in a position to buy 100 shares of Stelco in 1911 was by no means large, but some at least of the inside group in Stelco must have made a killing.

The merger of five companies from which Stelco emerged took place in 1910, engineered by Max Aitken, later Lord Beaverbrook, head of Royal Securities, assisted by Herbert Holt, later Sir Herbert, and president of the Royal Bank of Canada.

The Beaverbrook group owned Montreal Rolling Mills, one of the two major companies involved, and they received for it $4 million in Stelco bonds and preferred stock, and 36,500 shares of Stelco common, on top of an extra million dollars that Beaverbrook adroitly and legally drew out of the assets of his company before the merger, to the intense indignation of the Hamilton side of the merger and their Dominion Bank allies. In telling the story, the official historian of Stelco says that Beaverbrook ended up with 30,000 shares of Stelco common which he held for some time. His profits would not have been small.

The myth that high taxes have ended the great fortunes has never been taken very seriously even by the public relations experts who dreamed up the idea. The president of the Canadian Manufacturers Association, Mr. W. H. Evans, evolved a new angle in a radio-TV symposium in 1960, a theory of much-the-sameness, the idea that regardless of differences in income all Canadians live in "much the same" way:

> . . . what we now see is not merely a lesser gap between the incomes of the well-to-do and the not so well-to-do than ever before . . . but just as significant an equality of affluence in terms of what we eat, what we wear, how we live, and, to a certain extent, what we do. The wives of men on $4,000, $10,000 and $25,000 a year shop in the same supermarket, wear much the same kind of clothes, buy and eat much the same kind of foods, live in much the same way.
>
> Is Business Reshaping Society? The Canadian Institute on Public Affairs, Toronto, 1960, p. 10.

But these comforting remarks about "equality of affluence" do not have any effect in bridging the very real gap between $80 a week and $500 a week. And the $80 a week man will have income tax deducted calculated on the basis of his total wage, his only source of income, while the $500 a week man will almost certainly be receiving some tax-free benefits.

It might not be necessary to comment on the honesty of the tycoons were it not for the fact that extravagant claims are sometimes made for their unimpeachable integrity.

Thus in the course of one of the discussions at the same conference at which Mr. Evans took part, a leading chartered accountant, Mr. J. R. M. Wilson, undertook to defend the honesty of the tycoons:

> Contrary to the general belief, (!) big business is terribly honest. It is very difficult for it to be otherwise. The president of a well-known electrical company, or soap company, would find it absolutely impossible to pick up some of the cash receipts that are coming in the door and put them in his own pocket. In fact, he probably doesn't even know where the cash box is. (And you could contrast that with the small corner store operator who has much more temptation available to him).

> Is Business Reshaping Society? page 20.

Mr. Wilson clearly has a limited view of dishonesty. He had however been thoughtful in his choice of examples; he was taking part in a panel with the president of Canadian General Electric and the president of Proctor & Gamble Co. of Canada Ltd., and felt it necessary and possible to give them a clean bill of health. He was lucky in resting his case for honesty on presidents of companies. Only a year later (6 Feb. 61) the vice-presidents of two well-known electrical companies, General Electric and Westinghouse, began to serve gaol terms of 30 days each for price-fixing. But this may not have been included within Mr. Wilson's concept of dishonesty, although Henry Ford, a General Electric director, was quoted, apropos of the price-fixing, as saying that top executives should have "the plain guts" to admit that this is "our failure . . . it will not happen again."

Perhaps no one was intended to take Mr. Wilson's amiable nonsense too seriously although, along with Mr. Evans' contribution, it has been solemnly reprinted in booklet form. Mr. Wilson didn't stop to explain why a small corner grocer should take the trouble to steal from his own cash box, and he evaded an important question:

whether tycoons take advantage of their position and
inside knowledge to make fortunes for themselves instead
of for their companies, a point that has nothing to do with
the location of the cash boxes.

A month after Mr. Wilson's pronouncement, Canadians
received a lecture from the president of the Chrysler Corporation of Canada, R. W. Todgham, on the need "to
stop nonsensical wrangling and re-discover the meaning of
common effort for the good of all." (Globe & Mail: 19
Mar. 60). In the light of what follows it may be noted,
en passant and without comment, that Mr. Todgham's
appeal to Canadians to stop squabbling was in order that
they might better meet the threat of Communism.

The efforts of Messrs Wilson and Todgham to reshape
society came only a few months before new light was shed
on their speeches by the announcement that for some
months Chrysler Corporation auditors had been investi-
gating the activities of the president of the corporation, one
William C. Newberg, that Newberg had made a personal
profit of $450,000 through interests he had in two suppliers
who were selling parts exclusively to Chrysler, and that he
had been forced to resign as president.

The news stories referred sympathetically to Chrysler
Corporation's "traumatic summer on a couch of corporate
self-analysis." (Globe & Mail: 6 Sept. 60). But the Canadian Press has reported that the heads of Canadian
Chrysler are in the clear, and no doubt Mr. Todgham will
continue his lectures. In the meantime Mr. Newberg is
suing the corporation for damages, and the wrangling
continues, reaching a high point at the 1961 Chrysler
annual meeting. At it the "czarist tactics" of the current
president were denounced by angry shareholders; he too
resigned, to be demoted to the chairmanship of the Chrysler Corporation of Canada, where he can talk things over
with Mr. Todgham.

Another study in morality was presented before the
Supreme Court of Canada by a distinguished Canadian
criminal lawyer, Mr. J. R. Nicholson, arguing on behalf of

his client, R. E. Sommers, the former B.C. cabinet minister sentenced for taking bribes from lumber and paper companies. The interest in the argument arises from the fact that Nicholson himself had wide experience in business circles as the wartime head of Polymer Corporation Ltd. and as former managing director in Rio de Janeiro of Brazilian Traction, Light & Power Co. Ltd. Headlined "No Crime if Cabinet Takes Bribes," the argument, according to press accounts, went as follows:

> No cabinet minister has ever before been convicted under British law for accepting bribes, nor is it a crime under present Canadian legislation.
>
> Toronto Daily Star: 29 April 59

The judges were not impressed; one was quoted as remarking, "I would not imagine that a minister could accept $25,000 for granting timber licenses without committing an offence of some kind. I would be astonished if that were so."

CHAPTER IV

Structure of Control

THE FINANCIAL GROUPS dominant in Canada maintain their power through a complex institutional structure by means of which other people's money, the savings of the people, is centralized, mobilized and controlled on behalf of the financial groups.

It is through their control of the financial institutions that the financial groups maintain their control of the wealth-producing companies; it is the existence of the producing companies (or rather, the labor of the workers employed by them) that makes possible and profitable the manoeuvres carried out by the financial groups.

At the centre of this financial and industrial corporate structure lie the chartered banks, the members of whose boards of directors make up the "Who's Who" of the dominant financial groups.

Linked to the banks are the trust companies, the life insurance companies, the loan and mortgage companies, the investment trusts, to say nothing of the endowment funds, religious and charitable trusts, all in control of vast assets and contributing to the ability of the financial oligarchy to control the economy of the country. And playing an important part in the structure of control are the investment dealers and corporation lawyers and figures in the political world through whom the financial interests operate.

Canada's federally chartered banks are eight in number. The smallest, not for our purposes a significant factor, is

the Dutch-controlled Mercantile Bank of Canada, with
assets of only $35.7 million (end of 1958).

The other seven range from the Royal Bank of Canada
with total assets of $4,133.6 million down to the Provincial
Bank of Canada with assets of $326.0 million. As we are
dealing here with 1958 figures, the Royal stands first but
by mid-1961 the Canadian Imperial Bank of Commerce
had moved into first place.

Several bank mergers have taken place in the past
decade. In 1955 the Toronto-Dominion Bank was formed
as a result of a merger of the Bank of Toronto and the
Dominion Bank. In 1956 the Imperial Bank took over
the British-controlled Barclays Bank (Canada). In 1961
the Canadian Imperial Bank of Commerce, now Canada's
biggest, was formed from the merger of the Canadian Bank
of Commerce and the Imperial Bank.

The three big banks, Imperial-Commerce, Montreal and
Royal, far surpass the others in assets and in the number
of directorships held by their directors in the largest companies.

After the big three come two important banks, more or
less equal in size and importance: the Toronto-Dominion
Bank and the Bank of Nova Scotia.

Following the five leaders come two smaller banks: the
Banque Canadienne Nationale and the Provincial Bank of
Canada. (Until 1961, the Imperial Bank, now part of the
Imperial-Commerce, was in this size-grouping). It is the
two banks in which French Canadian capital predominates
that are now at the bottom of the list, much smaller in
assets and influence than their rivals.

We do not here attempt a complete analysis of the role
of the banks in the economy; our concern is with the banks
as the centre of the system through which the oligarchy
maintains control.

The banks sit astride a major proportion of the savings
of the people; they can direct how these savings are put to
use; they themselves own billions of dollars worth of securities and through their affiliated trust companies control

additional billions; they maintain connections with banks in other countries, bringing the Canadian financial oligarchy into touch with other groups; they play a vital role in financing trade with other countries.

The members of the boards of directors of the banks (mainly of the three largest banks) plus some of their close allies are then the men through whose hands run the strings that control Canada.

The most important bank directors hold directorships in the big trust companies, in the life insurance companies, in the important investment trusts. They appear on the boards of mining and industrial enterprises, transportation companies, utilities, department store chains; they are members of the boards of governors of universities and they own newspapers and radio stations. They sit on the boards of charitable foundations; they help administer the funds of churches. In short they are found wherever there is capital to control.

They are highly skilled people, even though most of their skills have no social value. Among them are experts in re-financing, in mergers, in take-overs, in the minimizing of tax liability, in the management of other people's money. They include managers and corporation lawyers, and even a few production men, although in general production is not their side of the business.

Their decisions range far beyond the boards on which they sit themselves; their decisions are carried into other companies by their associates.

The holdings of the banks in securities are large and are growing. The three largest banks (at the end of 1958) owned $2,873.7 million in securities of Dominion and provincial governments, and $1,045.0 million of other securities (municipal bonds, corporation bonds and stocks). It is when we relate these holdings to those of the rest of the financial institutions that we get the picture of the way in which control is maintained by minority ownership.

It has been and is argued that the day of finance capital is past, that whereas, say until the 1920's, the great industrial corporations lacked the capital needed to expand and had to get it from the banks on the bankers' terms, in recent years the big monopolies have generated out of profits the larger part of the funds they needed to expand. Hence, by this argument, the domination of the banks is ended, and the corporations now control their own decisions.

The point is not, of course, whether the banks dominate industry or industry the banks; it is that the same group of finance capitalists dominate both. And the role of the banks is not limited to lending money to the corporations, although that is still an important function; as we have said, the bank directors are the key figures in the financial superstructure through which control of the producing corporations is maintained. And the more widely diffused are the shares in the big corporations, the more important becomes the role of maintaining control, and the closer the links between finance and industry.

Again we can use Stelco to illustrate the argument on this point. The official history of the company tells us that the Stelco expansion program of the 1950's cost $250 million. Of this total, some $187 million came out of accumulated profits and reserves, $35 million from two bond issues, $28 million from the sale of new shares by means of rights to subscribe issued to existing shareholders. We are not told how much short-term financing within this program was handled by the banks, but from the information given it is clear that while the dependence of Stelco on outside financing was reduced, in fact the company was unable to finance from its own resources to the extent of $63 million (25% of the amount needed) and the success of the bond issues and the issue of the shares depended very largely on the support of the financial houses and, indirectly but very positively, of the banks. The Stelco board includes seven bank directors, five directors of the Montreal, one of the Royal, and one of the Imperial-Commerce.

What is true of Stelco is true for the leading companies as a group. Now, as in the 1920's, the boards of directors of the industrial giants and of the banks interpenetrate.

In Table III (page 239) we have set out the interlocking interests of the five leading banks and a group of the largest non-financial corporations.

Sixty-four corporations have been tabulated. We have assumed that the largest corporations are the most important and we have used assets (balance sheet figures) as a criterion of size. In the case of foreign-controlled subsidiary companies, we have used the Canadian subsidiary as the basis for interlocks, etc. Nine important companies are included whose assets are not available. Private companies with a limited number of shareholders are not obliged to publish financial statements. These companies may be Canadian-controlled (The T. Eaton Co. Ltd.) or foreign-controlled (General Motors of Canada Ltd.). The accounts of private foreign subsidiaries are consolidated with those of the foreign parent and are not available separately.

While there is no particular magic in a list established on this basis, it is completely clear that a similar degree of interpenetration and interconnection would be shown if the list had been based, say on the top two or three firms in each branch of industry, regardless of relative size, or restricted to the producing companies. (We have included the big merchandising enterprises).

In examining these sixty-four companies, we find that 28 at least are U.S.-controlled, six or seven are U.K.-controlled, and one at least is Belgian-controlled.

Of the remaining 29 or 30, some are Canadian, others are alliances of U.S., U.K., Canadian and other capital in varying proportions. The Canadian Pacific, Brazilian Traction, Algoma Steel, Shawinigan, are prominent examples in this category.

The links between the sixty-four companies and the leading banks are impressive evidence of the power of the oligarchy. (Our calculations are on the basis of interlocks at the end of 1958, before the Imperial-Commerce merger).

Twenty-five Royal Bank directors held 69 directorships in 37 companies on the list; 26 Montreal directors held 59 directorships in 24 of the companies; 25 Commerce directors held 47 directorships in 31 of the companies.

Thus directors of the big three of Canadian banking held 175 directorships in the sixty-four companies; directors of the five largest banks held 227.

We can show roughly the effect of the Imperial-Commerce merger in terms of interlocks by adding the Imperial directorships to those of the Commerce as of the end of 1958. At that time 8 Imperial directors held 15 directorships in 12 of the companies listed. That gives a combined Imperial-Commerce total of 33 directors holding 62 directorships in 34 companies, or the big three holding 190 directorships, and the five leading banks, 242.

Only seven companies among those tabulated had no bank directors on their boards of directors.

Only two of the seven are parent companies: The T. Eaton Company and Distillers Corporation-Seagrams Ltd. In the past the T. Eaton Company has had representation on the Toronto-Dominion board; Distillers Corporation-Seagrams has no direct banking interlocks, but Lazarus Phillips, a director of an important Bronfman holding company, is a director of the Royal Bank and Montreal Trust.

Of the five subsidiaries: Chrysler Corporation of Canada has an "inner" board; the main banking connections of the company are in the United States. Trans Mountain Oil Pipe Line Co. is owned by the leading oil companies and they do have banking connections; Loblaw Companies Ltd. is controlled by George Weston Ltd. linked to the Bank of Nova Scotia; Shell Oil Co. of Canada Ltd. also has an "inner" board but internationally the Shell group has important banking connections; Marathon Corporation is a subsidiary of American Can, a Morgan-controlled company.

Whatever conclusions one draws from the fact of these interconnections, it would be difficult to find support for the idea that the age of finance capital is past.

.   .   .

The trust companies are privately controlled bodies, usually with a comparatively small number of shareholders. In the past they have been controlled by Canadian capitalists with small participation of U.S. capital, but while control has been in Canadian hands, the controlling groups have been Canadians with a close relationship to U.S.-controlled companies.

Even this is changing. The president of the Royal Trust, Mr. Jack Pembroke, reporting to the annual meeting of his company in 1961, warned that Canadian trust companies were coming under the control of outside interests, no doubt referring to U.S. interests. The evidence for his warning was the sharp bidding going on for trust company shares that had forced prices above normal profit expectations.

The trust companies perform a number of functions that make them an important factor in the financial structure. They act as trustees of other people's property, for a fee. They are transfer agents for the big corporations, keeping an up-to-date record of stock ownership. At any given moment they have under administration billions of dollars worth of assets belonging to their clients; these assets include stock holdings in all important Canadian corporations. Thus at the time of Mr. Pembroke's speech, the assets under the administration of his company amounted to $2.5 billion.

The Montreal Trust, the other giant among the trust companies, prefers not to publish the total assets under its administration, someone with a sense of public relations having reached the conclusion that it is preferable not to appear before the world as a billion dollar corporation. It is comparable in size to the Royal Trust, and the total assets under administration must be about the same in amount.

The Bank of Montreal and the Royal Bank of Canada both have a satellite trust company working with them in continuous, intimate, harmonious contact. The Bank of Montreal is tightly linked to the Royal Trust Company (14 directors in common) and the Royal Bank is as closely linked to the Montreal Trust Company (15 directors in common).

The Canadian Imperial Bank of Commerce has nine directors in common with the National Trust Company Ltd. The relationship is not quite as exclusive as in the case of the first two examples; the National Trust board includes six Bank of Nova Scotia directors and three Toronto-Dominion. The Imperial-Commerce has connections with the Canada Trust Company (four directors in common) and with the Toronto General Trusts Corporation (four directors in common), but the Toronto-Dominion Bank predominates with eight directors of that bank on the board of Toronto General Trusts.

The Toronto-Dominion Bank has moved to strengthen and consolidate its position in the trust company field. It has increased its shareholdings in Toronto General Trusts (acting in co-operation with the Wood, Gundy investment house), has taken over the Canada Permanent Mortgage Corporation which controlled the Canada Permanent Trust Company (on whose board the bank already had seven directors) and merged the Toronto General Trusts Corporation and the Canada Permanent Trust Company to form the Canada Permanent Toronto General Trust Company. (Financial Post: 3 June 61). At the time of the purchase by the bank of more Toronto General Trusts shares, the president of the bank was quoted (Globe & Mail: 3 Jan. 61) to the effect that the interest of the bank itself in Toronto General Trusts will still be less than 50%, so as not to violate a provision of the Bank Act that forbids a chartered bank from engaging in another type of business.

In addition to the minority position it holds in the National Trust, the Bank of Nova Scotia is dominant in the

Eastern Trust Company (three directors in common) and, in co-operation with the investment dealers Burns Brothers & Denton Ltd., has arranged to purchase control of the Chartered Trust Company. No doubt for the same reason as given by the president of the Toronto-Dominion, the interest of the Bank of Nova Scotia was said to be less than 50%.

The Banque Canadienne Nationale is linked to the General Trust of Canada (five directors in common) and the Provincial Bank to the Administration & Trust Company (five directors in common).

The large amounts of common stock among the securities held under administration by the trust companies have of course voting rights, and these rights are exercised by the trust companies. Let us suppose that the Royal Trust, so closely linked to the Bank of Montreal and hence to the Canadian Pacific Railway, holds 100,000 CPR shares among the assets it is administering for a number of clients. Unless special and unusual instructions have been given by the clients, these shares are voted as a matter of form by the Royal Trust in support of the existing management of the CPR.

In this way, the control by the trust companies, within the terms of their trust, of billions of dollars of assets makes them an important force in the structure of control.

Table IV at page 244 lists the largest trust companies, those with assets of $100 million and up, and shows the ties between the trust companies and the banks as at the end of 1958.

Directors of the Royal Bank held 21 directorships in six leading trust companies (15 of them in the Montreal Trust); directors of the Montreal held 20 directorships in six trust companies (14 of them in the Royal Trust); directors of the Commerce held 25 directorships in eight trust companies (nine of them in the National Trust). If we add to the Commerce total the directorships held at that date by the Imperial Bank, the combined Imperial-Commerce

total becomes 33 directorships in eight trust companies
(nine in the National Trust).

Equally closely linked to the banks are the big life insurance companies, although here the links are often with
several banks, rather than predominantly with one bank as
in the case of the largest trust companies.

The life insurance companies receive in premiums billions of dollars to be invested on the decision of their directors (as limited by law) in stocks and bonds and mortgages.
The savings of the people are centralized and channelled
into the corporate investments the directors desire to promote; control of these vast sums of money makes control
of the life insurance companies extremely important. They
hold large amounts of federal and provincial government
bonds; their stock holdings give them influence on the
policy of the corporations.

Of the 80 life insurance companies doing business in
Canada in 1958, 32 were said to be Canadian, 14 British,
and 34 were shown as foreign, mainly from the United
States.

Metropolitan Life, largest in the world, Rockefeller-controlled, and the Prudential Insurance Company of America (a Morgan company) are the two largest U.S. companies doing business in Canada; Standard Life Assurance
Company is the largest of the British companies. The largest Canadian company is the Sun Life Assurance Company of Canada, almost three times as large in terms of assets as its nearest Canadian rival, the Manufacturers Life
Insurance Company.

The Bank of Montreal and the Royal Bank share influence in the Sun Life; the president of the Sun Life and
three other directors of the company are directors of the
Bank of Montreal, matched by four others who are directors of the Royal Bank. There is no Imperial-Commerce
participation.

The Manufacturers Life is associated with the Toronto-
Dominion Bank; in 1958 nearly half the outstanding shares

in the company were said to be owned by the M. Ross Gooderham estate.

Bank of Montreal forces have a commanding position on the boards of the Mutual Life Assurance Co. of Canada (four directors in common) and the Standard Life Assurance Company (two directors in common with the parent company, three with the Canadian subsidiary).

The Metropolitan Life is linked to the Royal Bank (two directors in common) and to the Montreal Trust Company. The Royal Bank has three directors in common with the North American Life Assurance Company, and two with the Canada Life Assurance Company although influence on the Canada Life board is shared with the Imperial-Commerce (four directors in common) and the Nova Scotia (five directors in common).

As an illustration of the way the structure of control functions, the Canada Life owned 60,000 shares in the National Trust (a $3 million holding), 37,500 shares in the Bank of Nova Scotia, and 45,110 in the Commerce.

If we take the fifteen largest life insurance companies doing business in Canada, those with assets of $100 million and up, we find (Table V, page 245) that directors of eight banks held between them 86 directorships on the boards of those life insurance companies.

Directors of the Royal held 14 seats on seven boards; Montreal directors held 16 seats on seven boards; Commerce directors held 16 seats on nine boards, and so on. If we combine the Commerce and Imperial directorships as of 1958, then the Imperial-Commerce held 27 seats on the boards of eleven companies.

The holdings of the Sun Life and the interlocks of the members of its board with other companies illustrate the role of the life insurance companies in maintaining control.

The invested assets of the Sun Life at the end of 1959 amounted to almost $2.25 billion, divided as follows:

In bonds, government and municipal	59.0%
In mortgages	24.8
In policy loans	4.1
In preferred stocks	1.3
In common stocks	7.0
In real estate, etc.	3.8
	100.0%

The total Sun Life holding in stocks, common and pre-ferred, was $184.6 million, up $21 million over 1958, the larger part, as the tabulation shows, in common stocks.

Some of the more important Sun Life holdings were as follows:

No. of shares	Company	Market value shares held, end 1959	
41,782	Bank of Montreal	$2.3	million
28,166	Royal Bank of Canada	2.3	”
49,975	Steel Co. of Canada Ltd.	4.3	”
117,018	Alminium Ltd.	3.8	”
94,719	Imperial Oil Ltd.	3.5	”
39,381	Bell Telephone Co. of Canada	1.7	”
52,180	Shawinigan Water & Power Co.	1.5	”
50,000	Trans-Canada Pipe Lines Ltd.	1.3	”
8,700	International Nickel Co. of Canada Ltd.	0.9	”
91,876	Dominion Textile Co. Ltd.	0.9	”

Several points are to be noted. The banks influence the Sun Life and the Sun Life reciprocates by holding large blocks of shares in the two banks allied to it. The Sun Life also held a small block of Commerce shares.

These large Sun Life holdings in the companies listed do not by any means constitute control of the companies invested in, but they are a powerful aid to the control exer-cised by groups allied to the Sun Life; they are another illustration of the prevailing community of class interest.

Thus the president of the Steel Company of Canada who is a director of the Bank of Montreal, is a director of the Sun Life, and the Sun Life owns close to 50,000 shares in the Steel Company of Canada.

Two directors of Aluminium Ltd., one being its senior vice-president, are directors of the Bank of Montreal; the Bank of Montreal has four directors on the board of the Sun Life, and the Sun Life owns 117,000 shares of Aluminium Ltd.

J. R. White, president of Imperial Oil Ltd., is a director of the Royal Bank; the Royal has four directors on the Sun Life board, and the Sun Life owns 95,000 shares in Imperial Oil.

Three directors of the Bell Telephone Company of Canada are directors of the Sun Life; the Sun Life owns almost 40,000 shares of Bell Telephone.

J. A. Fuller, president of Shawinigan Water & Power Co., is a director of the Royal Bank and of the Sun Life; the Sun Life owns 52,000 shares of Shawinigan.

A former general manager of the Royal Bank is a director of Trans-Canada Pipe Lines Ltd.; the Sun Life owns 50,000 shares in Trans-Canada.

The Bank of Montreal has four directors in common with International Nickel Company of Canada Ltd., one of whom is also a director of the Sun Life; the Sun Life owns close to a million dollar interest in International Nickel.

G. Blair Gordon, president of Dominion Textile Co. Ltd., is a director of the Bank of Montreal; the Sun Life owns 90,000 shares in Dominion Textile.

An important fact emerges from this analysis. We can see how Canadian savings are used by the tycoons to support and extend the control of their U.S. allies over companies operating in Canada.

The Sun Life holdings (product of Canadian savings) in Aluminium Ltd., Imperial Oil, Bell Telephone, Trans-Canada Pipe Lines, International Nickel, all support the control of the existing U.S.-dominated managements and so enable U.S. financial groups to expand their influence over wider sectors of the economy with the support of Canadian capital.

In recent years control of several Canadian life insurance companies passed to U.S. interests. In 1957, the Lin-

coln National Life Insurance Company of Fort Wayne, In-
diana, took over the Dominion Life Assurance Company;
in 1960, the Glens Falls Insurance Company of New York
took over the National Life Assurance Company of Canada, and Aetna Life Insurance Company of Hartford took
over the Excelsior Life Insurance Company.

Loan and mortgage companies, general insurance companies, play a role in the apparatus of control similar to
that of the life insurance companies, although their stock
holdings are smaller. In the field of general insurance the
advance of outside interests has been rapid. No less than
nine Canadian general insurance companies were taken
over by foreign (U.S. and U.K.) companies in the first nine
months of 1961.

.   .   .

The corporations known as investment trusts are in
theory a means by which small investors can invest their
savings at a minimum of risk. The would-be investor with
a little money buys shares in an investment trust; the trust
uses the money of its shareholders to buy shares in a number of corporations, thus spreading the risk of any decline
in the stock market. The income of the investment trust is
derived from dividends on the shares it holds; after payment of expenses, etc., the balance is distributed in dividends to its own shareholders.

Investment trusts can take many organizational forms
but we are concerned here with the way in which the stock-
holdings of the trusts help the oligarchy to maintain control of the corporate structure.

In theory the investment trust has nothing to do with
control of the enterprises in which it invests its money.
Thus the head of Investors Group Canadian Fund Ltd.,
one of the leading investment trusts (U.S.-controlled) operating in Canada is quoted as saying that "the fund will
not invest in companies in order to exercise control."

We are told that eight U.S.-controlled Canadian investment
companies are convinced that they have at least a

"partial answer to fears of U.S. domination of the Canadian economy." (New York Times: 16 Feb. 58). Their answer lies in stepping up the tempo of portfolio investment through investment trusts "since the portfolio investor is interested primarily in assets and returns, and not in exercising control."

Clearly not very much would be changed if all U.S. investment in Canada was divided into smaller packets and re-labelled as "portfolio investment". And whereas the individual investor in an investment trust doesn't have any interest in control, the people operating the investment trust very definitely do.

The investment trusts, as they get bigger and as their stock holdings increase, play an increasingly important role in the corporate structure, and, as might be expected, the oligarchy are in tight control of the investment trusts.

We find the Boston-controlled investment trusts managed by Maxwell Meighen buying up shares of Argus Corporation to the point where Maxwell Meighen has become a director of Argus, sharing in the control of the tightly oganized group of Argus companies.

The theoretical difference between the investment trust and the holding company is supposed to lie in the fact that the holding company is specifically formed for the purpose of maintaining control over the companies in which it owns stock. Canadian examples are Argus Corporation, Power Corporation of Canada, and McIntyre Porcupine Mines Ltd., the latter originally a gold-mining company, now turning itself into a holding company as it uses its gold profits to buy large or controlling interests in other companies.

The distinction between the investment trust and the holding company is one of degree; the influence of the investment trust is less direct than that of the holding company but it is also vital to the question of control.

The investment trusts operating in Canada are often incorporated in the United States: they may own shares in companies operating in Canada or anywhere else. In many

cases the U.S. parents of Canadian-incorporated investment trusts also own large blocks of shares in Canadian
companies. And we see Canadian-incorporated investment
trusts that have substantial holdings in West German banks
and corporations.

In some cases the same financial group operates through
a whole series of investment trusts. One trust may control
the others associated with it, or the connection may simply
be in the fact that the same individuals control all the
trusts.

We shall consider mainly three of the most important
groups of investment trusts operating in Canada, all three
groups under U.S. control. Incidentally, it should be borne
in mind when a given company gives information on the
number of its Canadian shareholders and the number of its
shares held in Canada, that these figures include Canadian-incorporated but U.S.-controlled investment trusts
and their holdings, Canadian in form, U.S. in fact.

The three leading groups of investment trusts operating
in Canada are: 1) the Investors group and its affiliates
(Canadian Imperial Bank of Commerce ties), 2) the Massachusetts-Meighen group and its affiliates (Royal Bank
ties), and 3) the Calvin Bullock group (Bank of Montreal
ties).

All three groups are U.S.-controlled, although the Investors Group does not admit it, all three are connected with
several financial groups and own large holdings in companies in which their directors or the allies of their directors are interested. All three as we have seen have been
able to obtain the participation of persons prominent in
government and official circles. Three ex-prime ministers
of Canada have been associated with the groups: Mr. St.
Laurent with the first, and in the past Arthur Meighen and
Sir Robert Borden with the second and third respectively.

The Investors group companies are, in terms of their
Canadian assets, one of the most important investment
trust set-ups and the one in which control is most difficult
to unravel. The group is centred on Investors Diversified

Services Inc. of Minneapolis. The assets of this company
at the end of 1958 were shown as $180.3 million but it con-
trolled Investors Mutual Inc. with assets of $1,248.7 mil-
lion, and a group of associated companies, including four
Canadian investment trusts: Investors Syndicate of Canada Ltd. (assets $130.8 million) which manages Investors
Mutual of Canada Ltd. (assets $163.7 million) and Inves-
tors Growth Fund of Canada Ltd. (assets $8.2 million).
Also associated is Investors Group Canadian Fund (assets
$168.9 million).

The control of this complicated corporate set-up and its
huge assets has been the subject of struggle and litigation.
Investors Diversified Services (IDS) was formerly controlled by the late R. R. Young, a Cleveland financier, through
the Alleghany Corporation, a holding company that also
controlled the New York Central Railroad. The Murchison
oil interests of Texas (of Trans-Canada Pipe Line fame)
have been engaged in a much-publicized battle for control
of Alleghany with Alan Kirby, one of the heirs to the Wool-
worth millions. The Murchison brothers were ousted from
the Alleghany board in 1960 (Globe & Mail: 21 Sept. 60);
they bought, fought and manoeuvred themselves back into
at least temporary control of Alleghany in 1961.

Investors Syndicate of Canada Ltd. (ISC) claims not to
be controlled by IDS and Alleghany; its relation with IDS
is "simply one of close friendship" an ISC spokesman is
quoted as saying. (Financial Post: 20 May 61).

The fact is that in October, 1956, IDS, then in control
of ISC, distributed its controlling shares in ISC to IDS
shareholders as a stock dividend. As a result of this "spin-
off", the group that controlled IDS also controlled ISC,
even though technically the companies themselves were not
connected.

How this situation has been affected by subsequent dealings in ISC shares is unknown, but IDS and ISC remain
closely connected, with key directors in common. A prominent member of Investors group boards is R. W. Purcell,

described as financial adviser to the Rockefeller brothers, and it is more than likely that Rockefeller interests hold the balance of power.

Investors Syndicate, Investors Mutual, and Investors Growth Fund each have one Royal Bank and three Imperial-Commerce directors on their boards; Investors Mutual and Investors Growth each have in addition one Toronto-Dominion director who is also a director of the fourth trust, Investors Group Canadian Fund, and is the only bank director on that board.

Mr. St. Laurent is a member of the board of Investors Syndicate, the senior company in the group, but not of the others. W. J. Bennett, one-time private secretary to C. D. Howe, sits on the Investors Syndicate board. Bennett had formerly been a director of Investors Mutual. He had to resign from that board early in 1957 because of criticism in the House of Commons that it was improper for Bennett, then a civil servant and head of Eldorado Mining, to be also on the board of a company investing in uranium shares. Bennett is now back in a more senior position.

S. M. Wedd, one of the three Imperial-Commerce directors on the boards of this group, is also a director of McIntyre Porcupine which has heavy investments of its own.

Both the U.S. and the Canadian sides of this group of investment trusts own important blocks of shares in Canadian banks and corporations as well as in the U.S. parents of subsidiaries operating in Canada.

In Table VI at page 247, we show a sample of the key holdings of Investors Mutual of Canada Ltd. and Investors Group Canadian Fund. The combined holdings of the two funds include an investment in stocks of the three largest banks amounting to more than $17 million; a holding in shares of Canadian steel companies of over $14 million; a holding in a group of mining and metal companies of $16 million; in three big oil companies of $10 million; and last but not least interesting a holding in companies controlled by the Taylor-Argus group of $20 million. This compares with the Argus holding in the same companies valued at $98.8 million.

The Investors Group holdings in the Argus companies are a substantial re-inforcement to the controlling position of the Argus group. While there are no direct interlocks between the Argus board and the Investors Group boards, there are points of contact: three Imperial-Commerce directors sit on the Investors Mutual board and seven on the board of Argus, an example of the co-ordinating role possible to bank directors. Investors Group Canadian Fund has a Toronto-Dominion director on its board, so does Argus.

The Massachusetts-Meighen group of investment trusts, so-called for our convenience since the control is Massachusetts and not Meighen, is based on the Boston financiers and insurance companies that control the huge Massachusetts Investors Trust (assets $1.4 billion, end '58) with which are associated a number of smaller investment trusts including the Boston Fund Inc., Century Shares Trust, and Massachusetts Growth Stock Fund Inc.

The Massachusetts Investors Trust is in business in a big way, as the size of a few of its shareholdings indicates:

423,000 shares Aluminium Ltd. valued at $14 million,
116,800 shares International Nickel valued at $10.3 million,
227,570 shares International Paper valued at $26.8 million.

The trust also holds a $45 million interest in Standard Oil of New Jersey, parent of Imperial Oil Ltd.

The Canadian side of the operation starts with Canada General Fund (assets $91.9 million) of which Arthur Meighen had been chairman and his son, Maxwell Meighen, vice-president. Of the eighteen directors, nine were residents of the United States who were directors of the U.S. parent and associated companies.

The board is a high level one and included the president of Shawinigan Water & Power (J. A. Fuller), the president of Consolidated Paper (G. M. Hobart), the senior vice-

president of Aluminium Ltd. (R. E. Powell) and a retired
vice-president of Imperial Oil (O. B. Hopkins).

The holdings of the trust reflected these interests. It
held, among other securities, 109,000 shares in Shawinigan,
40,000 Consolidated Paper, 15,000 Aluminium Ltd., and
51,000 shares in Imperial Oil.

The Massachusetts group are also linked to Canadian
General Investments Ltd. (assets $31.4 million) and Third
Canadian General Investment Fund (assets $4.3 million).

The Canadian General and Third Canadian owned 32,-
300 Argus shares at the end of 1958; this holding was increased to 84,000 shares during 1959 and to 161,000 shares
by the end of 1960, worth some $5.8 million, and as a re-
sult Maxwell Meighen won promotion to the Argus board
and later to the Royal Bank.

The third major investment trust group in terms of its
operations in Canada, although it does not have behind it
the same kind of giant U.S. parent as do the first two, is
that based on the New York investment house of Calvin
Bullock.

The largest trust in the group appears to be Dividend
Shares Inc. with assets of $250.6 million. Frank Pace Jr. of
General Dynamics, parent of Canadair, Ltd., is one of its
directors.

The Canadian members of the family are Canadian
Fund Inc. with assets of $45.6 million, and Canadian In-
vestment Fund Ltd. with assets of $87.3 million, but own-
ing securities with a market value of $120.2 million.

The ten directors of Canadian Fund Inc. all appear on
the board of Canadian Investment Fund (the investment
trusts have problems in finding differing yet related names
for the various branches of their undertakings), plus the
president of the Canadian Pacific Railway, N. R. Crump.

Graham Towers, a Royal Bank director, is chairman of
the two boards, Canadian Fund and Canadian Investment
Fund, and a powerful group of tycoons is associated with
him, mostly connected with groups dominant in the Bank

of Montreal. (The funds have four directors in common
with the Montreal and one more with the Royal Trust).

Two other members of both boards, not directly connected with the Bank of Montreal, are Henry Borden, president of Brazilian Traction, and a director of the Canadian
Imperial Bank of Commerce, and Philippe Brais, corporation lawyer and director of the Banque Canadienne Nationale, Montreal Trust, Sun Life, and CPR.

These links are as usual reflected in the shareholdings of
the investment trusts. The Calvin Bullock trusts hold 27,-
000 shares of the Bank of Montreal and 32,000 of the
Royal Bank. They have important holdings in companies
within the Bank of Montreal orbit: 109,000 shares CPR,
67,000 Cominco, 64,500 Inco, etc. They have no holdings
in Argus-controlled companies although they held 70,000
shares in Price Brothers, a company close to the Bank of
Montreal in which the Taylor forces have a non-controlling interest. They have 127,000 shares in Shawinigan.

Some of the principal corporate shareholders of International Nickel Co. of Canada Ltd. are shown in Table VII,
page 250.

The listing even though incomplete gives a graphic picture of the extent to which a handful of large investment
trust shareholders are in a position to influence the policies
of the group in control. To maintain a sense of proportion
it should be said that, at the date referred to, Inco had
some 14,500,000 shares outstanding; our table shows the
ownership of 800,000 shares only. We do not show the
main centre of control, the Morgan-Rockefeller holdings
and those of their U.K. allies; we are illustrating the important supporting role of the investment trusts. The figures given are for the end of 1958; the trusts are buying and
selling but it is unlikely that the over-all picture has
changed appreciably since then.

Other investment trusts operate in Canada. The Scudder Fund of Canada Ltd. (assets $61.6 million) is an im-
portant one; there is a group of smaller trusts associated
with the Montreal investment house of Nesbitt, Thomson

and the Power Corporation interests; another group associated with the Wood, Gundy interests; the Mutual Accumulating group of British Columbia is growing; W. A. Arbuckle, a director of the Bank of Montreal and Standard Life, is a director of thirteen or fourteen companies classifiable as investment trusts.

A less important role is played by the capital forming part of endowment funds or invested in foundations of one kind or another.

The privately owned universities have endowment funds administered by the boards of governors of the universities and these boards always include figures prominent in the financial oligarchy.

McGill University had, at the end of 1958, endowments amounting to $76.5 million. Of this total, 37%, or some $28 million, was invested in common stocks. Queens University funds amounted to $17.8 million, of which 23.7%, or some $4 million, was invested in common stocks.

Here again stock holdings in funds controlled by tycoons help buttress the control of the tycoons over the economy.

.   .   .

The big investment houses, the stock exchange firms who promote and carry through mergers, underwrite issues of new securities and market them to the public, who execute the stock market deals involved in shifts of control, are a group who play a profitable and important role in the inner circles of the oligarchy.

By tradition it is rare for the heads of these firms to become bank directors, but their links to the tycoons are close. Many tycoons have begun in this field and then moved into direct control of industry.

E. P. Taylor was helped along the road to fortune by the connections he established while working with the investment firm of McLeod, Young & Weir.

Jules R. Timmins, of Hollinger Consolidated Gold Mines Ltd., Noranda Mines Ltd., Iron Ore Company of Canada, etc., is head of J. R. Timmins & Co., Montreal investment dealers.

C. L. Gundy and other partners of Wood, Gundy & Co. and the partners of Nesbitt, Thomson of Montreal, the latter controlling Power Corporation, hold a long list of important directorships.

The partners in A. E. Ames & Co. hold directorships in Falconbridge Nickel Mines Ltd., in Russell Industries Ltd. and in Dominion Foundries & Steel Co.

With most of these firms it is easier to learn something of their past activities than of their present-day operations.

The Price Spreads Report of 1937 threw some light on the profits and methods of the Thirties; there is little reason to suppose that any essential change has taken place.

The Report referred to the promoters' profits in the 1928 re-organization of British Columbia Power Corporation, in which the Power Corporation has a substantial interest. The promoting group paid $57 million for the securities of the predecessor company and then sold securities of the new re-organized company to the public to the amount of $60 million. But the gross cash profit of $3 million was not the main point. The promoters "also" ended up owning the Class B shares in the company, giving them control.

The Wood, Gundy house of Toronto, now headed by C. L. Gundy, son of the founder, participates in a number of companies. Gundy and his associates hold directorships in Dominion Steel & Coal, A. V. Roe Canada Ltd., Massey-Ferguson Ltd., Dominion Tar & Chemical Co. Ltd., Canada Cement Co. Ltd., Abitibi Power & Paper Co. Ltd., Simpsons Ltd., Simpsons-Sears Ltd., British Columbia Power Corp. Ltd., MacMillan, Bloedel & Powell River, Home Oil Co., etc., etc.

The Price Spreads Report sharply criticized Wood, Gundy on the 1925-29 re-organizations of Simpsons. The commission found that close to $3 million in "costs" written in to the corporate structure went to Wood, Gundy and 100,000 Class B shares, that this "remuneration" was "seriously out of proportion . . . to the social significance of their action, which indeed might be argued had little merit whatever."

In spite of these strictures, C. L. Gundy and his partner, W. P. Scott, are today both directors of Simpsons Ltd., and Gundy of Simpsons-Sears Ltd.

Both Wood, Gundy and Nesbitt, Thomson took an active part in the struggle for control of Alberta natural gas. Both were members of the "western group" that eventually formed part of Trans-Canada Pipe Lines Ltd. In 1957 each of the two firms owned, directly or indirectly, 84,919 shares in Trans-Canada, for which they had paid $8 a share. By 1958, date of the Borden report, Power Corporation interests (Nesbitt, Thomson) held 195,938 shares in Trans-Canada and Wood, Gundy 57,031. The report made no estimate of their profits.

Dominion Securities Corporation Ltd. has just celebrated 60 years of activity. This company was formed in 1901 by a group of Toronto financiers linked to the Canadian Bank of Commerce, including E. R. Wood, Sir William Mackenzie, and Sir Joseph Flavelle. Today, partners in the firm hold directorships that include Dominion Foundries & Steel Co., Maple Leaf Milling Co. Ltd., Canada Bread Co. Ltd., Salada-Shirriff-Horsey Ltd., etc. The relations of Dominion Securities to the 1928 reorganization of Burns & Co. Ltd. were investigated by the Price Spreads Commission. The Report denounced the activities of Dominion Securities as a "very flagrant case," "nearly fraudulent," because of the way in which depreciation reserves had been juggled and corporate assets re-appraised in order to make a good balance sheet.

In that re-organization, Dominion Securities, in addition to purchasing the bonds and preferred stock of the new company they were promoting at 92.80 and then selling the bonds to the public at 99.50 and the preferred at par, ended up with all the common stock of the new company.

The inability of the new company to bear the burdens imposed on it by the greed of the promoters forced another re-organization in 1934, when some of the water was pumped out.

The big law firms, "law factories," with their highly trained specialists in corporation law, act as confidential advisers to the tycoons, to the main financial groups and to the banks. Leading corporation lawyers like J. S. D. Tory, W. H. Howard, G. P. Campbell, Philippe Brais, etc., are prominent members of many boards of directors. Their fund of experience on what is legally possible, their technical understanding of how to manoeuvre through and around the Companies Act and Combines Investigation Act, on how to minimize tax liability and extract capital gains, are of great value to the financial groups. Corporation lawyers often do the negotiating behind the scenes with the politicians on behalf of the monopolies.

Corporation lawyers hold imposing lists of directorships but in most cases they do so as representatives or nominees of a given financial group and carry out the instructions of that group, although from time to time leading corporation lawyers become part of the inner groupings and active big shots in their own right.

Certain legal firms have been linked for years to a particular bank or group. In some cases members of law firms hold directorships in more than one bank: thus in 1958 one partner in the law firm of McCarthy & McCarthy of Toronto was a director of the Toronto-Dominion Bank and another of the Bank of Nova Scotia; J. A. MacAulay of Winnipeg was a director of the Bank of Montreal and one of his partners was a director of the Imperial Bank.

The Blake & Cassels law firm of Toronto has been for years closely related to the Canadian Bank of Commerce. Z. A. Lash, a one-time head of the firm, was a close associate of Mackenzie and Mann, the Canadian Northern Railway promoters and tycoons. For many years the Blake firm was prominent on the boards of Brazilian Traction, Mexico Tramways, Mexican Light & Power, Barcelona Traction, etc.

Allan Graydon, present senior partner in the firm, is a director of the Canadian Imperial Bank of Commerce, of

Abitibi, Stelco and Russell Industries Ltd. He is also, as members of that firm have been for fifty years, a director of Mexlight although the company is now under the control of the Mexican government, and of Barcelona Traction. Another partner in his firm, D. G. Guest, is a director of Magnum Fund Ltd., the investment trust in which the proceeds of the sale of Mexico Tramways to Mexican interests have been invested. Another partner in the Blake firm is a director of National Steel Car and of the Southam Co. Ltd., another of American Can Company of Canada and of Canadian Shell Ltd.

The board of directors of the Royal Bank of Canada is especially rich in corporation lawyers: W. H. Howard, a vice-president of the bank and head of the Howard, Cate law firm of Montreal; J. S. D. Tory of Toronto, with an imposing list of Canadian, British and U.S. clients but a power in his own right and a point of contact for a number of powerful forces — Argus, McIntyre Porcupine, Abitibi, Simpsons-Sears Ltd., etc.; J. E. L. Duquet of Montreal, a director of Canadair, Asbestos Corporation, etc.; Lazarus Phillips of Montreal, a director of Webb & Knapp (Canada) Ltd.; he and one of his partners are directors of Cemp Investments Ltd., an important Bronfman holding company; H. R. Milner of Edmonton, with wide oil interests; F. M. Covert of Halifax holding a number of directorships in Maritime province firms.

Other leading lawyers are on the boards of other banks. Senator G. P. Campbell of Toronto is a vice-president of the Canadian Imperial Bank of Commerce. He has important connections with U.S. interests as a director of Canadair Ltd., Stone & Webster Canada Ltd., and United Funds Canada Ltd., the latter a duPont investment trust. A partner in his firm is a director of de Havilland Aircraft, now controlled by the Hawker Siddeley group who also control A. V. Roe Canada Ltd.; another partner is a director of Mannesmann Tube, owned by the West German interests associated in Algoma Steel; a fourth member of the Campbell firm is also a director of United Funds Canada.

J. Y. Murdoch, mining magnate and a vice-president of the Bank of Nova Scotia, started his career as a corporation lawyer and still heads a large Toronto law firm. A partner is a co-director with Murdoch in two of the Hollinger companies associated with the Iron Ore Company of Canada; another is a director of Patino of Canada, Canadian outlet for the funds of Patino, the Bolivian millionaire and tin magnate.

Philippe Brais of Montreal is a director of the Banque Canadienne Nationale; we have already noted some of his directorships.

Perhaps the most significant example of the role of the large law firms over a period of years is provided by the Howard firm of Montreal.

Over the past thirty years, this firm has provided three vice-presidents to the Royal Bank of Canada to which it is counsel, at least three Quebec judges, one of them a Chief Justice, a senator, an ambassador, a member of parliament, a president for Dominion Steel & Coal, etc., etc.

The late Senator A. J. Brown, former head of the firm, was legal adviser to Sir Herbert Holt, in his time Canada's most famous tycoon. For many years Holt was president of the Royal Bank; some of the old Holt connections can be seen in the directorships held today by members of the Howard firm.

W. H. Howard, as well as being a vice-president of the Royal Bank, is chairman of the Montreal Trust. The law firm of which he is the head now comprises over thirty lawyers. (A 1960 accession to their ranks was a former federal assistant deputy minister of justice.)

Interlocks between several financial groups operate or are strengthened in operation through the directorships held by Howard and other members of the firm. Thus Howard and F. C. Cope, another member of the partnership, are both directors of Sogemines, the Belgian-controlled holding company. Howard is a director of

Algoma Steel, Cope of Dosco. The Howard firm has had long connections with Dosco; the late L. A. Forsythe, former Dosco president, was a member of the law firm. Other members hold directorships in Canadian International Paper (a former member of the firm is general counsel and a vice-president of CIP), Gatineau Power, Northern Electric, Gutta Percha, Dominion Bridge, etc., etc.

Howard is as well a director of several investment trusts, of five pulp and paper companies, of Canada Cement, Canada Steamships, etc. In many cases he appears to be representing British and European capital seeking profitable outlets in Canada.

Thus the members of a single law firm, associated with one of the largest banks, include directors of two of the three largest steel companies, of six important pulp and paper companies, a large power company, and have links to U.S. interests as well as to U.K. interests and the Belgian Sogemines group.

.   .   .

The picture here sketched is one of relationships between financial groups and their adherents and agents by means of which the Canadian tycoons and the U.S. financial interests to which they have subordinated themselves maintain control over the country's economy. This or that group, or this or that individual may gain or lose influence, but the oligarchy as a whole maintains itself in power.

The discussion of the way in which large blocks of stock can be mobilized by the tycoons and their agents in support of their position through control of the financial structure is a demonstration of the unreality and indeed impossibility of corporate democracy, whether company annual meetings are attended by 100 or 1,000 shareholders.

It is probably also a sufficient answer to the propaganda put out a few years ago by the Canadian Chamber of Commerce and Du Pont of Canada.

The Chamber advanced the old chestnut that "nearly every adult in Canada is an investor" adding, prudently but ambiguously, "either directly or indirectly." This was all explained, "in humorous light-hearted vein," or so we are told, in a 14-minute animated technicolor film entitled "The Story of Creative Capital". (The Telegram: 1 June 57).

Apparently the project had limited success; two years later even the Financial Editor of The Telegram was admitting:

> People's Capitalism is a concept with an aura of never-never land about it. In its final, beautiful perfection it would have the same people, and all the people at that, owning, working for, and being the masterful customers of, all economic activity.
>
> The Telegram: 17 June 59

As the Financial Editor well understands, the structure of control is not designed to function for that purpose, and no matter what the oligarchy might like us to believe, they are in tight control.

CHAPTER V

A Tangled Web

THE IMPORTANCE OF THE STRUCTURE of control through the financial institutions that we have been describing lies in what is controlled—the producing companies, source of the country's wealth.

In this chapter we shall examine the way in which rival groups of producing companies are related through the banks and see how the producing companies in the key branches of industry have direct or indirect relationships with companies controlled by rival groups and are able to develop a common approach on major problems.

The boards of the banks, particularly of the three biggest banks, represent nearly always a coming together of several related financial groups, and at the same time an important group may and often does operate through more than one bank.

The Royal Bank of Canada is a meeting place for U.S., Canadian, British and European capital.

The Rockefeller interests, as we have indicated, have a strong and close connection with the Royal through Metropolitan Life and Imperial Oil. In recent years the president of the bank has been a director of Metropolitan Life, and the senior vice-president of Metropolitan Life has been a director of the bank. The only banking connections maintained by Imperial Oil are with the Royal Bank, and the Imperial president has a seat on the bank board.

The Mellon interests are also connected with the Royal, as they are with the Montreal and Nova Scotia. W. E. Phillips, a Royal director and one the leading lights in Argus

Corporation, is chairman of Canadian Pittsburgh Industries and a director of Pittsburgh Plate Glass, both Mellon companies.

We have seen something of the interests of W. H. Howard, a Royal Bank vice-president, and his links to Belgian and British groups, particularly with the Rothermere newspaper group of Britain; the ties of the Royal Bank with Abitibi Power & Paper, Shawinigan Water & Power, Canada Cement, also reflect Canadian, U.S. and U.K. interests, including the Beaverbrook interests.

Traditionally the members of the board of directors of the Bank of Montreal have regarded themselves and been regarded as the most important centre of financial and industrial power in Canada. It is however a centre of power in which U.S., Canadian and U.K. interests interpenetrate.

The Morgan interests have a close relationship with the Bank of Montreal. H. S. Wingate, a director of J. P. Morgan & Co., is a director of the bank as well as of the CPR and has been president of International Nickel. Canadian General Electric, closely linked to the bank and interlocked with the Steel Company of Canada, is Morgan-controlled.

The Morgan-Rockefeller alliances that control Bell Telephone and International Nickel operate through the Bank of Montreal but not exclusively through that bank; in the case of the Bell Telephone the alliance also operates through the Royal Bank, in the case of International Nickel through the Toronto-Dominion as well as the Montreal.

The Mellon interests that control Aluminium Ltd. and the Aluminum Company of Canada and British American Oil also operate through the Bank of Montreal.

The connections of the Montreal with British capital are probably more important than those of any other Canadian bank, going back to the building of the CPR in the 1880's. The bank has three directors in common with Canadian Industries Ltd., owned by Imperial Chemical Industries Ltd. of Britain, thus establishing a double relationship with the British capitalists who have an interest in Inco. The bank is also linked to the Bowater pulp and paper

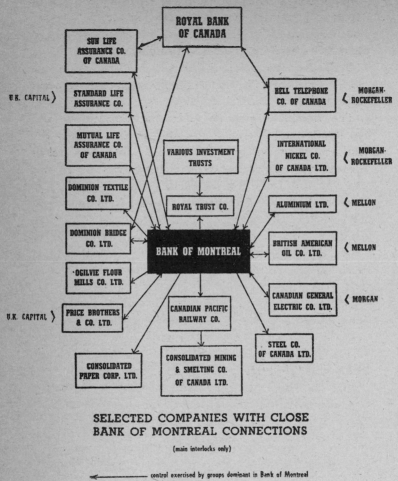

**SELECTED COMPANIES WITH CLOSE
BANK OF MONTREAL CONNECTIONS**

(main interlocks only)

← ─────── control exercised by groups dominant in Bank of Montreal
← ─────→ alliance with other interests

interests of Britain; in 1959 Bowater was the largest manu-
facturer of pulp and paper products in Europe and the
third largest manufacturer of newsprint on the North
American continent. Bowater interests extend to Australia,
New Zealand and South Africa as well as to Britain,
Europe, Canada and the United States.

Another link between British capital and the Bank of Montreal is through the British Newfoundland Corporation in which Rothschild and Rio Tinto capital is associated with other British interests, including Bowater.

Much the same picture is disclosed when we look at the outside (mainly U.S.) influences operating in the other major banks.

The Imperial-Commerce (then the Commerce) and the Royal worked together in the deals that brought the Hawker Siddeley group of Britain into a shared control of Algoma Steel and control of Dominion Steel & Coal Company. Sir Roy Dobson of the Hawker Siddeley group, president of A. V. Roe Canada Ltd., and R. H. Winters, president of Rio Tinto of Canada (U.K.-controlled) are both directors of the Imperial-Commerce but as in the case of the Royal and Montreal, the links of the Imperial-Commerce with U.S. capital are more important than their links with British capital.

Directors of General Dynamics, of Crown Zellerbach, of Johns-Manville Corporation, of Proctor & Gamble, of Celanese Corporation of America, all major U.S. corporations, sit on the Imperial-Commerce board, the directors involved, with one exception, being Canadian citizens.

Like the Bank of Montreal with the CPR, the Imperial-Commerce has had a particularly close and intimate relationship with Brazilian Traction ever since the enterprise was founded. And as in the case of the CPR, but here even more decisively, the basis of the financial alliance controlling Brazilian has been shifting in favor of U.S. capital, although the active operation of Brazilian remains in the hands of Canadian tycoons.

The Toronto-Dominion Bank has interesting and important links with the duPont interests. Four Toronto-Dominion directors hold directorships in duPont-controlled companies. R. S. McLaughlin is a director of General Motors Corporation, W. Dent Smith of U.S. Rubber, of its subsidiary, Dominion Rubber, and of United Funds Canada, H.

H. Lank is president and H. Lawson a director of Du Pont of Canada Ltd.

The Toronto-Dominion also has two directors in common with International Nickel: J. R. Gordon, the new president of the company, and R. S. McLaughlin.

In the case of the Bank of Nova Scotia, the most striking connection with U.S. capital of groups working through the bank is the participation of J. Y. Murdoch, a vice-president of the bank, in the Iron Ore Company of Canada operation dominated by Cleveland steel interests. J. R. Timmins, formerly a vice-president of the Imperial, now of the Imperial-Commerce, also participates in the Canadian side of the Iron Ore Company operation. The Nova Scotia has two directors in common with British American Oil and one on the board of its parent, Gulf Oil, Mellon-controlled.

. . .

We have said that the most important centre of financial power in Canada operates through the Bank of Montreal, but the statement while probably true is not susceptible of proof. It has been argued in recent years that Toronto financial interests have overtaken the Montrealers. Certainly strong Toronto interests operate through the Canadian Imperial Bank of Commerce and its associated companies, through the Toronto-Dominion Bank, and in fact through the Bank of Montreal and Royal Bank. But the centre of power based on companies closely associated with the Bank of Montreal still gives evidence of being the most cohesive and most important.

Around the Bank of Montreal is a cluster of closely linked companies over which several related financial groups exercise control, wrapped up in the group of financial institutions close to the bank described in the last chapter. (Royal Trust, Sun Life, Mutual Life, Standard Life, Calvin Bullock investment trusts, and the investment trusts in which W. A. Arbuckle is prominent).

The cluster (see chart, p. 102) is built around the Canadian Pacific Railway Company and its subsidiary, Consolidated Mining & Smelting. It includes Canadian-controlled companies: Ogilvie Flour, Dominion Bridge, Steel Company of Canada, Consolidated Paper and Dominion Textile; powerful U.S.-controlled companies: Aluminium Ltd., Bell Telephone, Canadian General Electric, International Nickel, British American Oil, Dominion Rubber, RCA Victor; and British interests: Canadian Industries Ltd., Bowater, British Newfoundland Corporation.

In September, 1961, Canadian General Electric took over Dominion Engineering Works, a subsidiary of Dominion Bridge, as the two firms were combining in a bid to build a $50 million steel mill in Argentina.

As is true of all corporate interlocks, the connection that unites the Bank of Montreal directors who take part in the control of these companies is basically a connection between corporations and group interests and not one between individuals.

The long intimate relations between the Bank of Montreal and the Canadian Pacific Railway do not depend to any decisive extent on the personality of the president of the bank or that of the president of the railway. And the same applies in the case of the Steel Company of Canada. C.D. Howe moved briefly into the inner circle of the bank after 1957. He was a powerful personal re-inforcement to any group of which he was a member, but his presence on the bank board was an expression of the existence of a community of class interest between big business and government, and his death made no change in the reality of solidly established corporate relationships. The ties of the bank with Aluminium Ltd., with Ogilvie Flour Mills, etc., continued to exist, as they had existed before Howe joined the bank board.

The corporate connections and interlocks, the class relationships, find expression however in terms of individual directorships held in common and it is in these terms that we examine them, bearing in mind that the corporate relationships are often deeper than the interlocks show.

To study the groups operating through the Bank of Montreal means to begin with the CPR.

The CPR is portrayed as the most Canadian of Canadian corporations; in fact for many years the majority of CPR shares were held in Britain, although the board of directors was and is predominantly Canadian. As U.S. capital gains ground in the CPR, as CPR oil and base-metal interests come into contact with U.S. groups, as U.S. influence in the Bank of Montreal and its related companies becomes stronger, the nature of the alliance that controls the CPR shifts towards stronger U.S. participation, and more and more decisions are taken in line with the orientation of U.S. capital, even though the company is operated by a board that is predominantly Canadian and retains its connections with British capital. The two U.S. directors on the CPR board are prominent figures: Howard C. Shepherd of the First National City Bank, and H. S. Wingate.

As of 1958, nine Bank of Montreal directors were directors of the CPR: the president of the bank (G. A. Hart), the president of the railway (N. R. Crump), the president of the Sun Life (G. W. Bourke), the president of the Mutual Life (L. L. Lang), the president of International Nickel (H. S. Wingate), the president of Consolidated Paper (L. J. Belnap), the chairman of Burns & Co. (R. J. Dinning), the president of British Newfoundland Corporation (H. G. Smith), the president of Dominion Textile Co. (G. Blair Gordon).

Five other banks have only six directorships in common with the CPR; the Bank of Montreal inner group is thus super-predominant in the railway.

The CPR controls Cominco; four Bank of Montreal directors are also Cominco directors: R. E. Stavert (chairman of Cominco), G. A. Hart, N. R. Crump, and L. J. Belnap, the last three being CPR directors as well.

Inco, whose centre of control is in New York, has three Bank of Montreal directors on its board: Wingate, Stavert, and H. C. F. Mockridge, Toronto corporation lawyer. Inco as we have noted, has links with the Toronto-Dominion Bank.

The Steel Company of Canada and Canadian General Electric also fit neatly into the Bank of Montreal picture. Five directors of the bank are also directors of the Steel Company of Canada: H. G. Hilton, now chairman of the company, R. A. Laidlaw, of the Laidlaw Lumber Company, chairman of the National Trust, G. A. Hart, L. L. Lang, and H. G. Smith. Hilton and Lang are as well directors of Canadian General Electric.

The connections of the bank with the Mellon interests have been noted; the bank also has two directors in common with the duPont-controlled Dominion Rubber, and two in common with RCA Victor. The Montreal and Royal each have three directors in common with the Bell Telephone Company of Canada; the president of the company (T. W. Eadie) is a director of the Montreal, the president of the Bell subsidiary, Northern Electric (R. D. Harkness), is a director of the Royal. The Commerce and Imperial, before their merger, each had one director in common with the Bell.

Up to this point, in discussing the Bank of Monteal inner group we have been dealing only with the most important companies related to the bank, where the influence of groups working through the bank is more or less dominant. Later we shall discuss the relationships between the bank and pulp and paper companies and oil companies, both of which can be better understood in relation to the forces operating in those industries as a whole.

Important as is the role of the groups working through the Montreal, there are fields in which it is weakly expressed. Bank of Montreal groups have no visible influence in Algoma Steel, Dominion Steel & Coal, Dominion Foundries & Steel; their influence in oil is weaker that that of groups associated with the Royal Bank. Royal and Imperial-Commerce influence is strong in A. V. Roe Canada, Canadair, Canada Cement, on whose boards there are no directors of the Montreal. The Royal and Imperial-Commerce interests predominate on the board of the Argus Corporation and its group of controlled companies. The Montreal has no interlocks with Argus but does have some connections with Argus-controlled companies.

The Royal and Imperial-Commerce and the alliances that operate through them present a more diffuse and even more complicated picture.

The interests of the groups working through the Royal Bank extend further into more companies than do those of the Bank of Montreal groups; in many cases control operates through an alliance of Royal and Imperial-Commerce interests.

The Royal-Imperial-Commerce alliance functions in Argus and was apparent in the complex dealings involving control of Algoma Steel and Dominion Steel & Coal.

Algoma Steel was headed and owned by Sir James Dunn who died on January 1st, 1956. Sir James owned 700,000 shares in the company, a majority of the shares outstanding. Dominion Steel & Coal, a somewhat uneasy alliance of U.S., U.K., Canadian and Belgian capital, was headed by L. A. Forsythe, a partner in the Howard law firm, who died on January 1st, 1957. The Dunn estate needed to raise money through the sale of Algoma shares in order to pay succession duties; Dosco was shaken by the need to find a president acceptable to all concerned; the way was open to a change of control in both companies.

At about the same time British and Canadian groups were working to get control of McIntyre Porcupine and its investment funds, and fighting off an attempt by Cyrus Eaton to get control. By mid-1956, control of McIntyre Porcupine was settled in favor of the British-Canadian interests; by mid-1957 the funds of McIntyre Porcupine were being used by a Canadian-British-U.S. alliance to buy effective control of the Ventures mining empire (previously under U.S. control) and a share in the control of Algoma Steel.

The Algoma Steel operation involved the co-operation of several groups: the Mannesmann steel interests of West Germany, the interests in control of McIntyre Porcupine, the Hawker Siddeley group of Britain, acting through their subsidiary, A. V. Roe Canada Ltd., and the executors of the Dunn estate, of whom C. D. Howe was the main force.

Of the 700,000 Algoma shares held by the Dunn estate, 500,000 were sold: 200,000 to the Mannesmann interests, 150,000 to A. V. Roe, 100,000 to McIntyre Porcupine, and 50,000 to the Royal Bank, acting for Locana Corporation, a British investment trust. (Algoma stock was split after the transaction, four new shares for each old one).

This deal had scarcely gone through when the Hawker Siddeley group, still acting through A. V. Roe, went ahead to buy control of Dominion Steel & Coal in spite of the opposition of a minority of Dosco directors.

This sudden and vigorous expansion of 1957 by the Hawker Siddeley group, bringing A. V. Roe and Dosco under common management with a substantial share in Algoma, was followed in 1958 by an equally sudden retreat from Algoma Steel.

In November of that year, after the change of government in Canada, the Hawker Siddeley group sold their Algoma shares to an undisclosed purchaser at a slight profit. It was denied that control had passed to the Mannesmann interests (Toronto Daily Star: 12 Nov. 58) but the impression remained that the West German influence in Algoma had increased.

The Mannesmann firm and the Dunn estate are now the largest shareholders in Algoma. Mannesmann is one of the major steel companies of the Ruhr, in existence since 1885. The association with Algoma had begun before the death of Sir James Dunn. In 1953 the Mannesmann Tube Co. (a subsidiary of Mannesmann Steel) had built a $20 million plant at Sault Ste. Marie, based on steel from Algoma.

W. Zangen, chairman of Mannesmann since 1934, was a former member of the Nazi party and of the SS; he was one of the group of big German industrialists who financed the Nazi rise to power and provided the armaments for the Nazi war machine. In the days of the Nazi invasion of the Soviet Union, Mannesmann opened short-lived affiliates in Kiev and Dniepropetrovsk. The Mannesmann board includes figures from the Deutsche Bank and Dresdner Bank of West Germany. Zangen is a director of Algoma Steel.

Just why the Hawker Siddeley group reversed themselves on Algoma Steel is not clear. They may have been influenced to enter the deal by C. D. Howe, with whom at that time they had close dealings, so as to provide, temporarily at least, more "British" capital (the money was provided by A. V. Roe Canada Ltd., from Canadian profits) and thus enable control to appear as British-Canadian. (Dunn had asked that if possible control of Algoma should be kept within the Commonwealth). Or the advance into Algoma may simply have been a case of over-optimistic expansion that called for drastic cutbacks once there was a hint that A. V. Roe might lose the Avro Arrow contract. The contract was in fact cancelled in February, 1959.

Algoma is not the only enterprise in which the McIntyre Porcupine group have an interest. McIntyre Porcupine and its subsidiaries held 156,000 shares in International Nickel, 118,545 in Bell Telephone, as well as 440,000 in Algoma Steel (after the 4 for 1 split) and another 440,000 in Ventures.

Following the hurly-burly of the Algoma-Dosco deals, the Royal Bank had four directors in common with Algoma Steel, two with A. V. Roe Canada Ltd., two with Ventures, one with McIntyre Porcupine and one with Dosco. The Imperial-Commerce had no interlocks with Algoma but had one director in common with Dosco, one with A. V. Roe, two with Ventures and two with McIntyre Porcupine.

Thus Algoma Steel and Dosco are under control of alliances of West German, British and Canadian capital and U.S., Canadian and Belgian capital respectively, working through the Royal Bank and the Imperial-Commerce. Stelco, as we have seen, is firmly within the influence of the inner group of the Bank of Montreal; Dominion Foundries & Steel, another important steel producer, is linked to the Bank of Nova Scotia (two directors in common) and Imperial-Commerce (one director in common), and to the investment firms of Dominion Securities and A. E. Ames & Co.

But the heart of the matter we have been discussing is that control of two of Canada's largest steel companies, affecting the future of the Canadian steel industry, was handed back and forth between financial groups, without consideration for the needs of Canadian development or the jobs of the miners and steelworkers involved.

.   .   .

The pulp and paper industry has been penetrated by a number of monopoly groups, among whose members bank directors hold leading positions. The interests involved have been U.S., Canadian and British, with other European interests, West German, Belgian and Swedish, beginning to move in.

U.S. groups, some established in Canada for many years, others entering the country for the first time, have been expanding operations in British Columbia as well as in eastern and Atlantic provinces in a drive to secure supplies of lumber and pulp sufficient for all time to come, either through buying timber lands or securing leases of Crown lands.

The size of these holdings can be judged from those held by two established companies. The Canadian International Paper Company happily announces that its Canadian timber holdings, owned and under lease, comprise 25,210 square miles. Abitibi Power & Paper controls 26,000 square miles of timber limits in three provinces.

Expansion in the industry, by no means confined to U.S. groups, has been reflected in intense rivalry between financial groups and among the individual tycoons involved, and has produced a situation in which relationships are fluid and mergers and re-organizations numerous.

In terms of the personalities involved some of the mergers have turned out unhappily. MacMillan, Bloedel & Powell River is a case in point. In December, 1959, MacMillan & Bloedel Ltd. merged with Powell River Company to form one of the largest forestry firms in Canada. Within a year and a half, cries of rage from former directors of Powell River echoed across the financial pages. According to M. J. Foley and H. S. Foley, formerly of the Powell River Company, president and vice-chairman respectively of the merged company, the understanding on the executive level had been for equal representation of the two companies on the merged board, with J. V. Clyne, formerly of MacMillan & Bloedel, as an impartial chairman. (Clyne being the B.C. judge who left the bench to become chairman of MacMillan & Bloedel).

The Foleys and other Powell River executives found him anything but impartial, and quit. Naturally the squabble among the directors on how to run the new company was not allowed to upset the merger. The dissident group had to go. H. S. Foley was a director of the Bank of Montreal; M. J. Foley moved to Anglo-Canadian Pulp & Paper as a vice-president and director.

U.S. groups have been pushing forward in British Columbia. Among them are Crown Zellerbach Canada (a subsidiary of the U.S.-controlled Crown Zellerbach), Rayonier Canada, formerly Alaska Pine & Cellulose (subsidiary of the U.S.-controlled Rayonier Inc.) Columbia Cellulose (controlled by Celanese Corporation of America), Scott Paper Company (Morgan control).

The Scott Paper interests are moving ahead both in British Columbia and in eastern Canada. They have taken over Westminster Paper Co. of British Columbia, acquired a large holding in B.C. Forest Products, now operated by a Scott Paper-Argus alliance in which Scott Paper is dominant, have an interest in a new company, Nova Scotia Pulp Ltd., formed by Swedish capital, and have close associations with the Minas Basin Pulp & Paper Co., also of Nova Scotia.

In Ontario, especially in northwestern Ontario, a number of U.S.-controlled companies operate, either to provide
newsprint for specific U.S. firms, or as extensions of pulp
and paper companies on the U.S. side of the border.

Thus Marathon Corp. of Canada (Marathon, Ont.) is
a subsidiary of American Can; Minnesota & Ontario
Paper (Fort Frances, Kenora, Ont.) is U.S.-controlled;
the KVP Company (Espanola, Ont.) is U.S.-controlled;
the Kimberley-Clark Corporation of the United States
controls Kimberley-Clark Pulp & Paper Co. (Terrace Bay,
Ont.) and, along with other subsidiaries, Spruce Falls
Power & Paper (Kapuskasing, Ont.) and has acquired a
35% interest in the Irving Pulp & Paper Co. of New
Brunswick.

The Spruce Falls Company is the source of newsprint
for the New York Times, and Kimberley-Clark supplies
newsprint for the Philadelphia Inquirer, Detroit News and
Washington Star.

The Ontario Paper Company (Thorold, Ont.) is controlled by the McCormick interests who own the Chicago
Tribune. The company also supplies The American (Chicago) and the Daily News of New York with newsprint.
The McCormick interests have expanded their holdings to
the province of Quebec where they control Quebec North
Shore Paper Company (Baie Comeau) and Manicouagan
Power Company. As an aside it should be mentioned that
through their control of Manicouagan Power the Chicago
Tribune interests have obtained a substantial minority
holding (40%) in Canadian British Aluminium Ltd. in
which Tube Investments Ltd. of the United Kingdom, and
Reynolds Metals of the United States, control the majority
interest, held through British Aluminium Ltd.

The giants in eastern Canada, in terms of over-all
operations are International Paper and the Bowater group
of the United Kingdom. Other important companies in
terms of their Canadian operations (they do not have
plants in other countries) are Abitibi Power & Paper;
Consolidated Paper; the group of companies controlled

by Argus Corporation through Dominion Tar & Chemical: St. Lawrence Corporation, Howard Smith Paper, and their subsidiaries; Price Brothers and the other U.K. interests — Anglo-Canadian Pulp & Paper, Anglo-Newfoundland Development — operating in Newfoundland and Quebec.

Most of these companies are connected with and operate in co-operation with Canadian financial groups. The exceptions are the U.S.-controlled companies in Ontario that act as extensions of their U.S. parent and have no interlocks with Canadian financial interests.

The pulp and paper groupings are united by a number of interlocks. Members of the Howard law firm (Royal Bank solicitors) hold directorships in pulp and paper companies in four of the main groupings: Canadian International Paper; Consolidated Paper; Howard Smith Paper (Argus); Anglo-Canadian and Anglo-Newfoundland.

The Bank of Montreal has directors in common with the Bowater companies operating in Canada; with Canadian International Paper; with Consolidated Paper (three directors in common); with Price Brothers (three directors in common); with the Dominion Tar & Chemical group: two directors in common with Dominion Tar, three with Howard Smith, and one with St. Lawrence Corporation.

A number of changes have taken place in the British-controlled companies associated with the Bank of Montreal and the Royal Bank. W. H. Howard is a director of Anglo-Newfoundland and of Anglo-Canadian — the first controlled by the Daily Mail interests of Britain, headed by Lord Rothermere, the second by the Daily Mirror interests headed by C. H. King, first cousin to Lord Rothermere. Rothermere, like Howard, was on the boards of both companies; E. M. Little was chairman of both.

King and the Daily Mirror group have shifted control of Anglo-Canadian to the Albert E. Reed & Co. Ltd. paper interests which they control.

The Rothermere interests have negotiated a merger between Price Brothers and Anglo-Newfoundland through an exchange of shares. Price Brothers has taken over Anglo-Newfoundland, and as a result Associated Newspapers Ltd. (the Daily Mail) will end up as the largest single shareholder in Price Brothers with the right to name six directors.

The interests of the Royal Bank and Imperial-Commerce groups are strong in the Argus-Dominion Tar & Chemical companies; the Royal has four and the Imperial-Commerce five directors in common with Dominion Tar & Chemical, the Royal has five and the Imperial-Commerce three in common with Howard Smith Paper, the Royal three and the Imperial-Commerce four in common with St. Lawrence Corporation.

The personal links of Argus directors extend beyond their own companies: P. M. Fox, of Argus, is president of the Argus-controlled St. Lawrence Corporation, and chairman of Great Lakes Paper Co. (Fort William, Ont.). The latter company was at one time part of the U.S. Backus-Brooks holdings that included the Minnesota & Ontario Paper Co. The Imperial-Commerce is represented on the boards of Great Lakes Paper and Minnesota & Ontario.

The board of Abitibi Power & Paper, one of the leading companies, is an amalgam of Royal Bank, Imperial-Commerce, Wood, Gundy and Argus forces. The board includes three Royal and two Imperial-Commerce directors; three of the five are directors of Argus Corporation.

Numerous points of contact exist between the giants in British Columbia and the companies operating in eastern Canada. H. R. MacMillan, honorary chairman of Mac-Millan, Bloedel & Powell River, is a director of Argus. He is also a director of the Imperial-Commerce, as is J. D. Zellerbach, of the parent Crown Zellerbach company. MacMillan is a director of Dominion Tar & Chemical, and so is R. T. Hager, a director of Crown Zellerbach of Canada. O. F. Lundell, a Vancouver lawyer, is a director

of B. C. Forest Products (Scott Paper and Argus control)
and Crown Zellerbach of Canada.

Canadian International Paper was at one time part of
the old International Paper & Power empire which also
included Gatineau Power, and several traces of the old
relationship can still be seen, indicating the continuing
parallel interests of the two companies. A member of the
Howard law firm is on both boards: J. G. Porteous on
Gatineau, J. A. Ogilvy on CIP; an Imperial-Commerce
director sits on the boards of both companies; two members of the Gatineau board sit on the Royal Trust board
and so do two members of the CIP board; two Toronto-
Dominion directors sit on the CIP board and two Gatineau
directors are connected with Toronto General Trusts,
controlled by the Toronto-Dominion Bank.

In dealing thus at some length with the pulp and paper
industry, we have been discussing a situation in which a
relatively large number of corporate units operate and
where the Gordon Commission studies indicated that only
two of the six largest companies were controlled outside
Canada. But we find that the corporate units controlled
by different groups are united by interlocks, that U.S.
interests are expanding, and are interlocked with other
groups, and that the most important companies, whether
controlled in or out of Canada interlock with the banks
and the financial structure.

.   .   .

In oil and gas where control of the industry is con-
centrated in far fewer corporate units the picture is
similar.

Imperial Oil, the huge Rockefeller company that dom-
inates all branches of the oil industry, is linked, as we
have seen, to the Royal Bank; British American Oil,
Mellon-controlled, has links with four banks — three
directors in common with the Bank of Montreal, two with
the Nova Scotia, one with the Royal Bank and one with
the Toronto-Dominion; Texaco Canada Ltd. (Texas Co.
control) has two directors in common with the Royal

and two with the small Provincial Bank of Canada. Control of the Texas Company lies between Chicago interests and the Hanover Bank of New York.

Canadian Petrofina (Belgian control) has connections with four Canadian banks: two directors in common with the Royal and Imperial-Commerce, one each with the Bank of Montreal and Banque Canadienne Nationale.

The Shell interests (British and Dutch control) show no interlocks with Canadian banks. British Petroleum (in which the British government has an interest) is now entering the Canadian field in strength; as chairman of the Canadian subsidiary it has Graham Towers, a director of the Royal Bank.

Canadian Oil Companies, related to the Power Corporation interests, has one director in common with three banks: Imperial-Commerce, Toronto-Dominion, Nova Scotia.

The main oil pipelines are controlled by the oil companies and their boards show no separate interlocks with the banks.

The two big gas pipeline companies, Trans-Canada Pipe Lines and Westcoast Transmission, are linked to the main financial interests: Trans-Canada to the Toronto-Dominion (four directors in common), Imperial-Commerce (two directors in common), Royal Bank and Bank of Nova Scotia (each with one director in common with Trans-Canada); Westcoast Transmission to the Royal Bank (two directors in common, including Frank McMahon, president of the company) and to the Imperial-Commerce and Nova Scotia (individual directors in common).

Here in a more tightly controlled industry, in which foreign capital (mainly U.S.) is in a far stronger position than in pulp and paper, the leading financial groups also co-ordinate their approach to common problems through the banks as part of the process of seeking to maximize their profit position.

The electrical industry, dominated by three U.S.-controlled giants, Canadian General Electric, Canadian Westinghouse, and Northern Electric, shows the same pattern of inter-relationships between groups that are in theory and sometimes in practice in sharp competition.

The Bell Telephone Co. of Canada, parent of Northern Electric, has three directors in common with the Royal Bank, three with the Bank of Montreal, and two with the Imperial-Commerce.

Northern Electric has two directors in common with the Royal, one with the Montreal, and one with the Toronto-Dominion Bank.

Canadian General Electric and Canadian Westinghouse both have a director in common with the Royal and Toronto-Dominion. The Bank of Montreal, as we have seen, is closely related to the Canadian General Electric.

Directors of the Bell Telephone, of Canadian General Electric and of Canadian Westinghouse, meet on the board of Brazilian Traction, as well as in other corporate capacities.

As will be noted, there is ample opportunity to adjust the differences of the various monopoly groups concerned.

. . .

An important area of influence of the financial groups operating through the Royal Bank of Canada lies in the relationships between Shawinigan Water & Power, British Columbia Power Corp., the Power Corporation of Canada and the Nesbitt, Thomson firm of investment dealers.

The Power Corporation is a holding company in which the Nesbitt, Thomson firm is the main force. Power Corporation assets at the end of 1958 were $49.5 million but the company owned securities with a market value of $79.2 million.

The company controls East Kootenay Power, Northern Quebec Power, and Imperial Investment Corporation, the latter controlling Laurentide Acceptance Corp. Ltd. With more awareness of the world situation than the directors of Canada's biggest, newest bank, the Power Corporation group decided to change the name of Imperial Investments to Laurentide Financial Corporation, since, as a spokesman explained, the name Imperial "has inherent disadvantages" . . . "disadvantages (that) could increase as the firm expands." (Globe & Mail: 29 July 61).

Shawinigan is, according to itself, one of the largest producers and distributors of hydro-electric power in the world, although in terms of total assets it runs some distance behind British Columbia Power.

Shawinigan controls Quebec Power, Southern Canada Power, and St. Maurice Power. It has an interest in the British Newfoundland Corporation project to develop the Grand Falls site in Labrador.

The Shawinigan board shows no direct connection with U.S. interests but such links exist through Shawinigan subsidiaries in which Shawinigan shares control with U.S. companies. British investors have a minority holding in the company.

Shawinigan Chemicals is a subsidiary of Shawinigan. In turn it has a number of subsidiaries that are joint operations (control equally divided) with U.S. companies: Shawinigan Resins is half-owned by Monsanto Chemical, Canadian Resins & Chemicals by Union Carbide, B.A.-Shawinigan by British American Oil.

Shawinigan has two directors in common with the Royal Bank, one of whom is J. A. Fuller, president of the company. British Columbia Power has one director in common with the Royal (the president of the company has been a Royal director) and two in common with the Montreal Trust, one of them being a former secretary to Sir Herbert Holt, Sévère Godin.

Shawinigan has two directors in common with British Columbia Power, while the Power Corporation has one director in common with Shawinigan and two with British Columbia Power. The Wood, Gundy interests, in the person of C. L. Gundy, also appear on the British Columbia Power board.

In addition to their connections with British Columbia
Power and Shawinigan, the Power Corporation group have
four directors in common with Bathurst Power & Paper
(including the chairman of the company), three with Canadian Celanese, three with Canadian Oil Companies (including the president of the company), and one with
Trans-Canada Pipe Lines. In all, directors of three banks
sit on the Power Corporation board, one each from the
Royal, Montreal, and Nova Scotia.

.   .   .

A number of facts emerge from or are confirmed by this
summary discussion of the connections between the financial groups that control the biggest producing companies.

Most of the important financial groups, U.S. or Canadian or other, have connections with more than one bank,
not always expressed in common directorships. And while
an important company like Imperial Oil has only one director in common with one bank, another giant in the same
industry, British American Oil, has a total of seven directors in common with four bank boards, and its parent company is itself directly represented on two bank boards.

A close relationship between a bank and a given company may be expressed in the fact that they have one
director in common; in other cases, relationships that are
no closer are expressed in an unusually large number of
common directors, as in the case of the Bank of Montreal
and the CPR, or the Imperial-Commerce and Brazilian
Traction.

Clearly defined areas exist where a financial group and
its allies have a dominant position, often to the exclusion
of rivals; in other cases influence is shared through complex interlocks among competing interests that indicate the
inevitability of future shifts of power and new mergers.

All groups and all banks and the forces working through
them are not equal; the Bank of Montreal is characterized
by the fact that within it exists a fairly cohesive inner
group; the Royal and Imperial-Commerce bring together
a wider range of interests than those represented on the

Montreal board. And although very important groups are represented on the boards of the Toronto-Dominion and the Nova Scotia, the total area of influence represented is considerably less than that represented on the boards of the three larger banks.

While the oldest and probably still the most important single centre of power is within the Bank of Montreal, other centres of power exist, and new groups are always in process of struggling for power and profit. The driving build-up of the Argus empire since World War II is a case in point that we shall examine in more detail.

More recently, important financial forces have been arising in British Columbia, in Alberta, in Winnipeg, mainly around oil and natural gas and the industries based on them. The boards of the largest banks have reflected this regional development by giving representation to forces outside the traditional financial centres of Montreal and Toronto so as to centralize and co-ordinate the activities of the newer groups. In this way they express the common interests of the financial oligarchy.

CHAPTER VI

"Not a Dollar that Costs Us Anything!"

A STUDY OF THE POWER and influence of Canadian capitalist groups (and of their relationships with non-Canadian capitalist groups operating in Canada) would be incomplete without an examination of Canadian investments abroad, how they have developed, and by whom they are controlled.

Canadian investments abroad are based on the export of capital from Canada, that is, the export of capital accumulated in Canada from profits produced by Canadian workers. In this real and important sense such investments are Canadian. But Canadian investments abroad can be and often are controlled by non-Canadian capitalist groups or by alliances of capitalist groups in which Canadian capitalists are a lesser force.

This is related to the fact that so many important sources of capital accumulation in Canada (factories, mines, mills) are themselves under the control of non-Canadian capital groups; it is not unexpected therefore to find Canadian capital exports under control of non-Canadians as well as of Canadians, or forming a part of alliances with stronger groups.

As a result of this control by non-Canadian (mainly U.S.) financial groups over sources of accumulation in Canada, capital is exported from Canada to expand the world operations of these groups without regard to the fact that alternative and more important uses for the capital exported may exist in Canada. The financial groups seek the most profitable outlets for their profits, not the ones that are most important for national development.

Canadian capitalists of course are not always or inevitably in a secondary position in every case of Canadian investment abroad, and, in a secondary position or not, they have been able to participate in large profits based on the export of Canadian capital.

The whole purpose of foreign investment, whether it be Canadian capital exported to other countries, or foreign capital invested in Canada, is that of "maximizing profit"; "an international company tries to achieve the maximum possible profit in its global operations." (The quotations are from a study prepared by the economists of the Gordon Commission). No financial group has ever exported capital for any motive other than profit; Canadian government loans and credits are no exception in that they are intended to and do result in indirect and substantial profit to Canadian capitalist groups.

This expansion of influence outside Canada through the export of capital in the search for the greatest possible realizable profit has involved expansion to economically underdeveloped countries (Mexico, Cuba, Brazil, of fifty years ago, British Guiana, Jamaica, Africa, today) as well as to the most industrially developed capitalist countries (U.S. and U.K.); in later years it has involved action by the Canadian government as well as by financial groups.

The movement of capital has sometimes been the result of tariff policy. U.S. companies that have set up subsidiary branch plants in Canada in order to avoid Canadian duties on the import of fully manufactured goods from the United States and take advantage of lower wage rates, have been able at the same time to penetrate the Commonwealth market in the guise of Canadian companies.

Thus the Ford Motor Company of Canada Ltd., a subsidiary of the Ford Motor Company of the United States and an example of U.S. investment in Canada, has its own sub-subsidiaries in South Africa, Australia, New Zealand and Malaya, classed, unrealistically, as Canadian investment abroad. The control of these enterprises is entirely in the United States; the capital originally invested in South

Africa, etc., many have come from profits made in Windsor or in Detroit or from borrowing on the credit of the U.S. or Canadian Ford company.

The picture of Canadian investment abroad is one of movement and change as financial groups expand at the expense of weaker rivals, or lose ground to more powerful forces. In the past Canadian railway promoters and bankers have gone heavily into enterprises like Mexican Light & Power, from which they were later all but displaced by more powerful groups; newer groups like the E. P. Taylor interests, the Roy Thomson publishing interests, and others have come forward to challenge for a share in the U.S. and U.K. markets by establishing or buying control of enterprises there, sometimes on their own, sometimes in alliance with U.S. and U.K. capital.

It is understandably difficult to express this complex movement of capital and control in statistical concepts; the figures for Canadian investment abroad are most useful as a means of indicating the rate of increase in such investment over the years and hence the increase in influence of Canadian and allied financial groups outside Canada. They do not tell us the actual capital outflow from Canada or how Canadian its control was.

Canadian investment abroad has increased from $1.3 billion at the end of 1930 to $5.5 billion at the end of 1959.

This is a substantial increase, on the face of it a more rapid rate of increase than that in foreign long-term investment in Canada.

There is, however, a difference. Foreign long-term investment in Canada is all private; Canadian long-term investment abroad includes $2.1 billion of government loans and advances, and government of Canada subscriptions to the International Bank of Reconstruction and Development (the World Bank), to the International Monetary Fund and to the International Finance Corporation.

The actual increase in private long-term investment abroad is from $1.3 billion (end '30) to $3.4 billion (end

'59). The total of $3.4 billion is made up of $2.3 billion direct and $1.1 billion portfolio.

As of the end of 1958, when the total was $3.3 billion, 66% of Canadian direct investment abroad and 69% of Canadian portfolio investment abroad was in the United States.

Two points should be noted: the importance of the government share (38% of the total of $5.5 billion) and the fact that the larger part of Canadian private investment abroad is in the United States.

Canadian long-term investment abroad ($5.5 billion) makes up the larger part of Canadian assets abroad ($8.8 billion, end '59). The larger figure includes additional items: Canadian government holdings of gold and foreign exchange, bank balances, and short-term commercial receivables.

.   .   .

The figure for total assets abroad does not include the large assets abroad of Canadian banks ($1,150 million, end '54) or of Canadian insurance companies ($2,047 million, end '53) although these foreign assets of banks and insurance companies are an important measure of the influence of Canadian financial and industrial circles outside their own country and owe their existence to the export of capital from Canada, an export, needless to say, much smaller in amount than the assets themselves.

The exclusion of bank and insurance assets from the total is based on the fact that these assets differ in character from the assets of companies engaged in production and are mainly held against corresponding liabilities.

These arguments have validity, but we are faced again with the real difficulty of measuring statistically the phenomena of investment and control. The reasoning that excludes bank and insurance assets tends to minimize the role played abroad by banks and insurance companies, a role based on business done, on the working control of large capital sums they do not own, rather than on the investment of Canadian capital.

As far as Canadian banks are concerned, their oldest, strongest, and most important connections abroad have been and still are with U.S. and U.K. banking interests. These deep-rooted associations have expanded as Canadian trade expanded and as the export of capital gained in importance.

The relationships of Canadian banks with other financial groups abroad are above all part of a system of doing business, within and without Canada. For example, to use an illustration based on Belgian capital, the Royal Bank of Canada is related to Belgian financial groups both through a loan to the former government of the Congo (export of Canadian capital) and through the activities of Belgian groups in Canada (export of Belgian, made-in-Congo, capital).

The same situation arises in regard to relationships with U.S. and U.K. groups. Canadian banks may be associated with the expansion of the E. P. Taylor brewing interests into the United States and Britain as with the expansion of U.S. and U.K. groups into Canada. Thus the relationships between groups in different countries are developing on the basis of a world-wide system of doing business that cannot always be divided accurately into internal and external sections. At the same time we can appreciate the influence of the Canadian financial groups better by examining separately their ramifications abroad.

While the connections of Canadian banks with U.S. and U.K. capital are most important, there are certain other areas, less developed economically than Canada, where Canadian banks have maintained a strong position. The most important such area has been in the Caribbean.

For many years six foreign banks dominated the economy of Cuba. Four were U.S. banks or banks dominated by U.S. capital, two were Canadian: the Royal and the Nova Scotia. In 1951 a World Bank report showed that the six held 54.5% of all deposits and controlled 52.3% of all banking assets in Cuba; no fewer than fifty small Cuban banks shared the rest of the business. In 1960 the Royal had 24 Cuban branches and the Nova Scotia eight.

These profitable relations with Cuba came to an end for the Canadian banks in December, 1960, when they sold their Cuban interests to the Banco Nacional de Cuba, the Royal on December 8th, the Nova Scotia on December 16th. The Royal Bank, according to its general manager, received $8.8 million for its Cuban assets; the Bank of Nova Scotia did not immediately announce what it had received although its president described the arrangements as "satisfactory." (Globe & Mail: 17 Dec. 60). At the bank's 1961 annual meeting the general manager said only that the sale had been made "without loss."

Other Canadian banks have followed the Royal and Nova Scotia to the Caribbean area. In 1958 we find the Bank of Montreal, influenced by the growing popularity and importance of tax-free Nassau as a business centre, joining with the Bank of London & South America to establish a new jointly-owned bank, the Bank of London & Montreal Ltd., (Bolam) with a Nassau head office. By 1960, Bolam had established 20 branches in the Caribbean, and A. C. Jensen, chairman of the Bank of Montreal, could optimistically forecast the development of the Bahamas, because of their "inviting" tax and corporate laws, as a "Switzerland in the Western Hemisphere." (Globe & Mail: 18 Feb. 60).

All told, Canadian banks had 61 branches in the islands scheduled to make up the West Indies Federation (Globe & Mail: 9 May 60), outnumbering the branches of British banks established there, and 24 in other Caribbean islands (exclusive of Cuba): Haiti, Puerto Rico, etc.

No doubt banking publicists would view this expansion simply as the unselfish provision of good banking services to the area; in real life it means that the control of a substantial part of the economy of the areas affected has passed to outside interests concerned to maximize the profits of their over-all operations.

Like Canadian banks, several Canadian life insurance companies do business outside Canada. Thus the Sun Life, Manufacturers Life and Confederation Life Association have particularly wide-spread interests.

All three, as might be expected, do business in the United States and Britain. All three do business as well in a number of present, or former colonies and countries subject to penetration by outside capital. One or the other or all of them operate in the British West Indies, the Netherlands Antilles, British Guiana, the Dominican Republic, Haiti; in Rhodesia, Nyasaland, South West Africa, Malaya, Singapore, Sarawak, North Borneo, Hongkong. (The list dates from 1958; some names refer to colonies that have since gained their independence).

The same penetration existed in the case of Cuba. The World Bank report on Cuba of 1951 to which we have referred, pointed out that the group of insurance companies classified by the bank as "British-Canadian" collected 37% of all insurance premiums paid in Cuba in 1949. According to the Financial Post (16 July 60), Canadian life insurance companies are writing 70% of all Cuban business, with policies in force amounting to $400 million. Here again the influence of these Canadian insurance companies on the economy of Cuba is not based on any spectacularly large Canadian investment but on their administration of large Cuban-generated savings which the companies invest, having in mind their own total profit position.

.   .   .

We have mentioned that 66% of Canadian direct investment abroad is in the United States, and in a certain sense this Canadian investment in the United States is the counterpart of the U.S. investment in Canada—they are both expressions of the same system of business. Apologists for U.S. investment in Canada never tire of pointing out that Canadian investment in the United States is per capita higher than U.S. investment in Canada. But economically and politically speaking, the effect of Canadian investment in the United States has been very different from that of U.S. investment in Canada.

Both are founded on the idea of maximizing profits; in some cases both may even be controlled by the same groups. But there is this significant difference: U.S.-controlled capital in Canada has behind it the whole weight of U.S. economic and political expansion. By its volume, direction, and rate of increase, it constitutes a threat to the independence of Canada.

Canadian investment in the United States does not involve any such threat to U.S. independence. This is not because of any special benevolence in the outlook of Canadian capitalists; it relates only to the balance of forces.

Canadian capitalist groups have never been in a position to dominate the U.S. economy, nor could Canada, vis-a-vis the United States, make use of any threat to use the big stick in defence of Canadian capitalist interests.

In order to improve their profit position, Canadian capitalists have exported capital to the United States; in doing so they have adjusted themselves, more or less comfortably, to the over-all dominant position of U.S. capital, in Canada as in the United States.

The picture becomes clearer as we look at some of the forms taken by Canadian investment in the United States and elsewhere.

The Canadian Pacific Railway Co. has very substantial interests in northern U.S. railway lines. The CPR controls and operates the 3,324 miles of the Minneapolis, St. Paul, and Sault Ste. Marie railway, as well as the Duluth South Shore and Atlantic, the Wisconsin Central, etc.

The Steel Co. of Canada Ltd. owns 14 U.S. iron ore properties and four U.S. coal properties.

Algoma Steel Corporation Ltd. owns four coal mines in Cannelton, West Virginia, leases 9,200 nearby acres, and owns limestone and dolomite deposits in the state of Michigan.

Distillers Corporation-Seagrams Ltd. has distilleries in the United States, a new 38-story building in New York, heavy gas and oil investments in the southern United States.

Hiram Walker-Gooderham & Worts Ltd. operates distilleries through subsidiaries in the United States, in Canada, in Argentina and Scotland. Its main plant is at Peoria, Illinois.

International Nickel Co. of Canada Ltd. is a particularly good example of how difficult the analysis of foreign investment in statistical terms can be. Inco is U.S.-controlled. Its operations are based on the ownership of 100,000 acres of nickel-bearing ore in the Sudbury area (the company now has other holdings in Canada and abroad).

Its mining, smelting and refining processes are carried on in Canada but Inco has rolling-mills, a refinery and research facilities in the United States, and a group of subsidiaries in the United Kingdom, with fabricating plants in Birmingham and Glasgow, refinery in Wales, etc., etc. There is strong minority representation of U.K. interests on the Inco board arising from the taking over by Inco of Mond Nickel in 1928. Inco directors are neatly divided geographically: twelve U.S., 6 U.K., and 6 Canadian.

The Inco example is an illustration of the export of Canadian-produced capital, under U.S. control, to the United States and to the United Kingdom.

The Taylor-Argus interests have moved strongly into the United States and the United Kingdom, as we shall see in dealing with the expansion of the Argus companies.

Canadian Breweries operates in the United States through Carling Brewing Co. Inc., now one of the major U.S. breweries, and in the United Kingdom through United Breweries Ltd.; the expansion through both companies being made possible in the first place by profits made in Canada. During 1960 United Breweries Ltd. was busy struggling for control of breweries and outlets in Scotland, Wales and England.

Another branch of the Taylor-Argus empire with large interests abroad is Massey-Ferguson Ltd., with important plants in the United States, Britain, western Europe, Latin America, etc.

Roy Thomson, owner of Canadian radio stations and a string of Canadian daily and weekly newspapers (some 30 dailies across Canada) moved into the British field to become one of the big four of British newspaper publishers. In 1953 he purchased The Scotsman, of Edinburgh; later he became chairman of Scottish Television, took over the Kemsley newspaper interests in 1959, made an unsuccessful bid for control of Odhams Press in 1961, took over the Odhams interests in the Union of South Africa, bought newspapers in Ethiopia, in Nigeria, in Trinidad, and with his family was reported to have a stake worth £20 million in British newspapers and television and £35 million in his total publishing empire in North America, Britain and Africa. (Globe & Mail: 25 May 61). In Canada, Thomson and J. S. D. Tory have worked together; in 1960 Thomson became a director of the Royal Bank of Canada.

. . .

The expansion of Aluminium Ltd., the U.S.-owned holding company that owns the Aluminum Company of Canada, one of the country's industrial giants, Saguenay Power, and about 50 other subsidiaries in some 28 countries, is a striking example of the use of Canadian-made profits to improve the world position of a giant U.S. trust under Mellon control.

Aluminium Ltd. was set up by the Mellon interests in 1928 to operate in Canada and in the rest of the world outside the United States. It is a twin brother of the Aluminum Company of America (Alcoa). In the technical, legal sense there is no direct link between the two companies as such; in fact both are owned by the same group of U.S. shareholders in which the Mellon-Davis interests predominate. For many years the presidents of the two companies were brothers: Arthur V. Davis of Alcoa, Edward K. Davis of Aluminium Ltd. In 1947, the thirty year old Nathanael V. Davis succeeded his father as president of Aluminium Ltd. The Davis family wealth, like that of the Mellons who have the major interest in the companies, is fantastic. In 1957, according to Fortune, Arthur V. Davis, then president of Alcoa, was one of seven persons with fortunes of between $400 million and $700 million. Four of the other six in that bracket were Mellons.

The parallel organization of the two companies, American and Canadian, both controlled by the same U.S. group, was an ingenious device by which to circumvent the U.S. anti-trust laws. Its ultimate success is still in doubt since somewhat half-hearted efforts are still pending in the United States to break up the trust.

The aluminum trust entered Canada after getting control in 1925 of the Duke-Price Power Co. which controlled highly valuable power sites on the Saguenay. At one time Shawinigan Power and Price Brothers held a substantial minority interest in Duke-Price Power but Aluminium Ltd. now holds over 90% of the stock of Saguenay Power which controls the upper development of the Saguenay as successor to Duke-Price.

Aluminium Ltd. is strongly based in Canada, with control of enormous power developments in British Columbia and Quebec, and a raw material base in Jamaica and British Guiana. The power plants it controls in Quebec and British Columbia have an installed capacity (1960) of 4,650,000 h.p., a very substantial fraction of the total capacity of Canadian waterpower installations.

Demerara Bauxite (Demba) is an important subsidiary operating in British Guiana. In 1956 Demba obtained a 50-year concession renewable for 25 years more covering bauxite sources there, and undertook to build an alumina plant. Demba owns 30,000 acres of bauxite land, leases 26,000 acres more and holds an exclusive mining licence over 1,460 sq. miles of possible bauxite-bearing land.

Alumina Jamaica Ltd., another subsidiary, owns 30,000 acres of bauxite land in Jamaica.

In 1957, Aluminium Ltd. was creating, through Bauxites du Midi, a French subsidiary, a new bauxite and alumina industry in French West Africa at a cost of $100 million;

its investment in Jamaica was said to be approaching the same figure. (The Telegram: 5 Feb. 57).

A few weeks later it was reported (Toronto Daily Star: 21 Feb. 57) that Aluminium Ltd. held a one-third interest in Sematan Bauxite of Sarawak, Borneo, in addition to its own subsidiary, South East Asia Bauxites, which operates in Malaya, and in which a Japanese Aluminium Ltd. subsidiary also participates.

In their plans for French West Africa, the Aluminium Ltd. interests appear to have miscalculated the sweep of the independence struggle. Prospects for the expansion of Mellon influence in what is now Guinea have faded as the government of Guinea put forward its own ideas on how to develop the country's resources. By the end of 1961, Aluminium Ltd. was admitting that $20 million already spent in Guinea (a company calculation) might have to be written off as a loss. The company's explanation for its decision not to go ahead was that international banks were unwilling to put money ino Guinea. (Globe & Mail: 1 Dec. 61).

In 1960, a $3 million expansion program in Ghana was announced, to be carried out by a subsidiary owned 60% by Aluminium Ltd., 40% by the government of Ghana. (Globe & Mail: 12 July 60). In the same year a new Dutch plant, owned by a subsidiary, was opened, flatteringly described as "Canada's first major investment in the Netherlands." (Globe & Mail: 18 Dec. 60).

By September, 1961, Aluminium Ltd. was able to announce the purchase of a modern aluminum foundry near Bremen in West Germany as part of a $12 million expansion program "regarded as an attempt by the large Canadian aluminum producer to capitalize on the Common Market." (Toronto Daily Star: 29 Sept. 61).

The expansion of the U.S. aluminum trust is U.S.-controlled Canadian investment abroad, made possible by huge profits extracted from the labor of Canadians, and by the ownership of water power sites and sources of cheap raw materials in Jamaica and British Guiana. It is investment abroad made not for any purpose even remotely connected with the national interests of Canada but simply to maintain and strengthen the world monopoly position of the Mellon-Davis group.

A U.S. group pursuing its own aims uses Canadian-produced profits to expand its own position and is by its very existence involving the Canadian government and people in its efforts to secure raw material sources around the world, in Africa, Asia, the Caribbean, all because the Mellon interests, to evade the U.S. anti-trust laws, have put on a Canadian corporate suit.

Only a few of the directors of Aluminium Ltd. have connections with Canadian banks and industry but the connections they do have are on the highest level. Nearly all the members of its 14-man board of directors are U.S.-born; one of the few exceptions is Earl Alexander, former Governor General of Canada, now a director of Barclays Bank of the United Kingdom, and of Aluminium Ltd.

In 1958 the two directors who had connections with other interests in Canada were both U.S.-born: R. E. Powell and C. D. Howe.

Powell and Howe were then both directors of the Bank of Montreal, the only Canadian bank with which Aluminium Ltd. has connections, although J. Alex Prud'homme, Q.C., a director of Alcan, the operating subsidiary, is a director of the Banque Canadienne Nationale.

J. H. Price, formerly a director both of Aluminium Ltd. and of Price Brothers, has survived only as a director of Saguenay Power.

The Aluminium Ltd. interests have enjoyed particularly favorable relations with Canadian governments in the past, especially in relation to writing off the costs of new power developments as a deduction from taxes in the way most favorable to the company, and it is safe to say that the company still has a comfortable relation with the politicos in Ottawa, in British Columbia, and in Quebec.

Canadian mining interests have been staking claims for themselves abroad with some vigor. The Noranda interests

(J. Y. Murdoch, J. R. Timmins and their associates) own a gold mining subsidiary in Nicaragua (Empresa Minera de Nicaragua). Noranda owns a 48% interest in Anglo-Huronian, a holding company in which the interests of Antenor Patino, Bolivian multi-millionaire, also participate. Anglo-Huronian has an 11% interest in Rhodesian Asbestos, a company controlled, at least until 1958, by the Johns-Manville Corp. of the United States.

The McIntyre Porcupine-Ventures group also have extensive interests, potentially of enormous value, outside Canada.

The Ventures mining empire includes companies in North America, South America and Africa. Important subsidiaries are Falconbridge Nickel, Frobisher Ltd., Giant Yellowknife. The unwieldy corporate empire, with a complicated interlock of subsidiaries and sub-subsidiaries has been undergoing a tidying up process (in spite of protests from minority shareholders) through which various subsidiaries are being consolidated while the inner group realize the customary tax-free capital gains.

Ventures controls La Luz Mines Ltd., a Nicaraguan gold mine; through its subsidiary, Frobisher Ltd., it controls Kilembe Copper Cobalt Ltd. and Sukulu Mines Ltd., both holding Uganda concessions. Frobican Exploration Co. Ltd., another Frobisher subsidiary, is described as the company's "vehicle for exploration in Africa". Frobisher itself operates the Connemara gold mine in Southern Rhodesia. Geoil Ltd., another Frobisher subsidiary, has an interest in several large oil concessions in Peru.

Quebec Metallurgical Industries Ltd., controlled by the Ventures group, is another holding company with wide interests in and outside Canada, including a small gold mine in Brazil, a platinum prospect in the Transvaal, and nickel and cobalt interests in New Caledonia.

The expansion abroad by Canadian capitalists based on the export of capital is closely related to the development of the Canadian economy: the growing concentration of production, the centralization of capital and credit—in fact, to the growth of monopoly—that began to assume importance in Canada in the early 1900's.

The completion of the Canadian Pacific Railway in 1886 and the later period of railway building in the early years of the century and the fortunes amassed by the railway builders formed a "new starting point" for Canadian capitalists, one that they vigorously took advantage of to develop large-scale industry at home through mergers and re-organizations, and to export capital to exploit profitable concessions and franchises in other countries.

The history of these early ventures is instructive for the light it sheds on the export of capital in general. This first ruthless surge of expansion from Canada came as profits accumulated in fewer hands, and as the trustification of the economy got under way. Over and over again, the names of the railway builders appear in connection with concessions or investments in Cuba, Mexico, Brazil, the West Indies.

The whole sequence was clearly and more or less accurately described by the board of directors of Brazilian Traction in 1923 in a tribute to their late chairman, Sir William Mackenzie, who had just died. Sir William, a member of the famous Canadian railway-building partnership of Mackenzie & Mann, was a notable railway promoter and capitalist. His fellow directors summed up his career in these words:

> Shortly after building the first section of the Canadian Northern railway system, which grew, under his presidency, to nearly 10,000 miles of line, and in keeping with his experience in electrifyng the street railway systems of Toronto and Winnipeg, he saw the opportunities for Canadian investment in South America; and was thus a pioneer in demonstrating that in the initiation of enterprises his country had reached an international status.

The words are nicely chosen. "Reached an international status" is a polite way of saying that monopoly had developed in Canada, that surplus profits were available in the hands of a small group who sought even greater profits through the exploitation of concessions in less developed countries.

There is perhaps intentional irony in the listing of Sir William's achievements. He had done much more than electrify street railways in Toronto and Winnipeg; in another sense he had electrified Canada by his bold attempt (with Mann and their legal adviser, Z. A. Lash) to build a whole transcontinental railway system, the Canadian Northern, entirely on other people's money, while retaining full ownership. The genial idea was to finance on government advances and on the sale of government-guaranteed bonds while the promoting group kept all the common stock (absolute ownership and control) in return for "services rendered."

As early as 1888, Donald Mann, who with Mackenzie had just built the CPR short line from Saint John to Montreal, took a jaunt through the Panama area, Ecuador, Peru and Chile, in the search for new and profitable railway-building projects. His unsuccessful search took him as far afield as Imperial China, and though he obtained no concession he achieved a status as an expert on Chinese railway problems.

Ten years later the process was in full swing. Mackenzie and his group in 1899, took the first step in what was later to be Brazilian Traction by incorporating under Ontario law the Sao Paulo Light & Power Co., having obtained a "perpetual concession" to provide Sao Paulo, at that time Brazil's second largest city, now the leading industrial centre in South America, with electric power.

Associated with Mackenzie in this enterprise and later in Mexico was a young U.S. engineer, F. S. Pearson, onetime chief engineer of Dominion Coal Co. Ltd., of which Sir William Van Horne, also a member of the Brazilian and Mexican enterprises, was a director. Pearson refused the presidency of Dominion Coal to become an expert in discovering situations that could be developed profitably.

His exploits included Winnipeg, Niagara Falls, Barcelona, Sao Paulo, Mexico City, and Rio de Janeiro.

In 1900, Sir William Van Horne who had just retired as president of the CPR (he continued as chairman until 1912) began a series of highly profitable ventures in Latin America and the Caribbean. Van Horne was a capable, ruthless organizer who knew where to go in order to get what he wanted. It is a hard reality that his "ability" to extract all-inclusive concessions from governments has left a legacy of political problems still to be solved—from the consequences of which people in several countries are still suffering.

Van Horne was by birth a U.S. citizen and had wide connections with financial circles in New York, London and Canada. His first point of attack was Cuba. At that time (January, 1900) following the defeat of Spain by the Cuban independence forces, the U.S. military forces under General Leonard Wood were in occupation and control. Taking full advantage of this fact and of his influence in U.S. financial circles, Van Horne, with the quick, vigorous action for which he was known, bought up the land needed for the right-of-way of a trans-Cuba railway.

With U.S. and European capital behind him, he began building before any Cuban government with power to approve or disapprove even existed.

That same year (1900) a syndicate headed by Van Horne acquired the electric railway and lighting franchises in three Caribbean centres: Port of Spain (Trinidad), Kingston (Jamaica), and Demerara (British Guiana). It was in the promotion of these enterprises that young Max Aitken, later Lord Beaverbrook, laid the foundation of his wealth. A Beaverbrook biographer has described these gainful activities as "youthful business excursions to the Caribbean area."

To anticipate in order to show the inter-relation between these "youthful excursions" and the process of building monopoly in Canada, one should remember that Beaverbrook, in his short residence in Montreal, approximately

1905 to 1910, created (according to his biographer) "every big trust that was created then in Canada." This creative activity included the formation and financing of the Steel Co. of Canada Ltd. in 1910, and the more celebrated Canada Cement operation of 1908. It was for this type of deal that the experience acquired with Van Horne in the Caribbean was a preparation.

In 1902 Mackenzie and Mann obtained a large concession on the Orinoco River in Venezuela, said to be rich in gold, rubber, and asphalt. At about the same time the colorful career of the Mexican Light & Power Co. Ltd. began. The company was organized in Montreal, with a subscribed capital of $12 million, to supply Mexico City with electricity by virtue of concessions granted by the dictator-president, Porfirio Diaz. According to the newspaper accounts of the time, the principal shareholders included the main railway figures and their banking allies: James Ross (a CPR contractor), E. S. Clouston (Bank of Montreal), Sir William Van Horne (CPR), all of Montreal, Senator George A. Cox (Canadian Bank of Commerce), J. H. Plummer, Sir William Mackenzie, and E. R. Wood, all of Toronto.

One of the chief promoters of Mexlight was F. S. Pearson, the engineer associated with Mackenzie in the Sao Paulo enterprise. Pearson it was who saw the possibilities in the Necaxa site in Mexico, interested his financial allies in Canada, the United States and Britain, and finally planned the largest earth dam and the longest transmission line then known.

Van Horne had still other irons in the fire. In 1903 he turned to Guatemala. Here he operated in association with Keith of the United Fruit Co. and General Hubbard of the U.S. Army, and they received what Van Horne described as "an admirable concession." The group took over a section of already constructed railroad and undertook to complete a line that would link Guatemala City with the country's Atlantic coast.

"We asked for everything we could think of, and we got all we asked for," was Van Horne's cheerful description of the terms of the Guatemala concession; with CPR experience behind him we can be sure that Van Horne was no mean asker. The line of railway built then (1903-08), International Railways of Central America, is still controlled by United Fruit and is still Guatemala's only outlet to the Atlantic, based on the concession so lightly conferred in 1903. One of the aims of the Arbenz government (overthrown in 1954 through U.S.-sponsored intervention) was to complete a highway across Guatemala so as to break the United Fruit transportation monopoly.

The year 1903 was a banner one in the growth of U.S. influence in Central America and the Caribbean (and in the creation of problems for future solution). It was in 1903 that the United States promoted the Panama incident (by which a U.S.-backed group declared the area of Columbia covered by the canal concession to be independent), and then prevented Columbia from re-establishing its sovereignty over the area. The scandalized Toronto Globe commented (4 Dec. 1903):

> There are two sides to the question, of course, but one side is very clearly that of right, while the other is that of expediency.

In that same month of December, 1903, U.S. marines occupied the area of the Guantanamo naval base in Cuba under the terms of an agreement extracted from a Cuban government that was, to put it mildly, only nominally independent.

In 1904, Mackenzie, Pearson and their associates extended their operations in Brazil through the incorporation and organization (under Canadian charter) of the Rio de Janeiro Tramway Co.

A revealing anecdote of this period is found in the memoirs of D. B. Hanna, later the first president of the Canadian National railway system and also a director of the then soon-to-be-organized Brazilian Traction. In 1905 (according to Hanna) Mackenzie, "an inveterate optimist", was interested in the idea of extending the Canadian Northern to Hudson Bay. Asked by a sceptical friend if he had ever been to the Bay, Mackenzie is said to have retorted:

> No, and I haven't been to Sao Paulo either, but I've taken a million dollars out of there within the last three years.

Now Sir William may have been boasting, but regardless of how many millions had in fact been taken out, he left no doubt as to his intentions. It would probably not have occurred to him to argue even as a joke that his purpose was to confer a benefit on the people of Brazil. Taking out was his aim, whether from Winnipeg or Rio.

Canadian financial circles continued to show strong interest in Mexico. Another important venture of the period in which Toronto and Canadian Bank of Commerce interests were involved was Mexico Tramways, also operated under a Diaz-granted concession; by 1906 other Canadian groups were seeking Mexican concessions and the Bank of Montreal opened a Mexico City branch. In that same year bonds of the Puerto Rico railway ($1.5 million) and of the Puebla Light & Power of Mexico ($1.6 million) were taken up in Canada.

In 1911 Pearson and his Canadian Bank of Commerce allies moved into Spain; the Barcelona Traction, Light & Power Co. was organized, with a Canadian charter, to supply electric power in northern and eastern Spain.

The development of the Brazilian enterprises continued. In 1908 the Sao Paulo Light & Power exchanged its Ontario charter for a Dominion one; four years later the Sao Paulo and Rio enterprises controlled by Mackenzie, Pearson and their allies were brought together under the control of Brazilian Traction, Light & Power Co. Ltd., a newly incorporated Canadian company with an authorized share capital of $120 million.

In this advance on Mexico and Brazil, the West Indies had not been overlooked, even though opportunities there were on a smaller scale. The Bank of Nova Scotia had

opened a Jamaica branch as early as 1889. Canadian
banking interests, later forming part of the Royal Bank of
Canada, entered Cuba during the U.S. occupation.

By 1912 we find T. B. Macaulay, later head of the Sun
Life Assurance Company of Canada, then president of
the Canadian West Indian League, advocating complete
union of the British West Indies and Canada.

All this aggressive expansion abroad by Canadian capitalists gave rise to complaints (especially in western Canada) that too much Canadian money was going out of
the country. (Had Sir William Mackenzie cared to do so,
he might have put matters in a different light; we are
told however that he was "sphinx-like in his attitude towards the public").

In 1913 the Canadian House of Commons Committee
on Banking and Commerce investigated the complaints.
Two eminent Canadian bankers were examined on the
point.

Sir Edmund Walker, president of the Canadian Bank
of Commerce, offered a realistic explanation and incidentally threw some light on the relationship between investment, ownership, and control:

> My own bank—we have been the bankers of the two most
> important South American enterprises—that is, the Rio and
> Sao Paulo enterprises. Our loans there have been loans on
> underwritings generally made in England . . . Regarding the
> South American enterprises as a whole, I think the situation
> today is that Canada has not a dollar of capital in them that
> has cost her anything. The money to build them—that is, the
> enterprises at Rio and Sao Paulo—was found in England, Bel-
> gium, Switzerland, and throughout the continent of Europe.
> The idea that money was found in Canada is a delusion. We
> lent money on those undertakings or on securities that were
> to be sold in Europe, but that is a very different thing from
> supporting the enterprises as such.

Sir Edmund said Canada when it is clear that he meant
the Canadian Bank of Commerce, and he emphasized
distinctions in order to meet criticism, but there was
obvious satisfaction for him in the fact that he and his

group had control (as they did have) of enterprises that one year later were to show combined assets of $230.5 million, and "not a dollar in them that cost (us) anything."

The general manager of the Royal Bank of Canada, Mr. Edson L. Pease, also appeared before the committee. He was asked if he considered his bank's West Indian business to be profitable. He was frank and to the point:

> Yes, it is, so much so that four or five years ago we received an offer from an American syndicate of no less than one million dollars for the good-will of the business, if we would retire.

Pease went on to defend the establishment of Canadian branch banks in Cuba, and pointed to the big increase in trade between Canada and Cuba since the Royal Bank had opened its Cuban branches.

These comments by promoters and bankers on the way in which Canadian investment abroad took shape in the form of raids on economically less-developed countries were made without the aid of modern public relations experts and hence without the hypocrisy that insists that investments of the type we have been talking about are intended to help the country in which they are made. Nothing could be more remote from reality.

Mackenzie, Van Horne, Beaverbrook's biographer, Sir Edmund Walker, Pease, are all witnesses in one form or another to the fact that the aim was to extract the maximum possible profit, and as far as the promoters were concerned, they succeeded. Beaverbrook's biographer notes that he (Beaverbrook)

> promoted electric light, tramways, and many other utilities, to his own substantial profit, and, incidentally, no doubt to the convenience of the inhabitants.

Quite incidentally — and rather an expensive convenience.

Apologists sometimes talk of the "risk" run by these courageous pioneers in foreign investment as a justification for the "taking out." But none of the gentlemen

144 ANATOMY OF BIG BUSINESS

involved were risk-takers, at least not with their own money.
They preferred to and generally did bet on a sure thing.

They were the people with the know-how and with
capital behind them; they were the experienced financial
operators; they knew how to profit both from the construction and operation of enterprises; their position rested
on perpetual or long-term franchises, tailored to suit them,
on government-guaranteed loans, and on relations with
governments that made it possible to set rates and prices
at a level that made success certain — and made it equally
certain that their successors in profit would find themselves faced with a rising tide of popular demands that
the enterprise be nationalized.

Not all the companies founded by the Mackenzie, Van
Horne, Pearson group in the early 1900's have survived.
In several cases while the promoters did well, shareholders
in later years did not. Mexico Tramways was taken over
by the Mexican government in 1946; Barcelona Traction
was declared bankrupt by a Spanish court in 1948 and
long-drawn-out legal proceedings have followed. The
Mexican government bought control of Mexlight in 1960.
Control of the Mexican and Barcelona enterprises had
passed from Canadian to Belgian hands, but Brazilian
Traction still has substantial Canadian participation.

Mexican Light & Power Co. Ltd. began as a Canadian-
controlled company although no doubt always with substantial participation from European capital, but for some
years prior to the take-over by Mexico, Mexlight had been
controlled by the 40% interest of Sofina, the Belgian trust
whose ramifications are world-wide including Argentina
and Spain as well as Mexico.

Sofina has always operated through an intricate chain
of subsidiaries, in the effort to keep its affairs as private
as possible. It was said in 1944 that Sofina, "created in
Belgium in 1928, registered in Panama, keeps its books of
account and its documents in Cuba, has its office in New
York and its technical experts in Lisbon."

Sofina announced during 1960 that it was selling its 40% interest in Mexlight to a mysterious "unknown" purchaser represented by the Central American Investment Trust of Vaduz, Liechenstein, operating through the Hong Kong & Shanghai Banking Corporation of Paris. Other shareholders were advised to accept a similar offer and sell their own shares to the "unknown" purchaser. Sofina solemnly maintained that it did not know the identity of the purchaser, meaning simply that it had undertaken to try and keep a secret.

In the event the purchaser was the government of Mexico, now, as a result of the purchase, free to plan the development of Mexican water power resources on a national basis.

An idea of the changed relationships within Brazilian Traction can be obtained by comparing the composition of its first board of directors with that of today's board.

The first president of the company was F. S. Pearson, and the first chairman of the board, Sir William Mackenzie. Of five vice-presidents, three were members of the Lash legal firm in Toronto, closely associated with Mackenzie. Ten of the fifteen members of the first board were prominent Toronto financiers or their legal associates, with close Canadian Bank of Commerce connections; two were from London, one from Montreal (Van Horne), one from New York (Pearson), and one from Rio.

Forty-five years later the Brazilian board is still predominantly Canadian as far as the geographical distribution of directorships is concerned but it is doubtful that this reflects the site of the controlling interest, and the Canadian members of the board are not all representing Canadian capital.

Today the board of Brazilian has twenty-three members, plus one honorary director. Of this number, fifteen, including the honorary director, are Canadians, three are from the United States, two from the United Kingdom, two from Belgium, and two from Rio de Janeiro (of whom one is a Canadian).

Brazilian and the Commerce, now Imperial-Commerce, still have five directors in common. The president and two vice-presidents of the bank are directors of Brazilian; the chairman and president of Brazilian are directors of the bank.

The Blake & Cassels law firm, active to the end in Mexlight, has given way in Brazilian to the law firm headed by Henry Borden, president of the company and a nephew of Sir Robert Borden, Canada's World War I prime minister. The honorary director of Brazilian, W. A. G. Kelly, Q.C., is also a member of the Borden law firm and a former director of the Canadian Bank of Commerce.

Directors of four other Canadian banks sit on the Brazilian board: W. E. Phillips of the Royal, G. Blair Gordon of the Montreal, Beverley Matthews of the Toronto-Dominion, and W. C. Harris of the Nova Scotia.

Brazilian directors have interests in a wide variety of Canadian companies. They are interlocked with four Canadian trust companies: National Trust Co. Ltd. (3), The Toronto General Trusts Corp. (3), The Royal Trust Co. (2), Crown Trust Co. (1), and with four life insurance companies: The Canada Life Assurance Co., Confederation Life Association, The Imperial Life Assurance Co. of Canada, The Mutual Life Assurance Co. of Canada, and with a number of investment trusts including the two Calvin Bullock funds: Canadian Fund Inc. (2) and Canadian Investment Fund (2).

In addition to these banking and financial connections, Canadian directors of Brazilian are linked to a number of important industrial firms, several of them U.S.-controlled. Henry Borden and J. A. Eccles are directors of The Bell Telephone Co. of Canada; W. E. Phillips is a director of Canadian Westinghouse Co. Ltd.; W. C. Harris of Canadian General Electric Co. Ltd.; Dr. R. L. Hearn, former chairman of The Ontario Hydro Electric Power Commission, is a director of British Newfoundland Corp. Ltd., of Venezuelan Power Co. Ltd., of Canada Wire & Cable Co. Ltd.; G. Blair Gordon of Dominion

Textile Co. Ltd., the Canadian Pacific Railway Co., and Canadian Industries Ltd.; J. A. Eccles is also a director of Imperial Chemicals of Canada, of The Shawinigan Water & Power Co., and of Canadian International Paper Co.

Clearly this group of Canadians are men with interests that reach into many corners of the Canadian economy; it is significant that so many of them, from Henry Borden down, hold directorships in U.S.-controlled firms operating in Canada (and one or two in U.K.-controlled firms). This is indicative of the relationship between Brazilian Traction and U.S. capital and (another way of saying the same thing) of the fact that Canadian exporters of capital are closely related to the U.S. and other foreign interests investing in Canada.

The United Kingdom interests in Brazilian are represented by Lord Bridges, former permanent secretary to the British cabinet, former permanent secretary to the Treasury, and a director of Babcock & Wilcox, and by J. G. Phillimore, a member of the British banking firm, Baring Brothers & Co. Ltd. Of the two Belgians, one is F. Van Langenhouve, former Secretary General of the Belgian Foreign Office and for ten years Belgium's permanent delegate to the United Nations.

There are now three U.S. members of the Brazilian board: Clarence Stanley, a vice-president of General Motors Corp.; W. L. Cisler, president of Detroit Edison, a direcor of Burroughs Corp. and of Fruehauf Trailers; and J. Peter Grace, president of W. R. Grace & Co., the leading South American shipping firm, and a director of the First National City Bank of New York, of Ingersoll Rand, Kennecott Copper, etc. Peter Grace is a director of Stone & Webster Inc., a U.S. holding company with a number of public utility subsidiaries; W. E. Phillips is a director of Stone & Webster of Canada.

Thus the Brazilian board, with its U.S., Belgian, U.K., and Canadian components, represents an alliance of several financial groups in which the most prominent although

not necessarily dominant role is played by a group associated with the Canadian Imperial Bank of Commerce, an
alliance in which in recent years there has been a steady
growth of U.S. influence, particularly First National City
Bank influence, to the point where the company is now to
all intents and purposes within the orbit of U.S. capital.

At the 1959 shareholders meeting, Brazilian announced
the distribution of its shares and shareholders. (The Telegram: 24 June 59). According to the information provided, 6.0 million shares were held by 30,000 Canadian
shareholders, 3.5 million by 5,000 U.S. shareholders, 1.4
million by 1,000 U.K. shareholders, and 100,000 shares
elsewhere. (Figures all rounded).

This is intended to suggest that control rests in Canada,
but the suggestion is not convincing. Many so-called Canadian shares are held by U.S.-controlled investment trusts
or by Canadian financial interests linked to U.S. capital;
we are not given any information on the distribution of
the large shareholdings; and to cap it all, the total number
of shares accounted for is less than 11 million when, as
of June 29th, 1958, there were said to be over 17 million
shares outstanding.

Brazilian Traction publishes the results of its operations
in dollars (in U.S. dollars at that, another indication of
the interests most concerned in it) and on the basis of
this calculation in dollars Henry Borden had a sad story
to tell the 1960 annual meeting (Globe & Mail: 29 June
60): net profits had dropped from $36 million in 1956
to $26 million in 1957, to $11 million in 1958, and to a
scant $10 million in 1959, and hence no dividends could
be paid.

But of course in Brazil the operating companies owned
by Brazilian Traction do not collect street car fares in U.S.
currency or send out hydro or phone bills in U.S. dollars.
They carry on business in the currency of Brazil, in cruz-
eiros, and in cruzeiro terms the company was doing very
well indeed — earnings for 1959 were up 19% over 1958.

The problem facing Brazilian Traction, a wholly artificial one arising from the non-Brazilian ownership of the
enterprise, was to change greater cruzeiro profits into U.S.
dollars, given a fall in the value of Brazilian currency and
the existence of Brazilian government controls over the
rate at which cruzeiro remittances can be converted into
dollars.

The foreign exchange difficulties of Brazil are directly
related to the system of which Brazilian Traction forms a
part: outside control and limited industrial development.
Until the government-owned oil company, Petrobras, can
make Brazil self-sufficient in oil, until Brazil produces even
more of the things she needs, until her exports are sufficiently diversified to lessen dependence on the fluctuating
price of coffee, in a word, until the over-all dependence
of Brazil on the United States is lessened, the currency of
Brazil will be weak in terms of the dollar, a weakness to
which the existence of Brazilian Traction and other foreign-
controlled enterprises contributes because of their demands
for U.S. dollars to send out of the country. Brazilian
Traction is helping to create the problem that causes it
trouble, trouble that would not exist if the company and
others like it were operated by Brazilians in the interests
of Brazil.

Brazilian Traction has struggled to maintain its position
against growing resentment in Brazil. The company is
seeking to get out of its street car concession in Rio on
which it claims to be losing money, and hold on to its
other interests. Lawyers for one of the Brazilian states
have asked that Brazilian's light concession in Rio be
cancelled, alleging that Brazilian has overcharged the
consumer and failed to provide service to growing sections
of the city.   .   .   .

Another Canadian financial group, that associated with
the Royal Securities Corporation and Montreal Engineering Co., has for years milked a handful of smaller public
utilities operating in five countries, in Venezuela (Maracaibo and Barquisimeto), in Bolivia (La Paz, Oruro), in El

Salvador (San Salvador and 32 municipalities), in Mexico (Monterrey), and in British Guiana (Georgetown). At one time the list included Puerto Rico and Newfoundland. The company operating in Puerto Rico was sold to the U.S. government in 1943 at what the then governor of Puerto Rico, Rexford Tugwell, felt to be an "outrageous" price, to be paid for by "the people of Puerto Rico" "over a period of twenty years in inflated rates," but "no one," said Tugwell, "showed any concern over that." The company operating in Newfoundland was, for tax reasons, given an independent corporate structure when Newfoundland entered Confederation although it remains under group control along with three other power companies operating in Canada.

The Latin and South American companies, many of them the product of Beaverbrook's youthful ventures and of Van Horne's eye for a bargain, have, since 1926, been operated through International Power Co. Ltd., a holding company controlled in his lifetime by I. W. Killam, Canadian millionaire power magnate, who himself owned 100,000 shares out of the total 197,500 issued by International Power.

Killam was president of Royal Securities Corporation from 1915 until January, 1954. He died in August, 1955. Since then a further level of exploitation has been added to an already complicated structure. The Royal Securities-Montreal Engineering group associated with Killam formed a new alliance, bought his holding, and in December, 1956, formed a new company to take control of International Power. The new holding company, Canadian International Power Co. Ltd., has taken over the old holding company which continues in existence to control the operating companies in the five countries mentioned. The two holding companies have identical boards of directors.

The income of International Power is based on the dividends declared by the operating companies in the five countries; the income of Canadian International Power is based on dividends declared by International Power.

Since 1957 these have been running at $12 a share. Since the operations all take place outside Canada, this income is tax-free in the hands of Canadian International Power.

We see as we examine the background of these transactions that the controlling group have made fabulous profits, not so much in dividends received from the operating companies as in the manipulation of the holding companies' stock and by taking advantage of Canadian tax laws. They have shown themselves real specialists in plunder.

The story has been told in part in The Power and the Money but it is repeated here because of the light it sheds on the way financial interests outside a country can take advantage of control of holding companies to make large gains at the expense, ultimately, of consumers within the country. The situation necessarily leads to a demand that the operating company or companies be nationalized so as to end outside control and resultant high costs.

Two instances of this legal robbery are conspicuous both for the profits they brought the insiders and the social uselessness of the actions taken.

The first took place under Killam's leadership during the years 1950 to 1954, the second under that of his successors and former associates in 1956-7. An examination of the procedure followed in the formation of the original companies and the take-over by International Power in 1926 would probably uncover other examples.

International Power had paid no dividends from 1926 to 1949 but had been piling up substantial reserves in undistributed profits. The declared policy of the company was that of "gradual expansion from retained earnings," but the Killam group took care to see that as little as possible was retained. By 1950 the time had come to divide the loot. Instead of using the reserves for expansion, a substantial chunk was used to make a huge tax-free gift to Killam and the other shareholders.

This was possible through the amendment to the Canadian Income Tax Act in 1950 which gave companies the right to pay a 15% tax on profits undistributed to the end of 1949 and then distribute the balance, tax-paid, to their shareholders.

The company paid the tax and had $8,415,000 on hand, taxes pre-paid, to distribute to the shareholders. The distribution took the form of a tax-free dividend of redeemable preference shares (5½%) issued to the existing shareholders on the basis of $43 worth of the new preferred for every share of common held. Killam owned 100,000 shares of common; he received as a bonus preferred stock with a face value of $4,300,000. Having issued the preferred stock, the company then proceeded to redeem it for cash over a three year period. The result of a complicated, socially wasteful operation was a tax-free gift to Killam of $4.3 million.

Beginning in 1949, the company began to pay dividends of $2.40 a share. Thus Killam, in addition to his tax-free gain, the most important benefit to him, was also receiving $240,000 a year in dividends (taxable) and 5½% on the preferred stock during the three years in which it was being redeemed, also taxable income.

After his death, his Royal Securities and Montreal Engineering associates devised a new coup. Needless to say, this project, like the former, was not in the least calculated to provide better service for the unfortunate consumers of power in Bolivia, El Salvador, Venezuela, British Guiana, etc. (The Jagan government of British Guiana has been trying to arrange a U.K. loan, said to be for $45 million, to take over Demerara Electric in the interests of the people of British Guiana.) (Globe & Mail: 2 Aug. 60).

The syndicate (Royal Securities-Montreal Engineering with three U.S. allies) bought the Killam holding of 100,-0000 shares of International Power for $24 million or $240 a share.

Their next step was to form a new holding company, Canadian International Power, with an authorized capital of $60 million in preferred shares and 2,500,000 no par value common shares. Both companies were controlled by the syndicate: International through the purchase of the Killam shares, Canadian International they had themselves formed.

The syndicate then offered the shareholders of International Power (they were themselves the majority shareholder) an exchange of shares — three of the $50 6% preferred shares and twelve no par value common shares of Canadian International Power for each share of International Power. This offer was accepted by shareholders owning 97% of the International Power shares.

At this point the syndicate, who, with their backers, had put up $24 million for the 100,000 shares that Killam formerly owned in International Power now held as a result of the exchange 300,000 6% preferred shares (par value, $50 each) in the new company plus 1,200,000 shares of the no par value common. This block of shares plus other shareholdings of syndicate members gave them absolute control of the new holding company.

It is clear that the syndicate through this complicated operation have got hold of a very good thing in which the potential profit is to be measured in millions; the amount depending on how many shares they held on to, and how many were sold to the public and at what price. At one point, six months after the transaction went through, the paper profit of the syndicate was as high as $10 million. One hundred thousand shares of preferred were offered to the public at $46 a share. By 1958 the common reached $27 a share. By the end of 1961 the market quotation of the common stock had sharply declined (at one point to $9 a share), and the paper profit had vanished, but no doubt the syndicate had sold at least a part of their holdings near the top of the market and the public, not the syndicate, was swallowing the loss on the common shares. The important fact was that the syndicate retained control of the lopsided corporate structure and could look foward to a fresh assault on the corporate treasury in the future.

The same Royal Securities-Montreal Engineering group have control of several utilities operating in Canada. G.

A. Gaherty, president of Montreal Engineering and a director of Royal Securities, is president of Calgary Power Ltd., and of Ottawa Valley Power Co.; Denis Stairs, vice-president of Montreal Engineering, is president of Newfoundland Light & Power Co. Ltd., and of Maritime Electric Co. Ltd.; Frederick Krug, vice-president of Montreal Engineering and a director of Royal Securities, is president of Canadian International Power Co. Ltd., and of International Power Co. Ltd. On the boards of each of these companies there is a preponderance of directors associated with Royal Securities or Montreal Engineering, or both.

The total assets (end '58) of the companies controlled by the group are as follows:

Calgary Power	$126.2 million
Can. Intl. Power	92.5 "
Newfoundland Light & Power	29.8 "
Ottawa Valley Power	13.2 "
Maritime Electric	9.4 "
	$271.1 "

Individual members of the group hold directorships in Nova Scotia Light & Power Co. Ltd. and in Trans-Canada Pipe Lines Ltd. There are no bank directors among its members but the group has Royal Bank associations judging from the facts that the Montreal Trust Co. acts as transfer agent for most of the companies and that the Howard law firm, solicitors for the Royal Bank, were consulted in reference to the Canadian International Power deal.

Again we see the close connection between the concentration of control in Canada and the export of Canadian capital. There is not a single reason founded on common sense or efficiency of operation why a small group of Montreal financiers and their U.S. associates, operating from 244 St. James Street West, Montreal, should control the distribution of electricity in Calgary, Fredericton, St. John's, Monterrey, La Paz, Maracaibo and Georgetown, a group that have given the minimum attention to providing service and the maximum to watering the stock of their companies.

The present day operations of Canadian International Power, like those of Brazilian Traction, rest on the franchises and concessions "secured" by the robber barons of the first decade of the century. The profits taken out by the promoters still form part of the capital structure of the companies, a non-existent asset that keeps down profits for today's shareholders (and keeps rates up), but today's inside controlling groups still have the opportunity to make sensational profits from re-financing as the case of Canadian International Power shows.

The fact that today's tycoons have been schooled to talk about "giving service" instead of taking out profit has not changed anything. Behind the new, elaborately contrived façades can be discerned the activities of the modern big shots, employing modern techniques for self-enrichment, just as profit-conscious as Mackenzie and Van Horne, and with equally small regard for the needs of the people in the countries where their companies operate.

.   .   .

In recent years the associations of Canadian capital with the International Bank for Reconstruction and Development (the World Bank) have assumed increasing importance and have proved extremely advantageous to the Canadian financial oligarchy.

The World Bank, fifteen years old in 1961, has a capital of $20 billion subscribed by the member nations, with U.S. capital in the dominant role; "The United States' capital subscription of $6.35 billion . . . is the major financial underpinning" (of the World Bank). (New York Times: 14 Feb. 60).

The bank, at least in the eyes of a Globe & Mail financial writer, is not entirely a disinterested body; to him "One Good Answer to Communism is World Bank." (Globe & Mail: 21 Sept. 61).

World Bank loans bring assorted benefits to the financial groups taking part in them. An example is a December, 1957 World Bank loan in which the Royal Bank and eight other banks from different countries participated. The loan was for $40 million to the government of the Belgian Congo, now the Congo Republic, for a highway building program, the money to be used mainly for imported machinery.

To the unwary, this Congo loan might appear to be a do-good operation and nothing more; when we examine the forces involved we see it more realistically as part of the system we have been describing, based on the exploitation, particularly brutal, of a particularly rich colony.

The Royal Bank of Canada and its associates were not just extending a helping hand to strangers in a far-off land. Quite the contrary. At the time the Congo was a Belgian colony whose administration and economy were dominated by the wealthy Union Minière du Haut-Katanga. The Union Minière achieved a certain notoriety in the '20's and '30's by obliging would-be purchasers of radium to pay $70,000 a gram, until competition from the Canadian Eldorado company forced the price down to a mere $20,000 a gram, a level at which both companies were able to make a profit. Union Minière profits were estimated by the Globe & Mail (26 July 60) to be three billion francs, something like $60 million, a year.

The Union Minière is owned by the Société Générale de Belgique, a rich pie in which several interests (including the Rockefellers and British capitalists) have their fingers but the Belgians run the show.

The Société Générale has been using its accumulated Congo profits to expand its holdings in Belgium and abroad, including Canada.

Their Canadian centre of operations is Sogemines Ltd., a Canadian-incorporated investment and holding company, closely linked to the Royal Bank of Canada. In 1959, James Muir, then president of the Royal, and W. H. Howard, Q.C., vice-president of the Royal, were both

directors of Sogemines Ltd., as was F. C. Cope, Q.C.,
a partner in the Howard law firm, the solicitors for the
Royal Bank. Six Sogemines directors are directors of the
Société Générale and two of them are also directors of
Union Minière.

Sogemines has a number of Canadian interests and this
brings us back to the earlier point that the relationships
between Canadian and Belgian capital are based on
alliances that operate both in Belgium or the Congo and
in Canada. Sogemines' most important Canadian interest
is in Canadian Petrofina Ltd. On the Petrofina board of
fifteen sit six Sogemines directors: W. H. Howard, Jean
Raymond, Jules R. Timmins, W. L. Forster, and two
Belgians, plus another Royal Bank director, D. W. Am-
bridge, president of Abitibi Power & Paper.

These are all important figures in the oligarchy. We
have already noted the connections of W. H. Howard.
Jean Raymond is a director of Banque Canadienne
Nationale, Canadian International Paper Co., Canadian
Celanese Ltd., Noranda Mines Ltd., Dominion Steel & Coal
Corp. Ltd., etc. Jules R. Timmins is a vice-president of the
Canadian Imperial Bank of Commerce, a director of the
Royal Trust Co., of Trans-Canada Pipe Lines Ltd., etc.,
as well as being a key figure in the Hollinger-Noranda
complex and the Canadian side of the Iron Ore Company
of Canada. W. L. Forster is a director of W. C. Pitfield
& Co., the Montreal investment firm.

Sogemines interlocks with Dosco, the A. V. Roe-control-
led steel producer, through the presence of F. C. Cope
and Jean Raymond on the Dosco board.

Sogemines and Dosco have been reported (Globe &
Mail: 7 July 60) to be joining in the construction of a
new $70 million rolling mill and integrated steel facility
on the south shore of the St. Lawrence, across from Montreal, although by 1961 the project was said to have been
abandoned.

Sogemines has been reported (Globe & Mail: 18 Feb.
60) to be investing $17.5 million to put into operation

the New Brunswick mines of Brunswick Mining & Smelting Corp. Ltd. in which the St. Joseph Lead Co. of the U.S., Morgan-controlled, has a heavy interest.

Sogemines has interests in cement, controlling Inland Cement Co. Ltd. and its subsidiary, Saskatchewan Cement. The Société Générale, through another subsidiary, United Cement and Brick (CBR), has paid $50 million to take over the cement and construction enterprises of the Miron brothers of Montreal. (le Devoir: 19 July 60). Mr. St. Laurent, former prime minister, is now chairman of la Compagnie Miron limitée.

Thus the Royal Bank loan to the Congo is more than a loan. It is on the part of the Royal Bank an opportunity to help and be helped by its Belgian associates. The full picture shows a large Canadian bank, linked at home with Sogemines Ltd. which is owned by the Société Générale the owners of the Union Minière, lending money to build roads in the Congo (to the undoubted benefit of Union Minière interests who have other more profitable uses for their money) while Union Minière profits find their way back through the Société Générale into Sogemines and interests connected with the Royal and other banks.

Everyone is happy; everyone is scratching everyone else's back at a profit—and the profits are extracted from the labor of Congo workers who up till recently have had nothing to say about the situation.

Another aspect of this system of doing business is shown by "certain precautions" taken by the Belgian government before handing over control to the new Congo government (Globe & Mail: 1 Aug. 60):

> The Congo's gold reserves were transferred to Brussels. The Belgian administration in the Congo carefully collected all the taxes it could up to the day of the hand-over. But it left many of its internal accounts unpaid for the first half of the financial year, and the new government has inherited these debts.

The Belgian friends of the Royal Bank give every evidence of knowing the tricks of the trade—but the Royal is no doubt able to deal with them on even terms, and in any case has been glad to take their money.

The whole transaction is part of the world-wide system we have been discussing by which financial groups vigorously drive for the maximum profit for themselves. The system finds an extremely profitable expression in the exploitation of less advanced countries by monopoly groups, that is, in the exploitation which is the essence of colonialism, or, put from an alternative point of view, of imperialism. In this exploitation Canadian financial groups (or financial groups based on Canadian holdings) take an active part, in co-operation with their financial allies.

These facts conflict with the point of view of those who like to speak of Canada's disinterestedness and freedom from selfish interests of any kind. People who think in those terms are usually careful to speak of the role of Canada, rather than, more accurately but less convincingly, of the role of the Canadian government or of Canadian financial groups.

But the policy of a country and its people can only find expression in the policies of its government, and no matter how gratifying it might be for Canadians to consider the government of Canada as one of the world's most disinterested governments, the facts are against us.

We cannot overlook the relationships of Canadian banks, insurance companies and industry with financial groups in other countries, primarily of course with groups in the United States, but also with U.K., Belgian and West German groups.

All these groups have their hands quite strongly on assets and resources in other countries as at home; their concern is with their world profit position; all of them, directly or indirectly, exercise powerful influence on the internal and external policies adopted by the Canadian government.

But James M. Minifie, in his interesting and valuable book, Peacemaker or Powdermonkey, (1960) repeats the

old, old story by quoting with approval the Hon. Howard
C. Green:

> Howard C. Green, the Secretary of State for External Af-
> fairs, has pointed out that Canada is peculiarly fitted to pro-
> vide (enlightened and selfless) leadership because its creden-
> tials are sound. Nobody fears Canada since it is without ter-
> ritorial ambitions. Nobody harbours resentment against Cana-
> da, because it has never held sovereign control over an alien
> people. Nobody suspects Canada of coveting national resour-
> ces—it has plenty of its own. (Page 3).

Minifie repeats the same thought later in the book. Canada, he says, is

> . . . free of the taint of economic and military imperialism
> which in Latin nostrils clings to the United States . . . (Page
> 40).

And the editors of the Globe & Mail, in saying what
Canada could do to help the Congo, could not resist adding (2 Aug. 60)

> As a Middle Power which has never held any colonies . . .
> Canada has an important role to play . . .

Now there is a sense in which these statements, or at
least some of them, are true.

The Canadian people don't have any imperialist ambi-
tions—nor for that matter do people in general.

But it is the role of governments and of the forces behind them that has to be considered, and there is a substantial difference between the picture of a selfless Canada
put forward by Messrs Green, Minifie and the editors of
the Globe & Mail, and the policies and actions of the Canadian government.

To boast, as Mr. Green does, that Canada has no colonies, is to make a formally correct political statement. But
to think of colonies and colonialism only in political terms
is to disregard the economic facts that we have been discussing. Mr. Green has ignored the profits coming into
Canada (into the treasuries of enterprises operating in

Canada) from the exploitation of less advanced econo-
mies. He has risen above a consideration of the plight of
Newfoundlanders, politically equal, economically colonized.
And he forgets about the position of Canada's Indian and
Arctic peoples, a point not irrelevant to a discussion of
selflessness and freedom from the taint of imperialism.

Perhaps the final word on Mr. Green's pleasant but unreal image was uttered by the Prime Minister of Canada
when he was reported as saying (Globe & Mail: 2 Aug.
60) that "Canada" was unable to promise capital assis-
tance to the new Congo republic "as Canada, in a stage of
great development, needed capital itself."

Now this is an indication of policy by the Prime Minister, speaking for the government and thus committing the
Canadian people. As a policy no doubt it has supporters
but the most determined of them would be unlikely to describe it as "selfless" or "enlightened."

The real point at issue, one that directly affects Canadians, is the right of countries whose development is frus-
trated or distorted by outside control of important resources, industries or sectors of industry, to assert their sovereignty and nationalize these resources or industries so as to
be able to develop their economy on the basis of national
needs.

CHAPTER VII

Room at the Top

THIS IS THE STORY of a small, closely organized financial group who own shares worth $30 million (they paid far less for them) and through that ownership control corporate assets worth one billion dollars.

It is the story of the able, ruthless men who form the group headed by E. P. Taylor, a story of insiders, of influence, of knowing the right people and being in the right place at the right time, of leverage, mergers and holding companies, and how men can make millions selling something to themselves.

It deals with their influence with government and their conflicts with the law—investigations, reports, trials—following which business went on as usual, their alliances and their struggles with other financial groups, their expansion into the United States and Britain.

What distinguishes this group and their story from that of other tycoons is simply the fact that more is known about Taylor and his associates, not facts involving personal dishonesty, but the doings that make up the annals of the rich, the normal, day-to-day dealings of a group of men intent on making the best of a very good thing for themselves.

Taylor and his allies are closely linked to the Royal Bank of Canada and the Canadian Imperial Bank of Commerce, the two largest of the big three banks. They coordinate their main activities through Argus Corporation Ltd., a holding company which they control and which in turn controls a group of important companies and their subsidiaries.

No other group has clashed so often with the Combines Investigation Act, Canada's anti-trust legislation. In 1954, Dominion Tar & Chemical, an Argus-controlled company, was named as one of a group of companies charged with fixing the prices of asphalt and tar roofing. In 1958, St. Lawrence Corporation and Howard Smith Paper Mills Ltd., both Argus-controlled companies, were charged with forming part of a group of pulp and paper companies that had agreed to limit the prices they would pay farmers and small producers of pulpwood.

The most recent clash ended with the trial (and acquittal) of Canadian Breweries Ltd., the brewing giant through which Taylor founded his empire, on a charge of operating a combine in the brewing industry.

It is a comment on the vigor with which the Combines Investigation Act is enforced to note that the government investigation of the alleged breweries combine began in 1951, that the report of the investigation is dated May, 1955, and that the trial of Canadian Breweries Ltd. on charges arising from the investigation began only in October, 1959.

The trial lasted 38 days and cost the government $153,526. The amount of the fees paid the lawyers of Canadian Breweries was not made public. The outcome was a decision by the Chief Justice of Ontario that there was no evidence to show that the public interest had been "detrimentally affected" by the activities of Canadian Breweries. The Minister of Justice announced that the government would not appeal the decision.

With this charge disposed of, Taylor returned to his expansion program in Canada, in the United States, and in Britain. Within a year Canadian Breweries had taken over the Calgary Brewing & Malting Co. No price was announced but a Financial Post writer (11 Feb. 61) estimated it at $6,750,000.

Following Taylor's victory in the Canadian Breweries case, the Globe & Mail (10 Feb. 60) exultantly reported

"No Crime to be Big," echoed in the Financial Post (13 Feb. 60) "Bigness isn't necessarily Badness."

There is of course more to the story than the question of bigness. We shall not discuss the evil of bigness but the consequences to Canada of the control of a group of enterprises by a handful of tycoons who, through a series of financial coups and the investment of relatively small amounts of their own money, have achieved control of a large capital belonging to others.

The bigness of the corporations is not the point. It is the fact that they are controlled by a small group in the interests of that group. Other questions arise: "What useful purpose does this group serve?" "Why should they be in a position to make big tax-free gains at the expense of the people who work for them and of the public?" "Is it sensible that beer, pulp and paper, chemical products, farm machinery, should all be produced under the control of a financial group whose main interest is focussed on maximizing their total profit position?"

While the Taylor group, thanks to government inquiries and a flood of newspaper and magazine articles, is the most publicized group of its kind in Canada, its weight in the economy is not as great as the volume of publicity would suggest. Taylor and his allies do have a place of increasing importance in the business hierarchy, but their companies are not as decisive to the economy as for example those controlled by the Bank of Montreal inner group or as a number of other giants operating in Canada.

The Taylor interests in pulp and paper are important and growing but they are less important than Canadian International Paper, the U.S.-controlled giant, or the Bowater interests of Britain. Massey-Ferguson and Dominion Tar & Chemical, two key Taylor companies, are not as basic to the economy as the Steel Company of Canada, as International Nickel, or Aluminium Ltd.

The comparison is not intended to suggest that the Taylor group is pure Canadian and, while smaller, "better" than the internationally-controlled giants. The fact is that the Taylor group while it is very conscious of the advantages of appearing to be national has strong ties with U.S. capital and does business around the world.

Taylor himself is a tycoon in the grand manner and his varied activities attract a stream of publicity. Thanks to his racing stable, his jovial face is often seen beaming, under a grey top hat, on the sports pages of the daily papers. Taylor is president of the Ontario Jockey Club Ltd. — profit $1.3 million in 1960 — and operates Windfields Farm and the National Stud Farm. We read of his chain of residences (Toronto, Montreal, Nassau), of his real estate development in the Bahamas ("$10,000 to $75,000 buys lot in E. P. Taylor's dreamland" — where income tax does not exist), of his interest in the arts (seen studying the financial statement of the Toronto Art Gallery). He is the financial expert behind the Duke of Edinburgh's Commonwealth Study Conference.

The foundation of his position as a tycoon and the basis of his rise to wealth and power in the oligarchy has been control of Canadian Breweries Ltd., the brewing monopoly of which Taylor was the chief architect.

Taylor started out in life with important advantages. His ability lay in knowing how to make full use of them, and this capacity to extract the maximum personal benefit from a given situation is a Taylor trade-mark.

He graduated from university in 1923. He stepped into a directorship in Brading Breweries of Ottawa, owned by his grandfather. And he joined the Ottawa office of McLeod, Young & Weir, an investment firm, as a security salesman under the eye of his father who was in charge of the office.

During his middle twenties we are told that Taylor attained his first, very practical, objective: "I tried to make $1,000 a year for every year of my life, and I succeeded."

By 1929, he was a full partner in the investment firm, had established important connections, and was ready to broaden his activities, using his interest in Brading Breweries as a starting point.

He needed a backer, someone with money, and he found one in the person of a U.S. promoter, Clark Jennison, who was advising a group of British investors. With the support of Jennison and capital from the British group, Taylor set up the Breweries Corporation of Ontario (the name was changed to Canadian Breweries Ltd. in 1937) with himself as president, a position he held until 1944, when he became chairman. He promptly set out to bring the brewing industry of Ontario under the control of his company, keeping the London Committee (his British backers) informed about his plans. Jennison died unexpectedly in 1931; the interest of the British investors was largely eliminated as a result of World War II.

The letters we quote from were made public either in the report of the investigation of Canadian Breweries or at the trial. They give a clear and intimate picture of Taylor at work, his close attention to details, his handling of governments, his rough and ready way with competitors.

The new company chose southern Ontario for its centre of operations because "it was not necessary to break the law to do business, as was the case in the north (of Ontario)."

In this early period, and no doubt later as well, considerable attention had to be paid to the problem of influencing Ontario government policy. On November 5th, 1931, we find Taylor writing to the general manager of John Labatt Ltd., his main competitor, about this thorny problem. Said Taylor, seeking to establish a brewer's united front:

> As you are aware, any contemplated changes in the liquor laws of the province will require the expenditure of a very considerable sum of money for propaganda to produce a favorable background for the government to take the necessary action. Having this in mind . . . I felt, some three or four months ago, that it was my duty to take the initiative . . . In order to ensure secrecy, I think it would be better to ask only

the following (the seven brewers then doing business in Ontario. Ed.) to subscribe to the fund.

Three years later, Taylor was reporting to his London Committee (10 April 34) that the amendments to the Liquor Control Act in Ontario are "quite satisfactory."

From 1930 to 1953, the new Taylor company expanded rapidly, buying out 23 rival breweries, 12 of which were promptly shut down.

In the words of the government report, "power was obtained and competition eliminated by deliberate, direct, intentional acts."

Taylor proudly informed his London Committee (12 June 33) that

> . . . with consolidation an accomplished fact, and half a million dollars cash in the bank, we would be in a position to make the operations of any one of the above listed companies (his main competitors. Ed.) so disastrous, that they would be forced to consolidate with us or go out of business.

And that was the tactic pursued with increasing success. An example will show how the technique worked. In 1934 Taylor was pressing with usual vigor for a merger with Canada Bud Breweries that would bring that company under his control. The Taylor offer was turned down by the Canada Bud directors; Taylor then appealed over their heads direct to the Canada Bud shareholders, asking them to exchange their Canada Bud shares for shares in Canadian Breweries.

To make this offer appear more attractive, Taylor took steps to increase the current price for Canadian Breweries shares. He urged his London allies

> to put a substantial volume of orders into the (stock) market between June 11th and June 14th (1934) as this is a critical period . . . and the market quotations on our shares is (sic) of paramount importance to the success of the deal.

The majority of Canada Bud shareholders accepted the Taylor offer, and control of Canada Bud passed to Canadian Breweries, that is to Taylor and his associates.

World War II was a turning point in the Taylor career. He was called to Ottawa by C. D. Howe in 1940, to become Canada's second-youngest dollar-a-year man.

But war activities did not distract him from personal postwar plans, and his war work presented him with exceptional opportunities to make useful connections that had highly profitable postwar results. Of these opportunities Taylor took full advantage.

He kept in touch with the affairs of Canadian Breweries Ltd. through daily news letters from the vice-president of the company and by flying to Toronto every second week-end. His correspondence during 1943 is full of references to plans to expand Canadian Breweries in western Canada. In a letter to his partner, J. A. McDougald, (26 April 43), Taylor painted a glowing picture:

> . . . there is a golden opportunity to repeat our Ontario performance. You will readily understand that there is a great advantage in being a truly national institution . . . We would of course produce our well-known Ontario brands in the western plants, and gradually soft-pedal the local brands.

By the end of the year (30 Dec. 43) Taylor was complaining to his associates that he should be relieved of his chores as president of Canadian Breweries and be made chairman of the board (a change that in fact took place in 1944)

> . . . to leave me free to do the really big things that have to be done with our company, not only in Canada but in the United States during the next five years.

All this time Taylor held important wartime positions, first as head of War Supplies Ltd., a Canadian crown corporation, and later as director-general of the British Ministry of Supply mission in the United States. As an article in Fortune pointed out, "for Taylor it was an incomparable chance to make friends in industry and to observe the good and bad in big company management. He made the most of it."

The restless Taylor, with his eyes on those "really big

things" and full of zeal to resume empire building in a
big way, resigned his wartime job early in 1944. "By then"
he is reported as saying, "I knew which side would win."

His first step after leaving government service was to
get started right away, a year and a half before the end
of the war, on an aggressive postwar expansion program.

This expansion was to take place on several fronts.
Canadian Breweries pushed into the markets of western
Canada, Quebec and the United States. More important
however was the organization by Taylor in 1945 of Argus
Corporation Ltd. as an investment holding company. Control of the company remained in the hands of Taylor and
his associates, but a considerable number of shares were
offered to the public, and from the proceeds of the sale
of these shares, plus borrowed money, Argus proceeded
to buy a controlling interest in several companies where
the possibility of making big capital gains looked bright.

In setting up Argus Corporation, Taylor had the support of Atlas Corporation, a U.S.-controlled holding company operated by Floyd Odlum, prominent U.S. financier.
Atlas took a five percent interest in Argus and for some
years was represented on the Argus board by two directors.
Odlum is a large shareholder in General Dynamics; W.
E. Phillips of Argus is a director of Canadair Ltd., subsidiary of General Dynamics.

To form Argus, Taylor brought together a group of
associates (the number of Argus directors has fluctuated
between 16 and 17) four of whom constitute the Argus
hard core. The four are Taylor himself ("Eddie"), W. E.
Phillips, J. A. McDougald ("Bud") and M. W. Mc-
Cutcheon ("Wally").

These postwar Argonauts were not strangers to one
another and had a good idea of where to find the golden
fleece they had in mind, as the story of their later achievements shows. Taylor had drawn Phillips into war service
under C. D. Howe to head Research Enterprises, a crown
company; McDougald was a brother-in-law of Phillips;

McCutcheon was a long-time associate in Canadian Breweries and had also been a co-worker at Ottawa as vice-
chairman of the Wartime Prices and Trade Board.

Before dealing with Argus and the companies it controls,
we shall follow the development of Canadian Breweries
Ltd., which since 1945 has been under Argus control.

Taylor believed in planning; under the influence of
world events he developed the habit of projecting a series
of Five Year plans for Canadian Breweries. His "Seventh
Revised Five Year Plan" of April 30th, 1945, visualized
a bold expansion into western Canada: British Columbia,
Alberta and Manitoba.

It took time for these plans to mature. In 1950, the
Taylor-Argus interests bought a minority interest in Western Canada Breweries Ltd. of British Columbia and placed
two men on the board of directors. In a few years the
Taylor-Argus group had secured complete control. In
1950, Taylor urged that W. R. MacKenzie be kept on as
general manager because "he knows how to handle the
political side with the provincial government."

The talents of MacKenzie (later a director and for a
time president of the company) were illustrated when he
reported to Taylor in April, 1952, on a plan to build a
small brewery at Prince George, to take over an existing
licence. Said MacKenzie

> The Attorney General has given his blessing to this. He is
> looking into the situation and if everything is clear will give
> us the okay.

Taylor himself took a hand in Alberta in 1950. We find
him writing to a colleague on the spot that "I would like
to see my friend the Attorney General, and if possible the
Premier." As Taylor wrote at the time, "we are now deadly
serious about obtaining some sale for our Canadian Breweries Ltd. products in Alberta."

The deadly serious mission apparently bore fruit and
expansion into the western provinces continued.

Through a series of confidential, inter-company deals, Grants Brewery Ltd. of Winnipeg was brought under control of Taylor, McDougald and McCutcheon.

Western Canada Breweries Ltd. set up a new company known as Grant-tor Ltd. and then subscribed for all the preferred shares in this new company. Grant-tor Ltd., using this money, bought all the issued shares of Grants Brewery Ltd. In the meantime, all the common (voting) stock of Grant-tor Ltd. had been sold to another company, Torcan Investments Ltd., the directors of which were Messrs Taylor, McDougald and McCutcheon. Thus Taylor controlled Torcan, Torcan controlled Grant-tor, and Grant-tor controlled Grants Brewery, all made possible by the money of Western Canada Breweries, also controlled by the Taylor group.

To the disgust of all concerned, this web of mystery and profit was pulled apart in the 1955 Report of the Restrictive Trade Practices Commission. McCutcheon sent MacKenzie a copy of the report on June 10th, 1955, warning him to say nothing to the press, adding gloomily

> I would draw your attention particularly to page 41 where the whole story of the control of Grants Brewery is set out. This means that there are no secrets about this at all now.

Open means of control could now be used. So we see Torcan Investments Ltd., its usefulness over, applying in 1959 to surrender its charter.

Headaches kept arising in Manitoba. In April of 1956, MacKenzie of Western Canada Breweries wrote a fellow-director, E. P. Andreae, of London, that he was not able to get away for a director's meeting "because the papers (in Winnipeg) claim we are making too much money . . . you will appreciate what we are up against." An investigation into brewer's profits was imminent, and MacKenzie asked the advice of Andreae on a plan to make profits look lower than they were. The reply from Andreae was to the point and practical:

You ask for my comments regarding your suggestion that it may be as well to keep profits down during the period of the Manitoba investigation. I couldn't agree with you more and I think it may be easy for you to give effect to your ideas in the manner you suggest, viz, by taking some extra depreciation in Winnipeg and also holding over some of the subsidiaries' dividends.

Needless to say, neither of these worthies had the slightest idea of actually reducing profit. The point was to increase profits while concealing the increase as far as possible.

Taylor had also been preparing, through Canadian Breweries, to invade the province of Quebec market, until then pretty well divided between National Breweries Ltd. and Molson's Brewery Ltd. National Breweries was headed by the influential Norman Dawes, a director of the Royal Trust, Consolidated Paper, Shawinigan, Dominion Bridge, etc. Molson's was controlled by the Molson family.

By 1951, Taylor was ready to enter this field and had selected National Breweries as his target. The first step was an offer to purchase made to the board of directors of National Breweries. It was turned down. Not in the least daunted, Taylor prepared to repeat the tactic that had been successful in the case of Canada Bud and others. In a letter to a brother director (18 June 51) Taylor wrote:

We have by no means lost heart. Norman Dawes is putting up a tremendous fight for personal reasons and on account of prejudice. We are giving his board a last opportunity next week.

Norman Dawes maintained his position. Taylor played his trump card, an appeal to National Breweries shareholders to exchange their stock for that of Canadian Breweries. This was effective, and after a year-long struggle Canadian Breweries took over. The name of National Breweries was changed to Dow Brewery Ltd., with Wilfrid Gagnon as its head. Gagnon had been a co-worker in the

Department of Munitions and Supply during the war; by 1961 he had moved up to the board of Argus. Norman Dawes was ousted, but one consequence of the battle for control was the government investigation of Canadian Breweries on the charge of operating a combine.

Taylor had developed a sensitive appreciation of the niceties of corporate behaviour, as has been shown in his correspondence with Wilfrid Gagnon.

In their annual report published in September, 1953, Molson's had been so unrefined as to refer with regret to the disappearance of the small local brewer as a result of mergers. Taylor, with an investigation of mergers and their results hanging over him, dashed off an angry note to Gagnon:

> The remarks in their annual report are stupid, childish and misleading.

And Gagnon was urged to slow down certain negotiations then pending with Molson's.

A further glimpse of Taylor's ideas of what constitutes proper behaviour, this time in relation to cash discounts, is seen in a letter to Gagnon (8 Dec. 54):

> During the early years of Canadian Breweries when there were many small companies . . . struggling for survival, we had to suffer the ignominy of making deals and concessions to those who re-sold our products. These practices were not only against the law, but they constituted an affront to our dignity . . .

The Taylor dignity is particularly susceptible to affronts when cash discounts offered by a rival are under discussion.

Canadian Breweries has not confined its activities to Canada. The elimination of rivals in Ontario ("the restoration of dignity" as Taylor might have put it), the expansion to British Columbia and the west and to Quebec, have been followed by expansion to the United Kingdom through a series of take-overs engineered by United Breweries Ltd., the new Taylor-controlled giant operating in Britain.

After a rapid and energetic push into the British market during 1960, Taylor began to meet stiff opposition and a series of temporary setbacks. By June 1961, he was busy denying that United Breweries was attempting to secure "an unduly large segment" of the British market. (Globe & Mail: 1 June 61).

The Taylor U.S. subsidiary, wholly owned by Canadian Breweries, is Carling Brewing Co. Inc. With plants in six states, a recently completed plant in Maryland, and a $20 million brewery projected for Fort Worth, Texas, the U.S. subsidiary has about half the total brewing capacity of the whole Canadian Breweries set-up. In ten years the U.S. Carlings rose from 62nd place to 5th place among U.S. breweries.

In 1956 the legislature of the state of Maryland was so ill-informed as to resent the extension of the Taylor monopoly to that state. A bill was passed prohibiting foreign-owned companies from brewing beer in Maryland.

But before the bill was signed by the governor, the U.S. State Department intervened successfully on the side of Taylor, pointing out to the governor of the state that it would be unwise to sign the bill "since there is some opposition to U.S. investment among certain elements in Canada, and an unfriendly attitude towards Canadian investments in the United States could easily stimulate greater hostility towards American enterprises in Canada."

The governor of Maryland took the point, and the attempt to keep Taylor out of the state failed.

According to a Toronto financial house, the brewing interests controlled by Canadian Breweries and its subsidiaries (controlled in turn by Argus Corporation, controlled by Taylor) are the largest in the world, with a total brewing capacity of 11.5 million barrels a year. The Financial Post (11 Feb. 61) estimated that the figure had risen to 13.3 million barrels as a result of expansion in the United States and Canada.

The earlier figure of 11.5 million barrels was divided as follows:

Ontario and Quebec subsidiaries	3.2 million barrels	
Dow Brewery Ltd.	1.8 "	"
Western Canada Breweries	0.9 "	"
U.S. subsidiary	5.6 "	"
	11.5 "	"

As long ago as 1954, the Taylor interests had a firm grip on the sales of beer in Canada, as can be seen from sales figures of the three main groups that year:

Total sales: Taylor group	96.72 million gallons	
Molson's	35.96 "	"
Labatts	27.07 "	"

The financial manuals are silent about the total number of workers employed in the Taylor beer companies, but in an article friendly to Taylor we read that Argus has an up-to-date labor policy: to know what the union wants and to grant concessions just a little ahead of the demands so as to head off any possible strike. However Argus, we are also told, will not allow itself to be "pushed around" by the union.

The two aspects of this policy came into conflict in the summer of 1958, resulting in a 40-day strike of the brewery workers, a trying interlude for the company which discovered that its thirsty customers turned to other beverages when beer was not available, and had to be won back to beer through an expensive advertising campaign. Another strike in 1961 that shut down Carling Breweries and O'Keefe Brewing seemed to suggest that the Argus labor policy is not all that up-to-date.

An idea of the influence exercised by Taylor on newspapers, magazines, radio and TV can be seen in the fabulous advertising budgets of the beer companies.

In 1954, Taylor explained to MacKenzie, then president of Western Canada Breweries, that

> We expect to be among the first six breweries in the United States within a ten year period (the expectation was correct. Ed.) . . . when this happens we will probably be spending $15,000,000 to $20,000,000 in advertising in the United States.

In Canada proportionately larger amounts are being spent. The directors of Canadian Breweries met on Nov. 10th, 1958, to authorize its subsidiaries to spend the following amounts on advertising in 1959:

Carling's	$4,500,000
O'Keefe's	4,350,000
Dow	5,000,000
	$13,850,000

At the same time the directors agreed that Dow should have the right to carry over the cost of the November, 1958, TV broadcasts of football games, amounting to $100,000 or $200,000 additional.

It can be reasonably clear that a group of companies that spends over $30 million a year on advertising will have a certain influence on the policy of the people from whom they buy advertising space or time.

.   .   .

Argus was designed as an investment holding company that would seek to exercise control over the companies in which it invested. The money with which to make the investments came from bank loans and the sale of shares to the public.

Taylor himself put into Argus his Canadian Breweries shares, receiving in return enough Argus shares to ensure him effective control of Argus in alliance with Phillips, McDougald and McCutcheon.

Some 1,400,000 shares of Argus common have been issued, owned by some 3,000 shareholders (many of whom are investment companies). However Taylor and his three closest associates hold, directly or through private investment companies, 40% of the outstanding common, with Taylor himself owning the larger fraction of this 40%.

Argus set about buying large blocks of shares in Massey-Ferguson (then Massey-Harris), in Dominion Stores, in Dominion Tar & Chemical, in St. Lawrence Corporation, in B. C. Forest Products, etc.

Again according to Fortune, Taylor has a three point

business philosophy, and the philosophy ascribed to him is certainly illustrated in the operations of Argus.

Taylor's three beliefs, says Fortune, are, first, a belief in borrowing — to acquire and expand enterprises through a judicious use of other people's money, second, a belief in bigness — that in every branch of industry five or six firms should dominate 90% of the business, third, a belief in the advantage of a situation where in a given company there is a dominant shareholder who has less than a majority interest (and hence, according to Taylor, always, of necessity, on his toes).

As a result of the application of this philosophy, we find that by the end of 1958 the Argus balance sheet showed total assets of $55.7 million, and that this figure "included" stocks with a market value of close to $100 million but carried on the balance sheet at only $52.7 million. By mid-1961 the market value of stocks owned had reached $140 million.

As we see from Table VIII, page 250, these Argus shareholdings represented, in 1958, an interest varying from 11.6% to 23.9% in the companies in which Argus had invested. With the exception of B. C. Forest Products (in which Argus has the 11.6% interest) the Argus holding, plus that of financial allies, gives effective control. In B. C. Forest Products the U.S. Scott Paper interests have a considerably larger holding than Argus.

Radio station CFRB of Toronto is controlled by the Argus group through Standard Radio Ltd. of which McDougald is chairman, McCutcheon and Phillips directors. McDougald is chairman and McCutcheon a director of radio station CJAD in Montreal. The CFRB group were unsuccessful applicants for Toronto's first private television station licence. In making the application, McCutcheon was obliged to put on record who owned what, protesting vigorously that there had been no attempt to conceal who owned Standard Radio.

There is a startling contrast between the market value of the Argus holdings ($100 million at the end of 1958)

THE ARGUS EMPIRE

(main interlocks only)

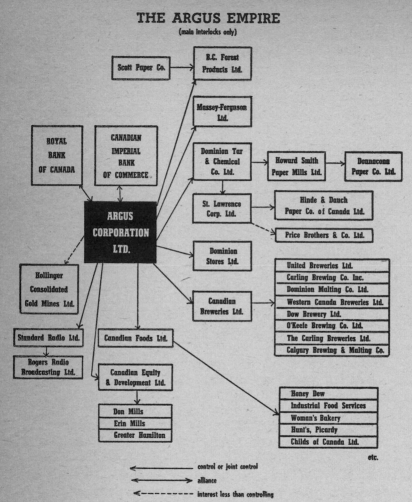

←	control or joint control
← →	alliance
← - - - -	interest less than controlling

and the total assets of the companies controlled which run close to one billion dollars, as shown in Table IX, page 251.

The control of this huge aggregate of corporate assets rests on the minority holdings owned by Argus, in turn controlled by the minority interest in it held by Taylor and his associates.

Through the ownership of the controlling interest in Argus, the Taylor group are able to exercise enormous leverage. If we assume the figures used by Fortune to be approximately correct, then the inner group of four own approximately 650,000 shares in Argus (40% of the outstanding shares).

Argus common was selling at $45 a share in October, 1961. At that price the value of the controlling interest in Argus was $29 million — although this can only be considered as an approximation.

The ownership of this $29 million in Argus shares (a figure much larger than the value of the assets originally put into Argus by Taylor and company) carries control of the $140 million (in 1961) Argus investments, and this gives the Taylor group (with the support of its allies) effective control of corporate assets amounting in 1961 to substantially more than one billion dollars.

The billion dollar holding is obviously not the personal property of the Taylor group. It is a figure that represents the value of the total assets controlled. It is a measure of power, not of wealth. Against these assets many obligations are outstanding, but the control of this huge capital enables the Taylor group to make large tax-free gains for themselves as individuals.

Taylor's personal wealth is a very different thing from the power he exercises through the control of this group of companies, but it is not insignificant. Fortune estimated it at $35 million. This is very considerably less than the estates left by some recently deceased tycoons. Taylor is one of Canada's very rich men but is not yet the richest.

Argus and its close-knit organizational structure cannot be considered separately from the whole financial network of which it forms part. Indeed Taylor and his group could not exercise the control they do without a whole system of alliances with other interests: insurance companies, trust companies, investment trusts. We have seen the large holdings of the Investors Mutual group in Argus companies; the Massachusetts investment trusts also have a

large block of Argus shares and a representative on the
Argus board.

Argus has sixteen or seventeen directors. Of those holding that position at the end of 1958, eleven were directors
of Canadian banks: Taylor, Phillips and Tory of the Royal
Bank; McDougald, McCutcheon, Bickle and MacMillan
of the Commerce; Black, Fox and Horsey of the Imperial;
Carmichael of the Toronto-Dominion, of which he was a
vice-president.

As a result of the Imperial-Commerce merger, directors
of the new bank greatly outnumber directors of other
banks on the Argus board, but it should be noted that of
the four key figures, two are directors of the Imperial-
Commerce, and two of the Royal Bank.

Argus directors are also directors of trust companies
and life insurance companies and have important connections with key industrial enterprises outside the Argus
companies. And it is precisely these far-reaching connections that help secure their control over Argus, secure,
that is, until a potentially more powerful group appears
on the scene to draw off the support of the allies and
challenge for power. (See Table X, page 252.)

Thirteen Argus directors held nineteen directorships in
some of the largest financial institutions in the country
including six life insurance companies (three of the ten
largest) and eight trust companies (the five largest). We
have listed these connections in Table XI, page 254.

The Argus group is closely connected with U.S. financial
groups and U.S.-controlled companies.

Taylor is a director of Texaco Canada Ltd. (formerly
McColl-Frontenac) controlled by one of the U.S. oil
giants, the Texas Company.

Phillips is associated with the Mellon interests as we
have seen.

Phillips and McCutcheon are directors of Avco of Canada of which McDougald is chairman. Avco of Canada is
a subsidiary of the Avco Manufacturing Company of

New York, and McDougald is a director of the parent
company. Avco controls Moffats Ltd., (kitchen appliances), Bendix Appliances, Crosley Radio & Television.

Two directors of Argus, one of them Phillips, have been
directors of Remington Rand Ltd.; General Douglas Mac-
Arthur is chairman of the U.S. parent company.

Other Argus directors, not of the inner group, also have
U.S. connections. P. M. Fox of Argus is a director of the
U.S.-controlled Montreal Locomotive Works Ltd.; Car-
michael of Argus is a director of Continental Can Co. of
Canada Ltd.; General Lucius Clay is chairman of the U.S.
parent company.

As a further indication of the orientation of Argus directors, it is of interest to note that during 1960 two Canadian life insurance companies on whose boards Argus
had representation were sold to U.S. interests: National
Life Assurance Co. of Canada of which McCutcheon was
chairman, and Excelsior Life Insurance Co. of which
Taylor was a director.

Argus directors meet other Canadian tycoons on the
boards of non-Argus companies: on the board of Abitibi
Power & Paper (three directors of Argus), Ventures Ltd.
(two Argus directors), etc.

Phillips and Senator G. P. Campbell, one-time fund
raiser for the Liberal Party, are both directors of the
Crown Trust, Confederation Life, Canadair Ltd., Stone
& Webster Canada Ltd., as well as meeting on the boards
of two Argus companies: Dominion Stores and Massey-
Ferguson.

.   .   .

In addition to Canadian Breweries, other Argus companies have been expanding rapidly, sometimes in terms
of taking over one another, a cannibalism that has often
resulted in substantial capital gains to the inner group.

Dominion Tar & Chemical, now co-ordinating the Argus
pulp and paper interests in eastern Canada, is a striking
example of the kind of expansion that has taken place.

At the end of 1955 its assets were $67.3 million; by the end of 1958 they had reached $172.5 million.

Dominion Tar & Chemical had controlled Howard Smith Paper Mills Ltd. for some years but in 1961 offered to purchase the minority interest as well. Through Howard Smith, Dominion Tar & Chemical also controlled Donnacona Paper Co. Ltd., a Howard Smith subsidiary. In 1959, Dominion Tar & Chemical took over control of Gypsum Lime & Alabastine Canada Ltd.

The next step for Dominion Tar & Chemical was to take over St. Lawrence Corporation, also an Argus company. This latest move has brought Howard Smith, Donnacona Paper, St. Lawrence Corporation, Hinde & Dauch Paper Co. of Canada, and Dominion Tar & Chemical under a unified, simplified management, but under Argus control before as well as after the transaction.

St. Lawrence had also been expanding before being taken over by Dominion Tar & Chemical. It had bought control of Hinde & Dauch of Canada from the West Virginia Pulp & Paper Co. in 1959. In 1956 it had borrowed money to finance the purchase of 225,000 shares in Price Brothers & Co. Ltd., the stock purchased being the property of the I. W. Killam estate and representing about 10% of the outstanding shares in Price Brothers.

However, as we have seen, in 1961 Price Brothers took over Anglo-Newfoundland Development Co. through an exchange of shares. To carry through the offer, Price Brothers would have to issue more shares; the result would be, according to a Financial Post writer, that the 10% interest of St. Lawrence in Price Brothers would shrink to 7%, while the former Rothermere controlling interest in Anglo-Newfoundland would hold a 17% interest in Price Brothers. (Financial Post: 22 April 61).

It remains to be seen whether the Taylor-Argus interests will withdraw from or be forced out of Price Brothers, or will seek to improve their position and achieve an alliance that will give them a share in control.

In British Columbia, as in Ontario and Quebec, the

pulp and paper interests of Argus, as we have seen, are closely associated with the Royal Bank and the Canadian Imperial Bank of Commerce. In the case of B.C. Forest Products Ltd. there is an example of the close connections between the Taylor interests and the U.S. financial groups, as well as of the process by which U.S. groups are penetrating the forest industry in British Columbia.

B.C. Forest Products Ltd. applied for and was granted a large forest management licence in British Columbia in 1955. (One of the charges against R. E. Sommers, former Lands & Forests Minister in British Columbia, was that B.C. Forest Products had paid more than $100,000 in order to obtain forest management licences).

After getting the licence, B.C. Forest Products made an agreement with Scott Paper (Morgan influence) by which Scott Paper agreed to buy one million shares in B.C. Forest Products at $15 a share, with the right to buy the whole production of the B.C. Forest Products Crofton mill until 1977.

As a result, the Taylor-Argus holdings in B.C. Forest Products (400,000 shares) have been dwarfed by the 1,000,000 shares held by Scott Paper. The fourteen-man board of B.C. Forest Products reflects an alliance between Scott Paper and Argus; it contains five U.S. directors, five Argus representatives, and four directors representing other British Columbia interests. Of the seven-man executive, three are from Argus, three from Scott Paper, and the seventh is Senator S. S. McKeen of Vancouver.

Massey-Ferguson, now said to be the largest manufacturer of tractors in the world, has been expanding rapidly since 1957. It has subsidiaries and plants in the United States, Britain, France, West Germany, Italy, Brazil, Australia, etc. as well as in Canada.

In 1959 it bought control of F. Perkins Ltd., a large diesel manufacturing concern in the United Kingdom, and took over the big Coventry tractor plant of the Standard Motor Co. Ltd. Two British financiers have been added to the Massey-Ferguson board: the Marquess of Abergavenny, and Lord Weeks. The latter was formerly chief of the Imperial General Staff, and later chairman, then a director of Vickers and a director of the Westminster Bank.

By the end of 1960, Massey-Ferguson had bought the long-established Landini tractor factory in Italy and established a new French plant in Paris. (Globe & Mail: 25 Nov. 60). By early 1961, senior Massey-Ferguson executives were busy studying languages so as to help "create a warm feeling towards the company" in France and Italy. (Globe & Mail: 24 April 61).

This may have seemed an easier task than creating a warm feeling towards Massey-Ferguson profits among Canadian farmers. A few weeks later the company "balked" at giving a House of Commons committee information on the cost of production of farm machinery. (Globe & Mail: 1 May 61); the Saskatchewan government suggested to the committee that nationalization of the farm machinery industry might be a solution to the problems of rising costs. (Globe & Mail: 20 May 61).

In 1961, Massey-Ferguson formed a new farm equipment company in Britain in partnership with the Butler Manufacturing Co. of Kansas City, the new company to be known as Massey-Ferguson-Butler Ltd.

With its seven plants in Britain, three in France, and one each in Italy and West Germany, Massey-Ferguson reported that it "welcomed" the move by the British government to join the European Common Market. (Globe & Mail: 1 Aug. 61).

.   .   .

Within the Argus companies there exists, as might be supposed, a web of interlocking directorships in which the names of Taylor, Phillips, McDougald and McCutcheon recur with regularity.

A certain division of labor exists. McCutcheon is the vice-president and managing director of Argus, chairman of St. Lawrence Corporation, chairman of the executive of B.C. Forest Products, and vice-chairman of Canadian Breweries.

Taylor is president of Argus, chairman of Canadian Breweries, of Dominion Tar & Chemical, of B.C. Forest Products, and chairman of the executive of Massey-Ferguson.

McDougald is chairman of Dominion Stores. Phillips is chairman of Argus and of Massey-Ferguson.

All the inner group hold directorships in the Argus companies whether or not they hold an office.

.   .   .

The process of building the Argus empire and of winning a place among the financial elite was not painless or devoid of struggle.

We have mentioned some of the battles that took place in the building of Canadian Breweries; the struggle for control of St. Lawrence Corporation was a long and bitter one. Taylor and McDougald won places on the board in 1951 after four New York directors had been removed from office. Now there are five Argus directors on the St. Lawrence board, although there has been U.S. representation in the persons of Nathan Pitcairn (like Phillips, a director in the Mellon-controlled Pittsburgh Plate Glass Co.), and Arthur Ross, a director of Rayonier Inc.

An interesting example of Taylor methods of struggle was the sudden and much discussed removal of James S. Duncan from the presidency of Massey-Ferguson (then Massey-Harris-Ferguson) in 1956. Duncan was a director of the Canadian Bank of Commerce, of Argus, of International Nickel, of Page-Hersey Tubes, and of Canada Cement. He had been with the Massey firm for 46 years and had managed it for twenty. In fact it was he who had induced Taylor to invest in Massey-Ferguson. During his tenure of office as general manager and president, Massey sales had multiplied thirty times in dollar value. Duncan had just been named "Canadian Businessman of the Year" when his Argus associates decided to ditch him.

An account of the dismissal that probably reflected the Argus point of view has appeared in Fortune. From this account we learn that Massey shareholders had never

186 ANATOMY OF BIG BUSINESS

realized how close the company came to bankruptcy in
1956. But the eagle eyes of Taylor and Phillips had noted
a dangerous increase in Massey-Ferguson inventories, up
to $182 million in May, 1956. They had a solution to this
piling-up of unsold farm equipment: close down the
plants, lay off workers.

But Duncan was "incorrigibly optimistic," and insisted
that sales in the United States would improve. He wanted
to keep the plants running.

In the face of this stubborn refusal to close down, the
Argus whip cracked. Duncan was swiftly voted out of
office by his brother directors, and a group of young, tough-
minded U.S. executives brought in. The new president,
Thornbrough, applied the remedy. He closed down Massey
plants in Toronto, Detroit, Racine, and began a bargain
sale of Massey products.

In four months these sales realized $50 million and the
plants were started up again.

At the 1957 annual meeting of the company, Phillips
sought to justify the dismissal of Duncan as "drastic surgery" "long over-due" without which the company "might
have perished." The change, he explained, was "part of
the price of streamlining and modernizing a large corporation." He expressed "regret" that some "necessary meas-
ures have unfortunate repercussions on personnel and on
communities."

But the famous crisis turned out to be short-lived in the
extreme. By May of 1957, Massey-Ferguson was starting
work to double the capacity of its Detroit plant and by
July of that year was prepared to pay the equivalent of $26
million to take over the Standard Motor Co. of Britain. In
fact the deal fell through at that time and it was not until
1959 that Massey finally bought the Coventry plant.

The new look in Massey-Ferguson was expressed in a
speech by Walter Lattman, vice-president, to the Canadian
Manufacturers Association. Mr. Lattman noted that Canada is steadily drawing closer to the United States, and
added:

I for one have felt for a long time that some form of economic integration between Canada and the United States is
more than a possibility. Defence considerations alone would
be an argument in favor of such tendencies.

Toronto Star: 9 June 59

Duncan, aside from the bitter loss of prestige, fell on his
feet, since he was understood to have received a substantial settlement. His resignation from Massey-Ferguson was
followed by resignation from the other boards of which he
was a member.

In announcing the resignation, he took refuge in a plea
of ill-health, but this myth was dispelled by the harsh
words of Phillips at the annual meeting.

.   .   .

The Taylor group are specialists in realizing tax-free
gains. This is one of the reasons why we find Taylor surrounded by a group of private companies of which he and
his three chief associates are both directors and shareholders.

Taylor is president, McDougald vice-president, and Mc-
Cutcheon a director of Taylor-McDougald Ltd., a private
company incorporated in 1951 with the object of promoting financial and industrial development and to enable the
incorporators to carry on business as "investors, capitalists,
financiers, brokers and agents."

The same three hold the same offices in Arbor Corporation, also a private company, formed in 1950 as an investment company. We have already come across Grant-tor
Ltd. and Torcan Investments; Heathview Corporation is
another, Taymac Investments Ltd. still another, and others
exist or have existed from time to time.

A classical example of how to set up a tax-free capital
gain is found in newspaper accounts of a 1955 transaction
involving three Taylor group companies: Argus, Arbor,
and St. Lawrence Corporation.

The transaction was nothing more than the purchase by
Argus of 200,000 shares of St. Lawrence Corporation that

had previously been owned by Arbor. Argus paid Arbor $75 a share, a total of $15 million.

The story came to light at the annual meeting of Argus (30 May 55) at which the purchase was approved under the watchful eyes of Taylor, Phillips, and McCutcheon, all three being directors of all three companies concerned. According to Globe & Mail stories of June 1st and June 3rd, "approximately fifty" Argus shareholders attended out of some 3,000 holders of common shares and some 2,200 holders of preferred.

The "approximately fifty," less than one percent of the shareholders, dutifully voted, 581,692 shares in favor, 1,404 shares against, to approve the proposal of the directors to buy the St. Lawrence shares.

On the surface we seem to be observing a perfectly normal proposal. Far-sighted, well-informed Argus directors in whom their shareholders have perfect confidence (almost) see the prospect for future gains to the shareholders and jump at it. The shareholders approve.

But the transaction also had its peculiar side, one that led the Globe & Mail reporter to "regret" that more questions were not asked by the too-submissive shareholders.

As the Montreal Gazette put it:

> This week's rites, giving Argus an 18% interest in St. Lawrence through purchase of 200,000 shares from the Taylor group merely finalized the relations that had gone on comfortably for some time.
>
> quoted in Labor Facts: June, 1955.

In other words, the Taylor group had controlled St. Lawrence before the transaction, and they continued to control it after the transaction. What had taken place was the sale of shares in a Taylor company (St. Lawrence) by a Taylor company (Arbor) to a Taylor company (Argus).

Practically speaking, nothing had happened. A share certificate had been moved from one pocket to another in the same suit.

But the transaction had a very real point. The money of Argus, in part subscribed by the "too-submissive" shareholders, was being used to give the inside group (Arbor: Taylor and his closest associates) a big tax-free capital gain. The problem of selling something to oneself at a profit had been solved.

The gain is channelled to Arbor, and the amount of the gain depends on what Arbor paid for the shares in the first place. Arbor was formed in 1950. In the intervening five years St. Lawrence had sold as low as $28\frac{1}{2}$; since we are dealing with a group of insiders it may not be too far off the mark to conjecture that Arbor bought the St. Lawrence shares for $30 a share. On that assumption the tax-free capital gain to Arbor was $45 a share, or $9 million.

The interesting fact is that in this transaction there was something for everybody. St. Lawrence stock went up to $90 a share, thus "justifying" the purchase by Argus at $75. The shares have since been split, four for one, and Argus as a result holds 1,000,000 St. Lawrence shares, worth some $18 million at the end of 1960.

What the 1961 take-over of St. Lawrence by Dominion Tar & Chemical means to the Argus group in terms of capital gains does not yet appear.

Pieces of paper representing control of St. Lawrence are moved from one Taylor company to another in a way that will net the insiders a handsome profit at the cost of the public and with no practical gain to the process of production. While the transactions are fictitious, the profits to the insiders are very real.

The smoothly working, highly profitable Taylor technique was used again in the 1961 purchase by Argus of a substantial interest in Hollinger Consolidated Gold Mines.

According to a Financial Post story (30 Sept. 61) based on an Argus prospectus, Argus holds 426,150 shares (an 8.7% interest) in Hollinger, worth, at that date, $11.9 million.

From whom and how did Argus buy these shares? Well, 250,000 of them were bought from Taymac Investments Ltd. for $7,125,000, or $28.50 a share. And who is Taymac Investments Ltd.? Why our old and much incorporated friends, E. P. Taylor, W. E. Phillips, M. W. McCutcheon and J. A. McDougald.

The unanswered question is just how much private profit was siphoned off to the bright-eyed four by this device. The Financial Post hints at $5 a share, or $1,250,000 as a non-taxable capital gain to Taymac Investments, on the assumption that Taymac bought the Hollinger shares as late as April, 1961. But the gain would be greater had Taymac bought earlier, since Hollinger shares had been selling at $19 a share at the end of 1960.

The money needed by Argus to pay Taymac Investments for the shares (and provide the inner group profit) was raised through a bank loan (we are not told how this business was divided between the two major banks linked to Argus) and the bank loan was repaid from the proceeds of a $10,000,000 issue of Argus redeemable preferred shares being sold to the public at par. In the meantime M. W. McCutcheon has joined J. A. McDougald on the Hollinger board of directors.

. . .

The Argus group is operating in a number of countries.

Thus Massey-Ferguson is competing with its giant U.S. rival, International Harvester, on a world basis—in Canada, in the United States, Britain, western Europe, Latin America, etc. Canadian Breweries has invaded the United States and Britain. The Argus pulp and paper companies, working through Dominion Tar & Chemical, are competing on the world market.

There is a sense in which the Argus group has a "Canadian" point of view. It is concerned with questions of trade and tariff policy and with Canadian government actions as they affect the position of the group. But the most important consideration for the group is the struggle to maximize the over-all profit position of its companies, taking into account all the countries in which they operate. And in this sense, apart from the citizenship of the majority of the Argus directors, there is very little that is Canadian or national about them.

The group is in a continuing state of re-adjusting its relations to U.S. financial groups and those of other countries, always on the basis of its world position.

All Canadian financial groups have not functioned a la Taylor. Argus is a relatively new creation, a newcomer pushing in vigorously among the giants already in existence; its story is therefore more dramatic, and for reasons we have mentioned, better known. A distinctive feature of Argus is its tightly knit organizational form; the groups operating through the Bank of Montreal, for example, do so on the basis of broad understandings and do not depend on a corporate structure like that of Argus.

But in the study of Argus and the corporations it controls, many typical features of Canadian finance capital can be seen: the secret agreements by which private profits are made by the insiders, the rigging of the market to make an offer look better than it is, the concealing of profits, the concentration on tax-free gains, the crushing of competitors, the overcoming of financial difficulties at the expense of the workers, millions of dollars wasted on advertising and public relations, connections with other financial groups, the inside track with governments (the bribing of cabinet ministers), the links with U.S. and other capital, the total emphasis on financial deals and maximizing profit, the lack of a national point of view.

These are characteristics not of Argus alone but of the whole financial structure.

CHAPTER VIII

Big Steal

THE INSIDE STORY of the relationships between governments and the big steel interests (mainly U.S.) that are
grabbing control of Canada's rich iron ore deposits will,
once it is fully known, make the Pacific scandal of the
MacDonald Tories and the Beauharnois Valley of Humi-
liation of the Mackenzie King Liberals look small and insignificant.

Not that mining and steel tycoons are "worse" than
others; the fact is that big concessions, exclusive mining
rights, have been and are being granted to large monopoly
enterprises, and they are not handed over for nothing.

Big mining companies want exclusive exploration rights
over thousands of square miles (where the mineral they
want is known to exist), with the right to get long-term
leases covering the best areas, and in return they want to
pay the lowest possible rental or royalty.

To achieve these results they require special acts of parliament from the province concerned and this involves
tough bargaining. It has been known to involve heavy con-
tributions to the funds of political parties in power.

The promoters have a simple argument: give us control
of this ore, we are prepared to develop it; we shall have
to spend so many millions of dollars in construction, and
this will mean jobs for your people—but it all depends on
the rental and royalties. If they are too high it won't pay
us to tackle the job.

The company looking for the concession tries to make
it appear that the only interest of their group is developing the country; in fact they will develop if they see a profit, and drop everything the minute a decline begins.

The millions they propose to spend will be largely borrowed money and a good part of it will go to construction
companies they control. In this way a substantial part of
the costs comes back to them as profit.

They have a reasonably clear picture of the future profit. If it was not going to be large they would not be starting the operation. U.S. companies count on increasing their
profit margin by taking advantage of lower wage rates in
Canada; the more cheaply they can secure the concession,
the greater the profit.

These negotiations generally have ended with big mining
companies in control of concessions for which they pay
sums that are minute in proportion to the profits involved;
even more serious than the loss of revenue to Canada is the
fact that control over the development of resources, control over the policy to be applied, control over future profits, has been lost.

This is all illustrated in the struggle for control of Canadian iron ore; here we can see most clearly what is
meant by the statement that Canadian tycoons are becoming junior partners to U.S. monopoly without regard to the
interests of Canada.

The iron ore story involves the immensely valuable ore
deposits in the Labrador Trough straddling the Quebec-
Newfoundland boundary, running from Ungava Bay south
to within 150 miles of the Gulf of St. Lawrence, as well as
the rich iron ore deposits in northwestern Ontario, in Newfoundland proper, on the Belcher Islands and at Great
Whale River, etc.

The basic question is a simple one: here is a valuable
asset of the Canadian people—for whose benefit shall it be
developed? Is it to be used to provide Canada with a huge-
ly expanded industrial base and provide jobs for Cana-
ians? Or is it to be used primarily to maintain the profit
position of existing steel combines in the United States,
West Germany, or the United Kingdom, and only second-
arily for industry in Canada? Will we be exporting jobs
along with the iron ore?

The assumption that primacy will be given to the outside interests, the assumption that is being acted upon, takes it for granted that Canada can continue indefinitely to export ore (and jobs), and import steel and finished steel products, that any expansion of the Canadian steel industry must be in line with and not disturb existing and future relationships in the steel industry of the capitalist world, and that steel plants outside Canada have an inherent right to make use of Canadian ore to maintain their world profit position and their exports to Canada.

In fact there is enough ore to provide both for a very greatly expanded steel industry in Canada and for exports to mills abroad. The problem is one of national policy, of priorities.

As things stand, the U.S. interests now get the ore, the profit on the ore, and the priority. A Canadian national ore policy would secure the profit and the priority for Canada, and then provide for exports of ore.

The Financial Post (5 Mar. 60) commented on the rapid expansion in the production of iron ore in Canada, from 2 million tons in 1950 to 25 million tons in 1959 (valued at $186 million). The Post, no doubt reflecting the current thinking-aloud of steel interests, then looked ahead to 1980; by that year it estimated that Canadian production of iron ore will be 96 million tons a year (at 1960 prices, worth about $715 million).

Who would be getting this ore? The Financial Post foresaw a possible division as follows, no doubt still based on financial gossip: 70 million tons to U.S. mills, 16 million tons "abroad", a euphemism for Krupp and other Ruhr magnates, possibly including a supply for British mills, leaving 10 million tons for use in Canada.

This estimate jumps even that of the U.S. experts of the Paley Report, Resources for Freedom, of 1952. The Paley experts foresaw U.S. iron ore imports during the 1965-75 decade of 40 million long tons a year each from Canada and Venezuela, this so that U.S. ore could be held in reserve against a war in which imports might be cut off.

The policy of putting Canada last in relation to iron ore
is one on which federal and provincial governments are
already embarked, and for which both levels of government
must share responsibility. The primary responsibility rests
with the provincial governments concerned—in the case of
the Labrador ores, the governments of Quebec and Newfoundland—but the policy of large-scale iron ore export
has been encouraged and acquiesced in by both Liberal
and Conservative federal governments.

Two former Liberal cabinet ministers have been linked
to iron ore interests; at least one U.S. cabinet minister was
personally interested in the sale of Canadian ore and led
the fight to get approval for the St. Lawrence Seaway so
as to provide cheaper transportation for Canadian ore to
Cleveland steel mills.

An idea of the forces at work can be obtained by listing
close to a dozen distinct operations now under way by
which financial groups have got or are getting control of
large areas of ore-bearing land in Canada, in nearly every
case with a view to exporting ore.

The first of these operations is still the most important.
Already producing ore at Knob Lake, shipping it out by
private railway to Sept Iles and thence to U.S. Lake Erie
ports via the Seaway is the Iron Ore Company of Canada.
Ioco is an alliance of seven inter-related U.S. steel mills
and ore companies, headed by the M. A. Hanna Co. of
Cleveland; the others are Hanna Coal & Ore, National
Steel, Republic Steel, Wheeling Steel, Youngstown Sheet
& Tube, and Armco Steel. With the M. A. Hanna interests
are associated two Canadian mining millionaires, J. R.
Timmins and J. Y. Murdoch, and a group of allies, who
hold a minority interest in Ioco.

Ioco is now building a 45-mile branch line west to its
new Carol Lake project in the Wabush Lake area, and expects to bring this new project into production by 1962
with an output of from 6 to 7 million tons of concentrates
a year.

U.S. Steel Corporation, the giant of the U.S. steel industry, controlled by Morgan interests, acting through Quebec
Cartier Mining Co., its subsidiary, has built its own railway
north from the Gulf of St. Lawrence to concessions in the
Mount Wright area. Production is scheduled for 1961-2.
Estimates of future output have varied from 8 million to
20 million tons a year.

The Steel Company of Canada, in co-operation with
U.S. firms (Pickands Mather, Mather Iron, Youngstown
Sheet & Tube, Interlake Iron) acting through a subsidiary,
Wabush Iron Co. Ltd., that is owned jointly by Stelco and
the U.S. side of the alliance, is developing leases in the
Wabush Lake area, and will share the costs of the Ioco
Carol Lake spur line. The U.S. companies in this project
are part of the Cleveland group; Youngstown Sheet &
Tube is interested both in Ioco and in the Wabush Iron
Co. Ltd.

By 1964 Wabush Iron Co. expects to be producing from
4 million to 6 million tons of concentrate a year.

Canadian Javelin, a U.S.-controlled company, which
holds big concessions from the Newfoundland government,
has transferred a large part of them to the Stelco-Pickands
Mather group but still has substantial interests in its own
name. No plans for production have been made public.
Javelin has been wracked by an internal struggle for control; its president, U.S. financier John C. Doyle, was arrested on a shareholders charge of conspiracy and theft of
1,350,000 shares of company stock valued at $4.8 million.
(Financial Post: 30 Jan. 60). After a series of legal battles,
Doyle, still president, finally agreed to pay the company
$3,350,000 as part of the settlement of various legal actions
taken against him. (Globe & Mail: 28 July 61).

Much further north, on the shores of Ungava Bay, two
powerful groups hold concessions and are deciding
whether the time is ripe for them to go ahead. One is the
alliance of Cyrus Eaton of Cleveland with five West German steel producers, headed by Alfred Krupp. Eaton also
controls the Steep Rock Iron Mines Ltd. operating in

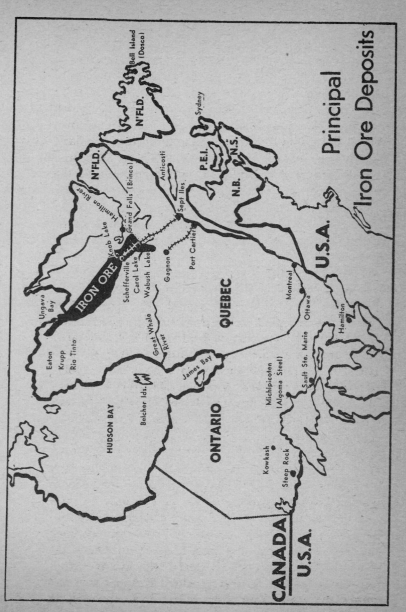

Principal Iron Ore Deposits

northwestern Ontario. The decision whether or not to go
ahead rested with the West German interests.

The second group interested in Ungava Bay is that
headed by the Rio Tinto Mining Co. of Canada, a subsidiary of Rio Tinto, the British mining company linked
to U.K. steel interests. The president of Rio Tinto of
Canada is R. H. Winters, former Liberal Minister of Public Works. C. D. Howe was also a member of the Rio Tinto
of Canada board.

The British Newfoundland Corporation and its subsidiaries hold important concessions from the Newfoundland government. Brinco concessions are in Labrador and
in Newfoundland proper; they include mining rights,
timber limits, and water power rights.

A group of Toronto promoters acting with R. C. Stanley
Jr. of New York (son of the former president of Inco)
hold iron ore concessions at Great Whale River and on
the Belcher Islands; these are still on the fringe of development.

Jones & Laughlin Steel Corporation and Cleveland
Cliffs Iron Ore (Cyrus Eaton is a director of Cleveland
Cliffs) have taken over the Mount Wright concessions of
Quebec Cobalt & Exploration Ltd., under a ninety-nine
year lease, and are preparing to develop them through a
subsidiary company, Normanville Mining Corporation.

In Ontario the powerful Anaconda Company (First
National City Bank of New York control) is taking over
concessions at Nakina in the Kowkash area, formerly held
by Lake Superior Iron and J. J. Gourd of Montreal.

The Cyrus Eaton interests control Steep Rock Iron
Mines Ltd.; Inland Steel is pushing the Caland ore development on ground leased from Steep Rock; Cleveland
Cliffs is studying a $30 million project in the Temagami
region.

This listing of companies entering the iron ore field in
Canada is not exhaustive. We are concerned to indicate
the extent to which great natural resources are passing
under foreign control, and the extent to which they will

be the basis for industrial development outside and not inside Canada. As can be seen, the process is very far advanced, but this does not mean that it cannot be stopped, or that it is irreversible.

Before dealing with the Iron Ore Company of Canada there are some points of interest in relation to U.S. Steel Corporation and Brinco.

Quebec Cartier Mining, wholly-owned by U.S. Steel Corporation, has built a 190-mile-long railway from Shelter Bay on the Gulf of St. Lawrence to Lac Jeannine in the Mount Wright-Mount Reed area, completed on December 10th, 1960. Two company towns, Port Cartier and Gagnonville, are to be built, as well as deep water harbour facilities, and a 60,000 h.p. hydro electric plant on the Hart Jaune River. The cost of the whole project is estimated at $275 million.

The company asked for and got a special act of the Quebec Legislature in December, 1957, to authorize it to construct a private railway from its mines to its harbour, the cost of the railway being estimated at $50 million. Canadian Javelin holds concessions in the same area; its representatives urged that the new railway be declared a common carrier, that is a normal railway, obliged to deal with all customers on an equal basis.

The late Premier Maurice Duplessis of Quebec categorically refused to accept such a suggestion, remarking cynically to the Canadian Javelin representatives as he gave an effective transportation monopoly to the U.S. Steel Corp.: "Nothing prevents your company (Canadian Javelin) from building its own railway."

Nothing presumably, but the lack of $50 million.

However the real point is the cold-blooded way in which the interests of U.S. Steel Corp. were looked after without reference to the future transportation needs of the area.

Brinco, British-controlled, Rothschild influence, was set up in 1953 "to explore and develop the natural resources of Newfoundland and Labrador, particularly minerals, including petroleum and natural gas, timber and water power."

The terms of the concessions granted to the company read like those granted in Tsarist Russia. The principal Brinco concession covers 35,000 sq. miles (22.4 million acres) in Newfoundland, and 7,000 sq. miles in Labrador. Sections of this satrapy are to be relinquished every five years up to 1973; the company will receive a ninety-nine year (or longer) lease on any areas not surrendered. Over and above this huge extension of land, the company holds five other concessions totalling over 11,000 sq. miles, and has an option, running until 1973, to take on the exclusive right for ninety-nine years to all uncommitted water power in Newfoundland and Labrador. The main plum here is Hamilton Falls, (Grand Falls), with a potential of four million h.p. and an additional two million h.p. on the same river. Shawinigan interests are sharing in development costs with Brinco and will share in the power produced. A new company, Twin Falls Power Corporation, controlled by Brinco, with Ioco and Wabush Iron as part owners, has been set up to supply power to the iron ore projects. (Financial Post: 2 April 60).

In return for all those privileges (and there are others as well) Brinco is to pay "certain royalties and rentals out of profits" (Financial Post, Survey of Industrials, 1959) and will spend not less than $1,250,000 on exploration in each five-year period.

In view of the size and importance of the concessions held, it is not surprising to find that Brinco is operated by a gilt-edged board of directors.

The leading influence in Brinco is the U.K. banking firm of N. M. Rothschild & Sons, also dominant in the Rio Tinto mining companies. R. L. de Rothschild is a Brinco director, so is J. N. V. Duncan of Rio Tinto of Canada. Other important U.K. interests participate in the Brinco consortium: the Bowater pulp and paper interests (three directors in common), the Rothermere interests through Anglo-Newfoundland Development (two directors in common), as well as English Electric and a lengthy list of other U.K. companies. (Globe & Mail: 17 June 57).

Among other Canadian connections of Brinco, that with the Bank of Montreal (one director in common) is probably the most important. Connections also exist with the Imperial-Commerce (one director in common) and there are interlocks with Brazilian Traction, Venezuelan Power, Newfoundland Light & Power, Canada Wire & Cable, and B.C. Telephone, as well as with the Montreal financial house of W. C. Pitfield & Co.

The balance sheet of Brinco shows total assets, as of March, 1958, of only $10.9 million, but this was before any of the Brinco projects had been brought into production; the value of leases and concessions was shown as only $35,001.

.   .   .

The only iron ore project in the Labrador-Quebec area that is actually producing on a large scale is that controlled by the Iron Ore Company of Canada (13 million tons in 1957, 7.8 million in 1958, 12.6 million in 1959).

The principal Canadian figures involved in this operation are J. R. Timmins of Montreal and J. Y. Murdoch of Toronto.

Timmins is a member of the well-known family of mining promoters — a nephew of Noah Timmins for whom Timmins, Ontario was named — and is head of a Montreal financial firm, J. R. Timmins & Co. He has been a vice-president of the Imperial Bank and is now of the Imperial-Commerce, and a director of the Royal Trust (Bank of Montreal); he is associated both with U.S. capital and with the Sogemines group and Canadian Petrofina (Belgian capital).

Murdoch is a lawyer turned mining tycoon. He is a vice-president of the Bank of Nova Scotia and is associated with U.S. capital and also with the Patino mining interests.

Both Timmins and Murdoch hold a long list of directorates. They and their associates control an extensive and complicated group of mining enterprises including Hollinger Consolidated Gold Mines (J. R. Timmins, president), Noranda Mines Ltd. (J. Y. Murdoch, chairman), Mining Corporation of Canada (Timmins and Murdoch both directors).

All these companies are surrounded by subsidiaries and related or controlled companies. Noranda in particular is the centre of an extensive empire. It controls Gaspe Copper Mines Ltd., Canada Wire & Cable, Kerr-Addison Gold Mines, and so on. Its profits are boosted by interests held in gold mines in Nicaragua.

In 1955 a Toronto Daily Star writer estimated that the interest owned by Noranda in ore reserves of various kinds was worth over $1 billion at then current prices.

The group in control of Noranda are known for their tough policy towards labor and their bitter opposition to the organization of their workers, whether at Noranda, Canada Wire & Cable, Gaspe Copper, or any other subsidiary. The 1957 Murdochville strike presented fresh evidence of that fact.

The Toronto Daily Star (23 July 57) attacked the policy of "the wealthy and powerful company" (Gaspe Copper) "that sought, in a backwoods region, to impose a type of arbitrary rule." In a later editorial (21 Aug. 57) the same paper recalled that "brute violence is of course nothing new in the history of Noranda Mines Ltd." and denounced the "company's adamant refusal to deal with the union" (the United Steelworkers). The Star added that "Noranda has been fully aided or protected in its position by the Duplessis government (of Quebec) and by a judge who issued a court order to stop certification of the union."

Two years later, the Globe & Mail (11 July 59) in a news story pointed out that the 1957 inquest into the death of a striker had never been completed, but that two law suits against the union were still pending: one taken

by Gaspe Copper Mines for $2,254,300 damages, the
other taken by a group of insurance companies for $75,000
— both seeking to hold the union responsible for actions
that had taken place during the strike.

When the company action against the union finally came
to trial in September, 1960, the claim for damages had
risen to $5,200,000. Court hearings lasted until February,
1962, but judgement was not expected until late in that
year. The inquest stood incomplete.

The story of the Timmins-Murdoch coup in iron ore
begins with the incorporation of two mining and exploration companies: first, in 1936, the Labrador Mining &
Exploration Ltd., (incorporated in Newfoundland), second, in 1942, the Hollinger North Shore Exploration Co.
(incorporated in Quebec). Behind these two companies,
both ostensibly Canadian, was the M. A. Hanna Co. and
the group of U.S. companies mentioned above.

The existence of a large body of iron ore in the Labrador Trough had been known for years. In 1894, A. P.
Low of the Geological Survey of Canada printed a report
on the ore body. Describing one of his trips, he wrote:

> For the next ten miles . . . exposures of iron-bearing rocks
> are almost continuous, and the amount of ore in sight must
> be reckoned by hundreds of millions of tons.

And in another report:

> Owing to their distance from the seaboard, these ores at
> present are of little value but the time may come when they
> will add greatly to the wealth of the country.

The writer was thinking of Canada. The time has come
indeed — but for Ioco, not for Canada.

These two exploration companies were financed by
Hollinger Consolidated Gold Mines and the M. A. Hanna
Co.; the Labrador Co. was 51% controlled by Hollinger
Consolidated — its job was to obtain concessions from
the government of Newfoundland; the Hollinger North
Shore Co. was 60% controlled by Hollinger Consolidated
—its job was to obtain concessions from the government
of Quebec.

A keen sense of public relations pervaded the operations from the very beginning; both these companies that were doing business with Canadian provincial governments were Canadian-controlled. At this point there could be no talk of handing over valuable resources to U.S. interests — unless one had been so unkind as to ask what those Canadian exploration companies intended to do with the iron ore they were seeking to acquire.

In fact the alliance between the Timmins-Murdoch group, using the accumulated profits of Hollinger Consolidated as a financial base, having the mining know-how and the approach to provincial governments, and the M. A. Hanna Co. of Cleveland, then headed by G. M. Humphrey, later to be Eisenhower's Secretary to the Treasury, with the group of U.S. steel companies, had already been formed.

The Hanna interests held the 40% minority interest in Hollinger North Shore and a 20% interest in Labrador Mining & Exploration. This is an example of a situation where the apparently smaller interest is in reality the more important; it was not good public relations for the U.S. group to show control at this stage, but the success of the operation from the point of view of Timmins and Murdoch depended on the deal with Humphrey and the Hanna interests.

The Hanna objectives were long-term leases from the governments of Quebec and Newfoundland covering the best ore-bodies. This required special acts of parliament from each provincial legislature—and these were obtained.

The negotiations were carried on over a good many years. In the case of Newfoundland they began in 1938 with the commission government — the British bankers' government to which in 1934 Newfoundland had yielded its right to self-government—and were concluded with the Smallwood government. Negotiations in Quebec began with the Godbout government before its defeat in 1944, and were concluded with the Duplessis government.

The 1944 agreement with Newfoundland (later amend-
ed several times for the benefit of the Labrador company)
gave the company exclusive exploration rights over an
area of 20,000 sq. miles. Each year, beginning at the end
of 1952, the company was to give up its exclusive rights
over a certain area. By 1963, it would be left with 1,000
sq. miles selected by it for a long-term lease. The lease is
for thirty years, renewable for two thirty-year periods, or
ninety years in all.

Rent was set at 50 cents an acre ($320 a sq. mile)
minus any amount paid that year as royalty on ore taken
out. Once the amount of the royalty exceeded the rent,
only royalty would be paid. The royalty is set at 5% of the
profit realized on the sale of iron ore and coal in the
previous year.

In 1946 the Duplessis government put through a special
act of the provincial parliament, the preamble to which
declared that since the Hollinger North Shore company
planned to spend $125 million in building a railway,
schools, in developing a new industry, it would be given
exclusive exploration rights over 3,900 sq. miles, and a
ten-mile-wide strip around this area would be withdrawn
from staking for ten years. The exclusive rights would last
until 1952 and would be renewable for two five-year
periods after that. The province in return received
$100,000 at once and would get $6,000 a year while this
arrangement was in force.

On any 300 sq. miles within this area, as selected by
the company, it would receive a twenty-year lease, renewable for three twenty-year periods, or eighty years in all.
For this lease it would pay $100,000 a year, starting in
July, 1958—the amount to be subject to revision every
ten years. Nearly eight million tons of ore were taken off
the Hollinger North Shore concession in 1957 — on that
level of production the rent is equivalent to 1¼ cents a
ton.

In 1960, Dr. A. O. Dufresne, who had just retired as
deputy Minister of Mines for Quebec, a job he had held

since 1941, was elected to the board of Noranda Mines Ltd. (Globe & Mail: 6 May 60).

By 1946, the concessions on which the deal was based had been acquired — by the "Canadian" companies — and the U.S. group prepared to take over.

The next step was to incorporate the politely named Iron Ore Company of Canada (it will be seen from the choice of name that the sense of public relations is still present). But this Canadian-sounding company is incorporated in the state of Delaware, with its head office at Wilmington, and is completely controlled in the United States. It has an authorized share capital of 6 million common shares, par value $10 each.

This new company, Ioco, incorporated in 1949, has made agreements with the two concession-holding companies. Ioco is to receive 7/8 of the first 400 million tons of ore produced, and 2/3 of the rest, in return for a royalty payment to the two exploration companies, who also received a block of Ioco shares.

The royalties to be paid by Ioco are fixed at 7% of the competitive market price of iron ore, f.o.b. Sept Iles, with 25 cents a ton as minimum. In one year at least the royalty paid was as high as 53 cents.

Thus the exploration companies have a fairly substantial quantity of ore available for sale on their own account. In 1957 this amounted to 1,500,000 tons for Hollinger North Shore and 900,000 tons for Labrador; in fact all sales seem to be handled through Ioco.

In addition to royalties on ore delivered to Ioco, and the proceeds of the ore sold on their account, the two exploration companies received a substantial payment in Ioco shares.

The Hollinger North Shore company received 300,000 shares of Ioco as a further consideration for handing over its concession rights to Ioco; it agreed to subscribe to another 300,000 shares if called upon to do so. The Labrador company received 200,000 Ioco shares on the same basis and also agreed to subscribe to a similar amount if called upon to do so.

Hollinger Consolidated and the M.A. Hanna Company, who control the exploration companies, each received directly a block of 500,000 Ioco shares in return for their expenses and for services rendered.

That accounted for 2 million Ioco shares; the remaining 4 million (66.6%) were assigned to six U.S. companies in the following proportions (the agreement also stipulated the percentage of ore to be available to each company).

Company	% Ioco stock	% Ioco ore
Hanna Coal & Ore	18	23
Republic Steel	16.6	23
National Steel	13.5	23
Youngstown Sheet & Tube	6.6	10
Armco Steel	6.6	10
Wheeling Steel	5	10
	66.6%	100%

Five of these companies (Hanna, Republic, National, Youngstown, Wheeling) are counted as under Cleveland group control, and one, Armco Steel, is controlled by family interests allied to the Rockefellers. Since M. A. Hanna Co. controls Hanna Ore and National Steel, and has a fairly substantial say in the shares held by Hollinger North Shore and Labrador, it can be seen that effective control of the operation lies with them.

As matters stand, Hollinger Consolidated Gold Mines is receiving far more profit from its participation in Ioco than from its gold mining operations. In 1957 it took in over $14 million net profit on iron ore—and only $220,000 from gold. The total net earnings of the company that year were $15.6 million.

The Ioco board of directors is composed of fifteen men. J. H. Thompson, president of M. A. Hanna Co. is president of Ioco; he is flanked by eleven representatives of U.S. steel mills and by four Canadians: J. R. Timmins and two associates — Leo H. Timmins and J. I. Rankin

— and J. Y. Murdoch. J. R. Timmins is vice-president of Ioco. All four Canadians are directors of Hollinger Consolidated.

It is a matter of some interest, in view of the important problems of national policy involved in the export of iron ore, that in 1959, C. D. Howe, former Canadian Minister of Trade & Commerce, a director of Rio Tinto of Canada, joined the Hollinger Consolidated board of directors. W. J. Bennett, Howe's former secretary, joined Ioco as a director and vice-president (9 April 60).

On the U.S. side, the enterprise had equally powerful political friends. For Ioco the completion of the St. Lawrence Seaway was essential if the greatest possible profit was to be realized on the Labrador ore; the steel interests had every incentive to join in the demand for the Seaway. Here George M. Humphrey played a key role. He was both chairman of M. A. Hanna Co. and president of Ioco. In 1949 the Hanna Co. announced that it had dropped its former opposition to the Seaway and now favored the project. (Globe & Mail: 26 Feb. 49). Humphrey resigned his directorates in 1953 to enter the Eisenhower cabinet.

Within the cabinet, Humphrey fought in March and April, 1953, to get U.S. approval for the Seaway:

> Humphrey maintained that access to Labrador ore deposits made the inland waterway necessary to national security. He emphasized that the Mesabi range in Minnesota no longer offered hope of rapidly expanding yields, whereas the Labrador deposits had the potential for the kind of expansion once possible in the Mesabi.
>
> Eisenhower, The Inside Story, by R. J. Donovan, New York, 1956, pages 76-8

Humphrey resigned as Secretary of the Treasury in May, 1957, and became chairman of National Steel, in which the M. A. Hanna Co. holds a substantial and probably controlling interest. When he entered the U.S. cabinet, Humphrey disclosed that he then held over $5 million of stock of M. A. Hanna Co. (at 1953 prices), as well as

12,471 shares in Hanna Coal & Ore, for which no valuation was shown. (New York Times, A.P.: 19 June 57).

To date the Ioco enterprise has proved highly profitable for all concerned, although it is a little difficult to get a clear picture of the amount involved because of the complicated legal structure surrounding the enterprise. Every device that skilled promoters, careful corporation lawyers, and experienced tax experts could think up has been employed to extract every last drop of profit at every level of the operation.

First of all there are the two exploration companies, Hollinger North Shore and Labrador Mining & Exploration, the concession holders, who receive royalties, a share in the ore, and dividends. Hollinger Consolidated and M. A. Hanna each have an interest in these two companies.

Hollinger Consolidated Gold Mines has two other subsidiaries: Hollinger Ungava Transport Ltd., to provide air transport for the iron ore development, and Ungava Power, to develop power for the mines.

Ioco has a subsidiary, the Quebec North Shore & Labrador Railway Co., to operate the 360-mile railway from the mines to deep water. Affiliated with Ioco is Gulf Power Co. (51% owned by Gulf Power & Paper, 49% by Ioco) formed to develop a 25,000 h.p. plant at Sept Iles.

So far this gives us six companies directly connected with the operation, all diverting a portion of the total profit to themselves.

The operation as a whole is the production of iron ore by a group of steel mills for use by themselves with surplus ore sold on the world market. But without the division into various corporate stages, the whole benefit of the cheap ore would go to the steel mills, and their profits would go up accordingly. Public relations comes in here. Steel profits are vulnerable; an increase might mean wage demands.

Then a way had to be found to give the Timmins-Murdoch group their percentage — not a share in the ownership of steel mills, but a share in the ore-producing end of the business.

Hence the solution: to let the major share of the profit go to Ioco, siphoning off as much as possible through other channels.

How artificial this whole corporate structure is can be seen by looking at the way it operates.

As it turns out, one man is the key to the whole business — one William H. Durrell. Durrell is general manager of the two exploration companies, he is a vice-president and director of the Quebec North Shore & Labrador Railway, and general manager of Hollinger Ungava Transport; he is general manager and a director of Ungava Power, and general manager of Gulf Power. In short he is in charge.

A few extra companies now appear: Durrell is president of Carol Lake Road Co., presumably building roads to or at the new Ioco Carol Lake project; he is president of the Labrador Supply & Equipment Co., and of Sept Iles Motors, Inc.

Obviously the ubiquitous Durrell could operate just as efficiently without this maze of inter-related companies but without them it would be harder for Durrell and his associates to make money buying from and selling to themselves.

This ability to do business with oneself at a profit has found ingenious expression in the final frill added to the Ioco corporate structure for the benefit of the promoting group.

In 1949, still another company, Hollinger-Hanna Ltd., was set up, owned equally by the Hollinger Consolidated and M. A. Hanna interests. The job of this company is nothing more or less than to manage Ioco, in return for a fee of 10 cents a ton on all ore sold. With Ioco sales running at 12 million tons a year, Hollinger-Hanna receives a tidy $1.2 million management fee.

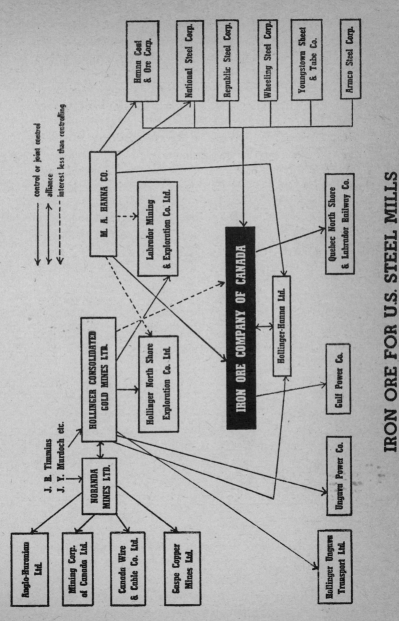

IRON ORE FOR U.S. STEEL MILLS

The absurdity of this deal was heightened by the fact that for some years (and as late as 1953-4) the same man, W. H. Durrell, to be sure, was general manager both of Ioco and of Hollinger-Hanna. Thus as general manager of Ioco he hired another company of which he was himself general manager to manage the company he was already supposed to be managing.

Either the multiplicity of offices proved too confusing or else the situation was felt to violate the principles of good public relations. Durrell is no longer shown as general manager of Ioco; he is still, as executive vice-president of Hollinger-Hanna, very much in charge of the show.

With this knowledge of the corporate structure of Ioco we can now try to see what happens to the profits. As a closely held company, Ioco makes public no detailed financial statement; its production costs are a trade secret. However in 1956 estimates of Ioco profits were discussed in the press.

A Globe & Mail writer, in a fairly detailed analysis that was apparently based on discussions with people aware of the facts, argued (1 Oct. 56) that on the basis of estimates prepared by Minnesota researchers, the Lake Erie port price for iron ore (then $10.85 a ton) would work back to $7.55 a ton at Sept Iles.

This was on the assumption that the Lake Erie port price would be the figure on which the price of all iron ore was based. In fact this meant that the price was to be determined by the cost plus profit of landing Mesabi ore, the most expensive ore in the picture, at Lake Erie ports.

On this calculation, the price at Sept Iles would have been the Lake Erie price of $10.85 a ton minus the estimated cost per ton of water transport from Sept Iles to Lake Erie, or $3.30 a ton, to give a Sept. Iles price of $7.55 a ton for ore.

The Globe & Mail writer then went on to estimate Ioco costs in getting the ore to Sept Iles. These costs he estimated at $5.25 a ton, giving a profit to Ioco of $2.30 per ton for ore.

"Which," as the reporter sagely remarked, "on 12 million tons is quite a lot of money." It is in fact $27.6 million.

The estimate was based on pre-Seaway shipping costs. If the completion of the Seaway meant a 10% reduction in ore shipping costs to Lake Erie, then on shipments of 12 million tons a year the result would be close to $4 million a year additional profit to Ioco.

The writer went on to break down the Ioco costs of $5.25 a ton as follows:

Mining and transportation of ore to crusher	$1.25	per ton	$15 million
Depreciation and interest	1.00	" "	12 "
Railroad freight to Sept Iles	3.00	" "	36 "
	$5.25	" "	$63 "

How many cents per ton (and hundreds of thousands of dollars) went to the various power companies, transport companies, all controlled by the promoters, is unknown.

We do see that the Quebec North Shore & Labrador Railway would receive $36 million freight revenue on shipments of 12 million tons of ore; it must have additional freight revenue from supplies going in to the mines. Total receipts would presumably cover running expenses, maintenance, depreciation, amortization of the cost of building the railway, and a profit on operations.

Interest payments other than those related to the railway are included in the $12 million allowed for depreciation and interest.

The figures in the analysis are a newspaper reporter's estimate, but the interesting point is the assumptions on which they are based. Even if the total profit is over-estimated by as much as 20%, it still represents a fantastic rate of return on the invested capital.

Ioco is always spoken of as a $250 million project and in relation to that amount the profit may not seem out of line. Then too there has been a propaganda barrage on the contribution of "risk" capital to the development of Canada and the higher rewards "earned" by it.

When we examine the Ioco financing we see that nearly 85% of the money required was raised by borrowing on the credit of Ioco bonds and debentures and only 15% was raised by the issue of shares. Ioco common shares exert exceptionally heavy leverage in that they control a large amount of capital in relation to the amount invested in the shares themselves.

The Ioco group issued Ioco bonds in three series at low interest rates ($3\frac{3}{4}$%, $4\frac{1}{4}$%, $3\frac{7}{8}$%) which were bought by a group of U.S. and Canadian insurance companies. The face value of these bonds was over $144 million.

In addition, Ioco issued 3% debentures amounting to $73.6 million, in the main subscribed for by the promoters and the steel companies concerned. The Timmins-Murdoch group, using the funds of Hollinger Consolidated Gold Mines, subscribed for $7.3 million worth.

The final source of funds was the capital stock of Ioco — the ownership of which controls the enterprise. We have seen that the authorized capital was 6 million shares, par value $10 each, and that all these shares were allotted: 2/3 to the U.S. companies, 1/3 to the promoters. This would have meant another $60 million or its equivalent to Ioco; in fact, at the end of 1957, only 4 million shares had actually been issued, representing $40 million, and not all for cash.

We now have the following picture of where Ioco got its funds, bearing in mind that the figures quoted are the face value of the bonds sold to the insurance companies.

Face value of bonds sold	$144,225,000
Par value of debentures issued	73,600,000
Common stock taken up	40,000,000
	$257,825,000

The estimated profit of $27.6 million stands therefore in relation to the $40 million "risk" capital, the actual investment of the controlling group, since as we have seen the cost estimates include (under freight costs and allowances for depreciation) funds to amortize the bonds and debentures outstanding. Of course we are dealing with an estimate, for one year, and on the basis of shipments of 12 million tons (over 13 million tons were shipped in 1959). But the inside group are controlling a $250 million enterprise on the basis of a $40 million investment plus loans covered by debentures that are being repaid. As the bonds and debentures are paid off, the value of the investment in Ioco represented by the common stock will sharply increase in value. The value of the owners' stake will thus continue to increase after they have taken out many times the amount of the original investment.

This whole operation with its massive profits is based on the labor of Canadian miners, engineers, railwaymen, using in the main Canadian equipment (and paid on an average something like 25% less than comparable workers in the United States), yet this labor of Canadians is hour by hour increasing the domination of U.S. financial circles over Canadian resources and holding back the development of Canadian industry based on those resources, simply by virtue of the fact that the concessions are controlled in the United States.

As a further point: Ioco was a project devoid of "risk." The ore had been known to exist, on the basis of geologists' reports, since 1894; once the M. A. Hanna group and the U.S. steel companies entered the picture, the project was a sure thing, even though difficult political and practical problems had to be solved.

The promoters had to get the concessions approved; they had to integrate their project with the policies of U.S. and Canadian governments. They wanted to be sure that the concessions covered the richest, easiest of access, ore bodies, on the terms most favorable to the promoters. When Timmins and Murdoch dealt with the governments of Quebec and Newfoundland they knew the value of what they wanted; they were prepared to pay and no doubt did pay accordingly. These were all problems — but the element of "risk" is not present.

W. H. Durrell, in his capacity as general manager of

the Quebec North Shore & Labrador Railway, appeared in
1956 before a Canadian House of Commons committee
to ask for an extension of ten years in the time within
which his company was obligated to extend the railway
north to Ungava Bay. In his evidence he described the
financing of the railway through the $145 million bond
issue, and the fact that he and his colleagues had hoped

> that a large part of it would be subscribed in Canada. Instead
> the company was forced to sell most of the bonds to U.S. in-
> surance companies because only $2 million worth were sold
> here to four Canadian firms. "This was a real blow to me, be-
> cause I'm a Canadian," Mr. Durrell said.

This curious reproach directed at Canadian insurance
companies for failing to buy the bonds of a U.S.-controlled
company in an operation where all available profits were
being grabbed by the insiders, seems to have been a
public relations idea—to blame Canadians for the U.S.
control of the enterprise. But the sale of the bonds had
nothing to do with control; the deal with the U.S. steel
mills giving them control had been made long before the
bonds were issued. We are not told whether that was a
"real blow" to Mr. Durrell.

Mr. Durrell made the news again in connection with
the Quebec North Shore & Labrador Railway, when he
appeared before the Board of Transport Commissioners
(Financial Post: 25 June 60) to argue for the right to
depreciate the assets of the railway over a period of ten
to thirty years. Ordinarily, according to the Financial Post,
the assets of a railway are written off over a period of thirty
to 115 years.

The aim of Durrell was to charge off as much depreciation as possible while profits were running high and so
show a smaller apparent profit. His argument was a claim
that Ioco and the railway had no real future after 1978
when the 25-year ore contracts signed with the steel companies run out. Other cheaper ore sources would then be
in production: Brazil, India, Liberia. Even thirty years
might turn out to be too long an estimate of the economic

life of the railway. Whatever Mr. Durrell was talking about, it was not the long-range development of Canada!

There would be more merit to this argument of gloom if Mr. Durrell had referred to the fact that the steel companies who might not renew their contracts are the owners of Ioco and of the railway; no doubt they would like to be in a position to write off the cost of the railway in ten years, thereby reducing their profit and their liability to taxes, so as to be free to give up the whole project at no loss to themselves, a real hit-and-run operation. Nor did Mr. Durrell mention that the famous Brazilian ore of which he professed to be afraid, was also to be developed by the same M. A. Hanna Company so influential in Ioco. (M. A. Hanna Co. was running into considerably more political difficulties in Brazil than it experienced in Canada; it is a question whether their Brazilian concession will ever be productive).

So the audacious argument is that one arm of Ioco should get tax concessions now because of what the other arm might do to it eighteen years hence.

Smaller U.S. iron ore producers have been demanding U.S. duties on iron ore imports. A U.S. tariff commission began the study of this question, and Canadian producers hastened to make representations. V. C. Wansborough, managing director of the Canadian Metal Mining Association, pointed out to the commission that

> Canadian exports of iron ore to meet the ever-increasing demands of the U.S. steel industry will continue to grow . . . Canada is a stable, secure, readily accessible and dependable source of supply.
>
> Globe & Mail: 21 Oct. 60

Durrell took over these politically more advanced arguments for a Toronto speech, saying that while other countries may have higher grade ore

> our (Canada's? Ioco's? Ed.) main selling point is our stability of government. This is something other countries do not have. Foreign investors . . . know that an agreement . . . with Canadian authorities . . . can be depended upon.
>
> Globe & Mail: 31 Oct. 60

So perhaps Ioco really won't close down in 1978.

M. S. Fotheringham, president of Steep Rock Iron
Mines Ltd. (a Cyrus Eaton company) apparently isn't so
sure about the stability and dependability. Speaking to
his company's 1961 annual meeting, he warned that plans
to finance a large iron ore mine in northwestern Ontario
may have to be revised "because of the Canadian government's attitude toward foreign investment." (Globe &
Mail: 11 Mar. 61).

.   .   .

The remarks of several of the members of the financial
group connected with the Ioco operation have had a
surprisingly naive flavor. Jules R. Timmins, one of the
main architects of the ore give-away program, has been
quoted (The Telegram: 30 May 55) as offering the following advice to young people: "Go west, east, north or
south, but stick with Canada."

O. W. Titus, president of Canada Wire & Cable, spoke
indignantly to the company's annual meeting in 1959
(Toronto Daily Star: 15 April 59)

> "Canadians are rapidly becoming economic colonists," O.W.
> Titus, president of Canada Wire & Cable Co. Ltd., told the
> company's annual meeting. This he attributed to unchecked
> import competition and foreign equity ownership of Canadian
> secondary industry and raw materials.

Mr. Titus was in a position to do something about his
fears. Canada Wire & Cable is a Noranda subsidiary; J.
Y. Murdoch and Leo H. Timmins, both directors of Ioco,
are his fellow-directors, and all the Canadian directors of
Ioco are also directors of Noranda.

.   .   .

The major interests of the Timmins-Murdoch group are
in mining, but they have other holdings.

J. Y. Murdoch, in addition to his mining and Bank of
Nova Scotia directorates, is a director of Canada Cement
(Royal Bank, Wood, Gundy and U.K. participation), of
British American Oil (Mellon-controlled), and of Rolland
Paper Co.

Jules R. Timmins, in addition to his Imperial Bank, (now Imperial-Commerce) Royal Trust and mining directorates, is a director of Sogemines Ltd. and Canadian Petrofina (both Belgian capital), of Montreal Locomotive Works Ltd. (U.S.-controlled), Great Lakes Paper Co., and Trans-Canada Pipe Lines Ltd. (U.S. control).

The interests of the Timmins-Murdoch group interlock with those of other financial groups. In particular they intersect those of the Argus group at several points.

J. A. McDougald and M. W. McCutcheon of the Argus inner group are directors of the Hollinger Consolidated Gold Mines. P. M. Fox of Argus is chairman of Great Lakes Paper of which Jules R. Timmins is a director; J. I. Rankin, a close associate of Timmins, and G. B. Foster, a Montreal lawyer, are directors of Noranda and of St. Lawrence Corporation, the latter controlled by Argus, and Foster is also a director of Howard Smith Paper, another Argus company.

Leo H. Timmins of the inner Timmins group holds only mining directorates; Noah A. Timmins Jr., associated with the Ioco project although not on the Ioco board of directors, is a director of the Bank of Montreal and a key figure in two companies controlled by English Electric Ltd. (He is chairman of the board of John Inglis Co. Ltd. and a director of Canadian Marconi). S. M. Finlayson, president of Canadian Marconi, is deputy chairman to Noah Timmins in the John Inglis Co.; Canadian Marconi owns Montreal radio station CFCF, and Finlayson holds the English language TV licence on Channel 12 in Montreal.

It may seem odd that the Timmins-Murdoch group, with their strong financial position (relations with leading banks and with other financial groups), with their control of ore sources, with the practical mining experience and know-how of their production force, did not themselves launch a steel mill in conditions where Canada produces far less steel than she uses.

In view of the profits being made in the sale of ore it

is doubtful that such a question ever presented itself to
them.

To form a new steel company would have meant chal-
lenging not just the dominant position of Stelco, Dosco
and Algoma in Canada, but also that of the steel giants
of the United States, since a rough and ready division
of the steel market in North America and Europe among
the U.S. steel interests and their chief competitors now
exists.

To disturb this balance by building a new mill and
blocking the U.S. acquisition of the Labrador reserves
would have meant running into head-on collision with the
strongest combinations of capital that exist. It would have
meant risking millions in most unequal battle.

In terms of their world outlook there was no choice.
They saw the opportunity to set up a continuing and very
profitable operation involving the sale of ore and they
took it. As a result Hollinger Consolidated Gold Mines
is back on its feet through income from the sale of iron
ore; the two exploration companies are highly profitable;
the inner group are benefitting from dividends and from
promoters profits, and future capital gains will be very
great. Their own position in the world of finance and industry has been greatly strengthened.

As a comment on another aspect of this operation, we
can do no better than bring up-to-date a statement quoted
in The Power and the Money. These news items dealing
with conditions in the company mining towns over a five-
year period, speak for themselves. Writing from Schefferville, (Knob Lake) on October 3rd, 1956, the Globe &
Mail's Robert Duffy reported:

> The ragged spectre at the rich industrial feast in Knob
> Lake is the little colony of Indians, to whose forefathers the
> whole country originally belonged.
>
> Encamped beside a lake . . . they are for the most part
> half-starved, inadequately clothed, housed in over-crowded
> huts and tents, hopeless and sick.
>
> Nobody here seems to know just what should be done for
> these people. Yet it is clear that something will have to be

done, and the urgency is beginning to prey on many con-
sciences.

"I don't know how long I could bear to watch these Indian women pawing over the town's garbage dump, when
there's so much money in this place" said a young student
employee of the Iron Ore Company who will be leaving his
vacation job shortly.

Three and a half and four years later there does not
seem to have been a decisive change for the better. Thus
another Globe & Mail reporter writing from Schefferville
(10 May 60) notes that two hundred Nascopie Indians
who used to inhabit "a tar-paper shack settlement" have
now (after three years) been housed in government-built
(note, government, not company-built) houses.

> It (the tar-paper shack settlement) was an unhealthy eye-
> sore but the Indians had to do something and the company
> was benign.

With the Nascopies in houses, still lacking fresh water
(the sewage disposal problem is "well advanced on drawing boards" but not apparently a reality) the problem of
the Montagnais Indians in the same town remained. For
the same number of years they had been living and in
1960 still were, in "a large shack town."

A later account speaks generally of Labrador in these
terms:

> There are two sides to Labrador today. One is the wealthy,
> progressive new mining area with its new homes, water and
> sewage facilities, churches and shops. The other is the collec-
> tion of disease-ridden, dirty tent villages inhabited by unedu-
> cated, primitive, Indians, who are looked down upon by their
> white brethren.
>
> The plight of the Indians has been brought to the atten-
> tion of the (Newfoundland) House of Assembly by Earl Win-
> sor, member for Labrador North . . . Labrador North includes
> the industrial areas of Carol Lake and Wabush and the great
> Hamilton Falls and Mr. Winsor describes it as probably the
> wealthiest area in the province.
>
> Globe & Mail: 4 Feb. 61

The writer forgot a third side, the most important one —the consequences to the country as a whole and to its future.

U.S. steel interests and their Canadian tycoon allies are making super-profits in Labrador based on the labor of Canadian miners on concessions obtained for a fraction of their value, and Canada has lost control, temporarily at least, over one of the country's great assets.

CHAPTER IX

Why Not Nationalize?

THE STRUCTURAL WEAKNESSES and distortion of the Canadian economy are reflected in the 1955-60 standstill, in the inability of the tycoons and their U.S. allies to develop manufacturing on a broad base, and in the sensationally unfavorable national balance of payments. They are also reflected in and reflect the gradual diminishing of Canadian independence and the failure of Canadian governments to confront urgent problems. They are related to and flow from the rule of the tycoons and their policy of subordinating the interests of Canada to those of U.S. monopoly capital in exchange for a share in monopoly profits.

The results of tycoon rule are becoming clearer as the problems of Canada become more acute. The one-sided partnership with U.S. capital that the tycoons have worked for and which has become the basis for government policy, is also the basis for the threat to Canadian independence and Canada's economic development.

It is this whole line of action and its consequences that have to be challenged; it is the sale of Canada that has to be stopped. Canadian independence cannot be secure, the economy of Canada cannot grow, until ownership and control of the key sectors of the Canadian economy is in Canada. Not until then can there be a national approach to Canadian problems.

To change the structure of the economy, balance the one-sided growth of semi-processed and raw material exports with the growth of manufacturing, modify the distorted pattern of Canadian trade and solve the balance of payments imbalance, raise living standards, all these things require what does not now exist: ownership and control in Canada of Canadian resources and Canadian factories.

But ownership and control put back in the hands of the tycoons who have parted with control is not the answer. The forces that led them to part with control in the past would lead them to do the same thing again.

The development of Canada, the preservation of independence, are only possible if ownership of the main U.S.-controlled enterprises operating in Canada, some 25 or so, is transferred to Canadian agencies under national control.

We speak of "U.S.-controlled enterprises" because the sector of the economy controlled by U.S. monopoly is the most important; circumstances might arise that would require an extension of national control to key enterprises that were not U.S.-controlled. It is however the U.S. control that constitutes the main problem with which we must deal.

Transfer to national control, or nationalization, might be the result of action taken by the federal government or by a provincial government with federal support. A nationalized enterprise might be operated by a crown company responsible to parliament and wholly or largely owned by the government concerned.

The benefits could be enormous.

The setting-up in Canada of a government-owned national oil and gas corporation to take over the existing U.S.-controlled reserves, refineries, pipe-lines and the industry based on them, would make possible the development of the whole industry on a national basis. Until such a step is taken, a national oil or energy policy for Canada cannot be a practical possibility. This national path of development has already been followed in Mexico with Petroleos Mexicanos (Pemex), the government-owned oil company that controls production and distribution, and in Brazil with Petroleo Brasiliero S.A. (Petrobras) in charge of production.

A Canadian national oil company could and would export surpluses above Canadian needs, setting its own prices based on its own costs, but it would put Canadian needs first and aim at the expansion of industry in Canada. It would only be the oil or gas that was exported, not oil and gas and profit and control.

A national east-west power grid to unite Canada's power resources, and especially the new sources of power to be developed in British Columbia, is under discussion. But such a grid is not complete until the large power resources owned, for example, by the U.S.-controlled Aluminium Ltd. and its subsidiaries are brought into the grid and made subject to priorities based on national needs.

Suppose the Iron Ore Company of Canada Ltd., the attractively named company incorporated by its U.S. owners in Delaware, really was the Iron Ore Company of Canada, and that Canadians could plan the development of the Labrador ores for the benefit of Canada's growing steel industry? No one would suggest that Canadian iron ore exports should come to an end, although a nationally-owned company might well decide to insert a Canada Preference clause in its sales contracts, reserving the right to give priority to the needs of Canadian mills. Canada would be exporting ore, but not at the expense of jobs in Canada, and the ore profits would be available for the expansion of the steel industry in Canada. To nationalize the steel industry would be a logical accompaniment, to include at least Algoma Steel and Dominion Steel & Coal.

Strong arguments exist in favor of the nationalization of other large-scale U.S.-controlled enterprises so as to transform them into independent Canadian plants, and end the branch-plant economy that holds back industrial development.

A nationalized Canadian auto industry making Canadian cars from made-in-Canada parts to meet Canadian needs could also compete on the world market.

A nationalized Canadian electrical industry, freed from dependence on U.S. patent agreements, could be a great source of strength to the Canadian economy and would be free to trade with the world.

To nationalize U.S.-controlled monopolies involves large problems as well as large benefits. Such an action would be feasible only when solidly supported by majority Canadian opinion. The national rights of French Canada are involved as are relations with the governments of other provinces. The principles upon which to base compensation would have to be worked out. Decisions would have to be reached on what enterprises to nationalize, in what order. The kind of national management and the principles upon which the managers operated would be continuing problems to be dealt with in relation to the political atmosphere that prevailed. All these problems would be manageable when there is agreement on the aim, and when they are tackled within the actual context of a crisis in the affairs of Canada.

Our concern here is to argue the proposition that nationalization in the terms suggested is the only visible way by which U.S. domination of the economy can be ended; that it is a practical proposal flowing from the realities of the situation.

The case for nationalization is not primarily that the Canadian tycoons are a socially unnecessary class (they are) or that they have extracted and are extracting huge profits from the exploitation of Canadian labor (as they have done and are doing); it arises as the answer to the whole complex of disastrous consequences (disastrous to the country, not to the tycoons) involved in the domination of the economy by U.S. monopoly interests.

Of course, if we accepted the idea that U.S.-controlled enterprises in Canada, the big important ones, are now being operated in the way most conducive to the growth and independence of Canada, then there would be no point in suggesting a change of ownership.

H. Scott Gordon, the Carleton University economist from whom we have quoted, can see no point in nationalization because it has never occurred to him that the need to change the policies of U.S. monopoly is the issue, and that the power to change the policy of U.S. enterprises in Canada will only exist as a result of nationalization. What difference would nationalization make, he asks plaintively, if policies are unchanged?

None at all. But ownership by U.S. interests of major Canadian oil resources (an obvious example but one of many that Professor Gordon might consider) has resulted in the operation of the big oil companies so as to maximize the profit positions of the Rockefeller and Mellon etc. oil interests. This style of operation cannot be ended until ownership by the U.S. monopolies is ended. The practical immediate step is to buy them out, to nationalize the companies and change the operational policy.

Other writers have sought to reduce the whole problem of U.S. domination to one of public relations. A McGill University professor has been advising U.S. corporations how to behave in Canada, telling them that only by acting in line with his suggestions can Canadian resentment against foreign domination be headed off. He has not stopped to consider that the problem is not behaviour and the solution is not in better public relations. What has to be ended is precisely the domination.

A striking weakness in the policies suggested by two well-known critics of U.S. investment in Canada is the failure to deal with the reality of U.S. ownership and control. Walter Gordon, prominent accountant and adviser to tycoons, and James E. Coyne, former governor of the Bank of Canada, have both evolved solutions short of nationalization; in each case the suggested solution would worsen the evil it is supposed to correct.

Gordon has made a kind of principle out of Canadian minority participation in U.S. monopoly. He is concerned by the fact that in a number of cases the Canadian participation is nil. In the report of the Royal Commission on Canada's Economic Prospects (1957) Gordon argued that "it would be desirable" that "larger Canadian subsidiaries (of foreign enterprises, Ed.) should sell an appreciable

interest (perhaps 20% to 25%) . . . to Canadian investors
and should include on their boards of directors a number
of independent Canadians." (Preliminary Report, page
90).

Coyne has made the latter point in enlarged terms:

> Why should not all Canadian corporations, or at least the
> larger and more important ones, have their entire boards of
> directors chosen from Canadian citizens?
>
> Calgary speech.

He goes on to argue that he is sure that such Canadian
directors would not be mouthpieces for foreign owners, and
that placing Canadians in positions of real responsibility
in the direction and management of foreign-controlled corporations would make these corporations more responsive
to the requirements of Canadian life.

The Gordon 20% to 25% participation proposal (others
have suggested different percentages, always well under
50%) has received wide support and in fact did not origi-
nate with him. It has been supported at different times by
the late C. D. Howe, by the present prime minister, by
nearly all investment dealers, and by a number of financial
editors.

But always the questions of control and policy are evaded. The 25% proposal may be attractive to investment
houses looking for securities to sell, or to financial groups
anxious to share insiders' profits, but it does nothing at all
to bring about any change in the policies of U.S. monopolies operating in Canada.

If Canadian capital associates itself with U.S. capital in
pursuance of the aims of the U.S. majority interest, the
result is that U.S. monopoly groups have larger resources
under their control and can keep on doing what they have
been doing with more vigor.

A Canadian minority interest now exists in International
Nickel; the Canadian directors are substantial men with
opinions of their own but no one would argue that the
policies of International Nickel have been affected in any

major way by this Canadian minority participation. The minority interests, Canadian and British, have not wanted to change basic company policies and could not do so if they did want to.

The Coyne proposals for the 100% Canadian board of directors are no more convincing than the Gordon 25% participation. As long as U.S. capital is in control and is dictating policy, the nationality of boards of directors is perfectly immaterial. And if the responsible Canadians in whom Coyne places confidence did disagree with the U.S. controlling interest, there is no doubt whose wishes would prevail. A sound argument is no substitute for power as Coyne found out.

As an adviser to and associate of tycoons, Walter Gordon has in his 25% proposal exemplified the essential and typical weakness in the approach of the most articulate spokesman of business. He has been unable to see beyond the kind of relationships with which he is most familiar.

Since 1949, Walter Gordon has been president of Canadian Corporate Management Co. Ltd., a privately incorporated company that appears to be a kind of investment trust or holding company. The oddly assorted board of directors of Canadian Corporate Management represents the kind of alliance of Canadian and U.S. capital responsible for the policies that have brought Canada to the critical situation she is in and which Walter Gordon talks about.

With Gordon on this board are associated a group of U.S. financiers: Godfrey S. Rockefeller, described as a textile executive, brother to James S. Rockefeller who is chairman and was president of the First National City Bank of New York; R. D. Stuart, director of Quaker Oats and assorted Chicago financial institutions, former U.S. ambassador to Canada; two partners in a Chicago law firm; a New York investment banker. Another participant is Lord Inchcape, a British bank director and shipping magnate; there are seven Canadians in addition to Gordon.

One of the Canadians is an employee of U.S. capital—head of several subsidiaries of Canadian International

Paper; another, J. G. Glassco, is a former partner of Gordon and is now executive vice-president of Brazilian Traction and a vice-president of the Imperial-Commerce; others are R. A. Laidlaw, chairman of National Trust (a Bank of Montreal director), Senator H. deM. Molson (Bank of Montreal, etc.), and J. Y. Murdoch (a vice-president of the Bank of Nova Scotia, prominent in Ioco, etc.).

From the participants in such an alliance no basic criticism of U.S. penetration and control could be expected. Gordon went as far as he could with his 25% proposal. His other colleagues might not have been as daring. Murdoch and his associates handed over control of their iron ore project to U.S. interests on the basis of something less than a 20% share in the profits.

R. D. Stuart, now Gordon's co-director, then U.S. ambassador in Canada, tangled with George Drew on this question in 1956. Drew had criticized U.S. control of the economy, called for a declaration of economic independence, and asked that Canadians be allowed to invest in U.S.-controlled firms. Stuart attacked him in a public speech. The Globe & Mail (18 April 56) gave Stuart a stinging rebuke for his undiplomatic interference in Canadian politics.

The point is that no proposal short of nationalization can be effective in dealing with the question of U.S. control. Either nationalization of U.S.-controlled monopolies in Canada or slow (perhaps not so slow) loss of independence.

Other critics of U.S. investment consider that nationalization, desirable or not, is impossible. Thus one of the contributors to Social Purpose for Canada, Professor G. Rosenbluth, expresses the opinion:

> Attempts to nationalize corporations having United States parent companies would be sure to encounter the resistance not only of these parent companies, but of the United States government as well. In view of the qualified character of Canada's political independence, it is likely that nationalization

of existing firms could not in fact be carried through on any appreciable scale.

Social Purpose for Canada, page 241.

Professor Rosenbluth did not feel it necessary to advance any arguments in support of his opinion. His judgement may be based on the existence of a cold-war atmosphere, although there is no point in assuming either an indefinite continuation of that atmosphere or that nationalizaion is impossible until world tensions have relaxed.

He has considered nationalization as an anti-U.S. step; his opinion might have been less negative had he considered whether nationalization might not lay the foundation for a firmer U.S.-Canadian friendship; whether it might not be a step in the long-run interests of both countries, making for better not worse relationships, and not necessarily repugnant to all citizens of the United States.

The approach for Canadians is surely to decide if nationalization is essential and in the national interest. If so then it is something to work for, not to reject as impossible.

Is it really so impossible for a Canadian government to exercise its sovereign rights?

Would not world opinion support action by Canada to assert its right to take independent action essential to its own interests?

Is U.S. opinion in the 1960's going to support an invasion of Canada to defend Imperial Oil, General Motors of Canada, the Iron Ore Company of Canada?

Is all the bargaining power on the U.S. side?

Is Canada today in a less favorable political situation than Mexico at the time of the 1938 expropriation of U.S. and British oil companies?

There is nothing politically impossible about the nationalization of U.S.-controlled enterprises in Canada once the will to carry through such a policy exists and finds expression. What is impossible is that things should be allowed to go on as they are.

The alternative to the proposals we have been urging is the kind of negative thinking illustrated in the 1961 annual report of W. Earle McLaughlin, president of the Royal Bank of Canada, to his shareholders. "Let nature take its course" was the battle-cry put forward: things will find their own level; Canada will go on exporting raw and semi-processed materials (the thing we do so well!), and, incidentally, living standards will decline. Bankers profits will presumably rise; independence and national identity are unlikely survivors.

Nationalization of U.S.-controlled monopolies in Canada is a measure designed to make further progress possible. It is not aimed at the United States but at U.S. monopoly domination. It discriminates against U.S. capital, not against the people of the United States. Friendship between Canada and the United States will have a substantial and lasting base when relations between the countries rest on respect in practice for national sovereignty and when Canadian industry stands on its own feet, free of U.S. control. That will be the time when integration can be discussed—between equals.

TABLES

Note

In Tables III, IV, and V, the chartered banks are referred to by the initials of their names.

TABLE I
(Text, page 21)

THE INTERNATIONAL INVESTMENT POSITION
OF CANADA
(End, 1959)

FOREIGN LONG-TERM INVESTMENT IN CANADA:

foreign direct investment (83% U.S.)	$11.8	billion
foreign portfolio investment (66% U.S.)	8.9	"
TOTAL, foreign investment	$20.7	billion

The U.S. share of the total
is 76% or $15.7 billion

CANADA'S GROSS LIABILITIES ABROAD:

foreign long-term investment in Canada	$20.7	billion
equity of non-residents in Canadian assets abroad	1.0	"
Canadian dollar holdings of non-residents	0.5	"
Canadian short-term assets of International Bank of Reconstruction & Development and of International Monetary Fund	0.4	"
short-term commercial payables	1.5	"
TOTAL, gross liabilities	$24.1	billion

CANADA'S ASSETS ABROAD:

Canadian long-term investment abroad	$5.5	billion
Government of Canada holdings of gold and foreign exchange	1.8	"
bank balances and other short-term funds abroad	1.1	"
short-term commercial receivables	0.5	"
TOTAL, gross assets	$8.8	billion

(Continued)

CANADIAN NET INTERNATIONAL INDEBTEDNESS:

Total, gross liabilities abroad	$24.1 billion
less Total, gross assets abroad	8.8 "
TOTAL net indebtedness	$15.3 billion

The figures are based on The Canadian Balance of International Payments, 1959 and International Investment Position, Dominion Bureau of Statistics.

Note: The increase in foreign (mainly U.S.) domination of the economy is shown in several related ways: by the rate of increase in foreign long-term investment in Canada, in Canada's gross liabilities abroad, and in net international indebtedness.

The net indebtedness figure has validity for balance of payments purposes but it is essentially a book-keeping concept and suggests that foreign investment in Canada will have to be paid off, when in fact it is here to stay, unless nationalized.

Investment figures include profits that have been reinvested as well as capital inflow (or outflow).

TABLE II
(Text, page 34)

CONNECTIONS BETWEEN U.S. CAPITAL AND LEADING CANADIAN BANKS
(End, 1958)

ROYAL BANK OF CANADA

FINANCIAL COMPANIES, U.S.-CONTROLLED, HAVING ONE DIRECTOR OR MORE IN COMMON WITH BANK:

Investors group investment trusts:
Investors Syndicate of Canada Ltd.
Investors Mutual of Canada Ltd.
Investors Growth Fund of Canada Ltd.

Massachusetts group investment trusts:
Canada General Fund
Canada General Investments Ltd.

Calvin Bullock investment trusts:
Canadian Fund Inc.
Canadian Investment Fund Ltd.

Metropolitan Life Insurance Co.
Excelsior Life Insurance Co.

NON-FINANCIAL COMPANIES, U.S.-CONTROLLED, HAVING ONE DIRECTOR OR MORE IN COMMON WITH BANK:

Avco of Canada Ltd.
Bell Telephone Co. of Canada
British American Oil Co. Ltd.
Canadair Ltd.
Canadian Chemical & Cellulose Co. Ltd.
Canadian Fairbanks-Morse Co. Ltd.
Canadian General Electric Co. Ltd.
Canadian Pittsburgh Industries Ltd.
Canadian Utilities Ltd.
Canadian Westinghouse Co. Ltd.
Duplate Canada Ltd.
Du Pont of Canada Ltd.
Ford Motor Co. of Canada Ltd.
General Motors Corporation
Gillette of Canada Ltd.
Hudson Bay Mining & Smelting Co. Ltd.
Imperial Oil Ltd.
International Utilities Corporation
Montreal Locomotive Works Ltd.

(Continued)

Northern Electric Co. Ltd.
Pittsburgh Plate Glass
Remington Rand
Simpsons-Sears Ltd.
Stone & Webster Canada Ltd.
Texaco Canada Ltd.
Trans-Canada Pipe Lines Ltd.
Webb & Knapp (Canada) Ltd.
Westcoast Transmission Co. Ltd.

BANK OF MONTREAL

FINANCIAL COMPANIES, U.S.-CONTROLLED, HAVING ONE
DIRECTOR OR MORE IN COMMON WITH BANK:

Calvin Bullock investment trusts:
Canadian Fund Inc.
Canadian Investment Fund Ltd.

Scudder Fund of Canada
J. P. Morgan & Co.

NON-FINANCIAL COMPANIES, U.S.-CONTROLLED, HAVING
ONE DIRECTOR OR MORE IN COMMON WITH BANK:

Aluminum Co. of Canada Ltd.
Aluminium Ltd.
American Radiator & Standard Sanitary
Bell Telephone Co. of Canada
British American Oil Co. Ltd.
British Columbia Telephone Co.
Brown Company
Canadian Celanese Ltd.
Canadian Chemical & Cellulose Co. Ltd.
Canadian Curtiss-Wright Ltd.
Canadian Fairbanks-Morse Co. Ltd.
Canadian General Electric Co. Ltd.
Canadian International Paper Co.
Dominion Rubber Co.
Goodyear Tire & Rubber Co. of Canada Ltd.
Hudson Bay Mining & Smelting Co. Ltd.
International Nickel Co. of Canada Ltd.
Northern Electric Co. Ltd.
Quebec North Shore & Labrador Railway Co.
RCA Victor Ltd.
Stone & Webster Canada Ltd.
Webb & Knapp (Canada) Ltd.

(Continued)

CANADIAN BANK OF COMMERCE

FINANCIAL COMPANIES, U.S.-CONTROLLED, HAVING ONE
DIRECTOR OR MORE IN COMMON WITH BANK:

Investors group investment trusts:
    Investors Syndicate of Canada Ltd.
    Investors Mutual of Canada Ltd.
    Investors Growth Fund of Canada Ltd.
Massachusetts group investment trusts:
    Canadian General Investments Ltd.
Calvin Bullock investment trusts:
    Canadian Fund Inc.
    Canadian Investment Fund Ltd.
United Funds Canada Ltd.
Excelsior Life Insurance Co.
Wells Fargo Bank

NON-FINANCIAL COMPANIES, U.S.-CONTROLLED, HAVING
ONE DIRECTOR OR MORE IN COMMON WITH BANK:

    Anglo-Canadian Telephone Co.
    Avco of Canada Ltd.
    Bell Telephone Co. of Canada
    British Columbia Telephone Co.
    Canadair Ltd.
    Canadian Admiral Corp. Ltd.
    Canadian Chemical & Cellulose Co. Ltd.
    Canadian Curtiss-Wright Ltd.
    Canadian International Paper Co.
    Celanese Corporation of America
    Crown Zellerbach Corp.
    Ford Motor Co. of Canada Ltd.
    Gatineau Power Co.
    General Dynamics Corp.
    Hilton of Canada Ltd.
    Hudson's Bay Oil & Gas Co. Ltd.
    International Business Machines
    International Nickel Co. of Canada Ltd.
    Johns-Manville Corporation
    Montreal Locomotive Works Ltd.
    Proctor & Gamble
    RCA Victor Ltd.
    Remington Rand
    Simpsons-Sears Ltd.
    Stone & Webster Canada Ltd.
    Trans-Canada Pipe Lines Ltd.
    Union Gas Co. of Canada Ltd.
    Westcoast Transmission Co. Ltd.

TABLE III

(Text, page 75)

INTERLOCKING INTERESTS OF FIVE LEADING BANKS AND A GROUP OF THE LARGEST NON-FINANCIAL COMPANIES AS SHOWN BY COMMON DIRECTORSHIPS

(End, 1958)

PULP & PAPER, LUMBER	ASSETS (millions)	RBC	BM	CBC	TDB	BNS
The Bowater Corp. of North Amer. Ltd.	$300.3	0	1	0	0	0
MacMillan & Bloedel Ltd.	192.3	1	0	3	0	0
Canadian International Paper Co.	N.A.	0	1	1	2	0
Abitibi Power & Paper Co. Ltd.	188.3	3	0	2	1	1
Crown Zellerbach Canada Ltd.	142.3	0	0	0	1	0
Consolidated Paper Corp. Ltd.	114.9	1	3	0	1	0
Minnesota & Ontario Paper Co.	109.5	0	0	0	0	0
St. Lawrence Corporation Ltd.	102.6	3	1	3	1	1
Price Brothers & Co. Ltd.	101.6	0	3	0	0	0
Marathon Corp.	N.A.	0	0	0	0	0

Note: Canadian International Paper and Banque Canadienne Nationale, Minnesota & Ontario Paper and the Imperial Bank, St. Lawrence Corp. and the Imperial Bank, each had one director in common. The head of the parent Crown Zellerbach was a director of the Commerce. MacMillan & Bloedel Ltd. and Powell River Co. Ltd. have merged to form MacMillan, Bloedel & Powell River Ltd. Marathon Corp. is now controlled by American Can; St. Lawrence Corp. by Dominion Tar & Chemical.

METALS & MINING	ASSETS (millions)	RBC	BM	CBC	TDB	BNS
Aluminium Ltd.	$1,272.7	0	2	0	0	0
The International Nickel Co. of Canada Ltd.	547.6	0	3	1	2	0
The Cons. Mining & Smelt. Co. of Canada Ltd.	180.8	1	4	1	1	0
Noranda Mines Ltd.	130.2	1	0	1	0	2
Iron Ore Company of Canada	N.A.	0	0	0	0	1

Note: Consolidated Mining & Smelting and Imperial Bank, Noranda Mines and Imperial and Banque Canadienne Nationale, Iron Ore Co. and Imperial, each had one director in common.

BASIC STEEL	ASSETS (millions)	RBC	BM	CBC	TDB	BNS
The Steel Co. of Canada Ltd.	$259.4	1	5	1	0	0
Algoma Steel Corporation Ltd.	175.4	4	0	0	0	0
Dominion Steel & Coal Corp. Ltd.	152.7	1	0	1	0	0
Dominion Foundries & Steel Ltd.	134.9	0	0	1	0	2

Note: Dominion Steel & Coal had a director in common with the Provincial Bank and with the Banque Canadienne Nationale.

OIL & PIPELINES	ASSETS (millions)	RBC	BM	CBC	TDB	BNS
Imperial Oil Ltd.	$861.3	1	0	0	0	0
The British Amer. Oil Co. Ltd.	511.7	1	3	0	1	2
Trans-Canada Pipe Lines Ltd.	282.8	1	0	1	3	1
Interprovincial Pipe Line Co.	241.4	0	0	0	0	1
Westcoast Transmission Co. Ltd.	223.8	2	0	1	0	1
Texaco Canada Ltd.	159.8	2	0	0	0	0
Canadian Petrofina Ltd.	158.1	2	1	1	0	0
Trans Mt. Oil Pipe Line Co.	130.6	0	0	0	0	0
Canadian Oil Companies Ltd.	117.8	0	0	1	1	1
Shell Oil Co. of Canada Ltd.	N.A.	0	0	0	0	0

Note: Trans-Canada and the Imperial Bank. Canadian Petrofina and the Imperial Bank and the Banque Canadienne Nationale, each had a director in common. Texaco Canada had two directors in common with the Provincial Bank. British Petroleum Co. of Canada Ltd. is now entering the field in strength. It has Royal Bank connections. Trans Mountain is owned by the leading oil companies.

TRANSPORTATION	ASSETS (millions)	RBC	BM	CBC	TDB	BNS
Canadian Pacific Railway Co.	$2,654.6	1	9	1	2	0

Note: The CPR had one director in common with the Imperial Bank and with the Banque Canadienne Nationale.

UTILITIES	ASSETS (millions)	RBC	BM	CBC	TDB	BNS
The Bell Tel. Co. of Can. Ltd.	$1,493.3	3	3	1	0	0
Brazilian Tract. L. & P. Ltd.	946.6	1	1	5	1	1
British Col. Power Corp. Ltd.	612.9	1	2	0	1	0
Shawinigan Water & Power Co.	373.7	2	0	0	0	1
British Columbia Telephone Co.	203.4	0	1	1	0	2
Gatineau Power Co.	160.4	0	0	1	0	0
The Consumers' Gas Co.	142.3	0	0	1	0	0
Calgary Power Ltd.	126.2	0	1	0	0	0

Note: The Bell Telephone and the Imperial Bank, B.C. Power and the Imperial Bank, Shawinigan and the Banque Canadienne Nationale, each had a director in common. Consumers' Gas and the Imperial Bank had three directors in common. For connections between Shawinigan and B.C. Power see text page 118, for Gatineau and Canadian International Paper see page 116.

(Continued)

STEEL FABRICATING	ASSETS (millions)	RBC	BM	CBC	TDB	BNS
Massey-Ferguson Ltd.	$312.3	3	0	4	1	0
A. V. Roe Canada Ltd.	310.4	2	0	1	0	0
Canadair Ltd.	N.A.	4	0	2	0	0

Common Directorships with

AUTO	ASSETS (millions)	RBC	BM	CBC	TDB	BNS
General Motors of Canada Ltd.	N.A.	0	0	0	1	0
Ford Motor Co. of Canada Ltd.	$270.0	1	0	1	0	0
Chrysler Corp. of Canada Ltd.	N.A.	0	0	0	0	0

Common Directorships with

Note: Graham Towers of the Royal Bank and R. S. McLaughlin of the Toronto-Dominion Bank are directors of General Motors Corporation.

ELECTRIC	ASSETS (millions)	RBC	BM	CBC	TDB	BNS
Canadian Gen. Elec. Co. Ltd.	$131.5	1	2	0	1	1
Canadian Westinghouse Co. Ltd.	79.9	1	0	0	1	0
Northern Electric Co. Ltd.	N.A.	2	1	0	1	0

Common Directorships with

CHEMICAL	ASSETS (millions)	RBC	BM	CBC	TDB	BNS
Dominion Tar & Chem. Co. Ltd.	$172.5	4	2	3	1	0
Canadian Industries Ltd.	146.5	0	3	0	0	0
Canadian Che nical & Cellulose Company Ltd.	134.8	2	1	1	0	0
Du Pont of Canada Ltd.	115.1	1	0	0	2	0

Common Directorships with

Note: Dominion Tar & Chemical had two directors in common with the Imperial Bank. It has become the coordinating centre for Argus Corporation pulp and paper interests in eastern Canada and controls St. Lawrence Corp., Howard Smith Paper, Hinde & Dauch Canada, etc.

CONSTRUCTION	ASSETS (millions)	RBC	BM	CBC	TDB	BNS
Canada Cement Co. Ltd.	$100.9	4	0	1	0	2
Dominion Bridge Co. Ltd.	96.8	4	5	0	1	0

Common Directorships with

Note: Canada Cement had one director in common with the Provincial Bank.

TEXTILE	ASSETS (millions)	RBC	BM	CBC	TDB	BNS
Dominion Textile Co. Ltd.	$138.7	0	1	0	0	0

Common Directorships with

(Continued)

BEVERAGES	ASSETS (millions)	RBC	BM	CBC	TDB	BNS
Distillers Corp.-Seagrams Ltd.	$544.3	0	0	0	0	0
Hiram Walker-Gooderham & Worts Limited	237.4	0	0	0	3	0
Canadian Breweries Ltd.	196.4	1	0	2	0	0

Note: Canadian Breweries had one director in common with the Banque Canadienne Nationale. Distillers Corporation-Seagrams has an indirect connection with the Royal Bank through a Bronfman holding company.

MERCHANDISING, MISC.	ASSETS (millions)	RBC	BM	CBC	TDB	BNS
The T. Eaton Co. Ltd.	N.A.	0	0	0	0	0
Loblaw Companies Ltd.	$195.3	0	0	0	0	0
Imperial Tobacco Co. of Canada Limited	184.6	1	0	0	0	0
Hudson's Bay Company	126.0	2	0	1	0	1
Simpsons Ltd.	115.3	2	0	1	0	0
Simpsons-Sears Ltd.	101.9	1	0	1	0	0
George Weston Ltd.	101.8	0	0	0	0	1

Note: The T. Eaton Co. Ltd. has in the past been represented on the Toronto-Dominion board. Simpsons-Sears is owned jointly by Simpsons Ltd. and Sears Roebuck, the U.S. giant. Loblaw Companies Ltd. is controlled by George Weston Ltd.

SUMMARY TABLE III
(Text, page 75)

Sixty-four companies have been tabulated. Twenty-eight are clearly under control of U.S. financial groups; six or seven are under British control, and one at least is Belgian-controlled.

Of the remainder, some are Canadian, as qualified in the text; some are alliances of U.S., U.K., Canadian capital in varying proportions.

In these sixty-four companies the directors of the three largest banks held 175 directorships, the directors of the five largest, 227.

Thus of the 64 companies tabulated:

No. of Directors	BANK	No. of Directorships	No. of Companies
25	Royal Bank of Canada	69	37
26	Bank of Montreal	59	24
25	Canadian Bank of Commerce	47	31
19	Toronto-Dominion Bank	30	21
15	Bank of Nova Scotia	22	17

At the end of 1958, eight Imperial Bank directors held 15 directorships in 12 of the listed companies. A rough idea of the effect of the 1961 merger of the Imperial and Commerce is given by combining the above Commerce and Imperial totals. The Imperial-Commerce then would have had 33 directors holding 62 directorships in 34 companies, the three largest banks 190 directorships, and the five largest, 242.

TABLE IV
(Text, page 79)

LEADING CANADIAN TRUST COMPANIES AND COMMON DIRECTORSHIPS WITH BANKS
(Trust companies with assets of $100 million and up)
(End, 1958)

NAME	ASSETS (millions)	RBC	BM	CBC	TDB	BNS	IB	BCN	PBC
Royal Trust Co.	$2,116.2	2	14	1	0	0	3	0	0
Montreal Trust Co.	90.6	15	1	2	1	0	0	1	0
National Trust Co. Ltd.	687.4	1	2	9	3	6	0	1	0
Toronto General Trusts Corp.	547.7	0	0	4	7	0	3	0	0
Canada Trust Co.	390.2	0	1	4	1	0	0	0	0
Administration & Trust Co.	261.7	0	0	0	0	1	0	1	5
General Trust of Canada	207.1	0	0	1	0	0	0	5	1
Crown Trust Co.	203.4	1	1	3	0	0	2	0	0
Eastern Trust Co.	190.9	1	0	0	1	3	0	0	0
Guaranty Trust Co. of Canada	186.5	0	0	0	0	0	0	1	0
Canada Permanent Trust Co.	160.5	0	1	0	7	0	0	0	0
Chartered Trust Co.	147.0	1	0	1	1	2	0	0	0
		21	20	25	21	12	8	9	6

Notes:

(1) The Montreal Trust Co. does not include "assets under administration" in its balance sheet. It is more or less equal in size and importance to the Royal Trust Company.

(2) The Bank of Nova Scotia has strengtheend its control over the Chartered Trust Co.

(3) The Toronto-Dominion Bank has strengthened control over the Toronto General Trusts Corp. and over the Canada Permanent Trust Co. and the two trust companies are in process of merging. The Canada Permanent Trust Co. had been owned by the Canada Permanent Mortgage Co. As a result of the merger, the Toronto-Dominion Bank will control the Canada Permanent Mortgage Co., which in turn will control the new merged trust company, Canada Permanent Toronto General Trust Co. (Financial Post: 3 June 61).

(4) The Canada Trust Co. is owned by Huron & Erie Mortgage Co.

(5) Traders Finance Corp has acquired a 20% interest in Guarantee Trust Co. of Canada. Traders Finance is a subsidiary of Canadian General Securities Ltd.

TABLE V
(Text, page 81)

LEADING LIFE INSURANCE COMPANIES OPERATING IN CANADA AND COMMON DIRECTORSHIPS WITH BANKS
(Companies with assets of $100 million and up)
(End, 1958)

NAME	ASSETS (millions)	RBC	BM	CBC	TDB	BNS	IB	BCN	PBC
Sun Life Assurance Co. of Canada	$2,212.5	4	4	0	0	1	0	1	0
Manufacturers Life Insur. Co.	820.9	0	0	1	0	0	1	0	0
Metropolitan Life Insur. Co. (U.S.)	787.0	2	0	0	0	0	0	0	0
Great West Life Assurance Co.	638.8	1	2	2	0	0	2	0	0
London Life Insurance Co.	667.2	0	0	1	2	0	0	0	0
Canada Life Assurance Co.	638.3	2	1	4	2	5	0	0	0
Mutual Life Assurance Co. of Can.	589.8	0	4	2	0	0	2	0	0
Confederation Life Association	411.4	1	1	1	2	0	4	0	0
Prudential Life Ins. Co. of America (U.S.)	392.4	0	0	0	0	0	0	0	0
Crown Life Insurance Co.	276.9	0	2	2	0	2	0	1	1
North American Life Assur. Co.	258.9	3	0	0	3	1	1	0	1
Imperial Life Assurance Co.	256.4	0	0	2	1	2	0	0	0
Standard Life Assur. Co. (U.K.)	222.7	0	2	0	0	0	0	0	0

(Continued)

NAME	ASSETS (millions)	RBC	BM	CBC	TDB	BNS	IB	BCN	PBC
Dominion Life Assurance Co.	176.6	0	0	0	0	0	1	0	0
Excelsior Life Insurance Co.	101.7	1	0	1	4	0	0	0	0
		14	16	16	14	11	11	2	2

Notes:

(1) In the case of Metropolitan Life, Prudential Life, and Standard Life, the assets shown are Canadian assets only, the total assets of the three companies being much greater.

(2) Companies are shown in order of assets, not of business in force.

(3) Dominion Life has been sold to Lincoln National Life of United States. Excelsior Life has been sold to Aetna Life Insurance Co. (U.S.).

(4) The Bank of Montreal has two directors on the board of Standard of Edinburgh, three on the Canadian subsidiary.

TABLE VI
(Text, page 88)

SAMPLE HOLDINGS TWO MEMBERS
INVESTORS GROUP
(End, 1958)

	Number of shares owned by each:		
	INVESTORS MUTUAL OF CANADA LTD.	INVESTORS GROUP OF CANADIAN FUND	mkt. value (millions)
Three leading banks			
Royal Bank of Canada	67,937	27,700	$ 7.0
Bank of Montreal	51,563	22,900	4.0
Canadian Bank of Commerce	82,532	35,974	6.5
			$17.5
Steel and related companies			
Algoma Steel	30,375	120,000	$ 5.4
A. V. Roe Canada		62,500	0.7
Steel Co. of Canada Ltd.	44,690	30,000	5.0
Dominion Foundries & Steel	90,887		3.4
			$14.5
Argus Corp. companies			
B.C. Forest Products		200,000	$ 2.5
Canadian Breweries	59,935		2.1
Dominion Stores	62,577		4.6
Dominion Tar & Chemical	128,667	300,000	6.2
St. Lawrence Corp.	60,200	200,000	4.3
Howard Smith Paper	12,545		0.5
			$20.2
Mining and metal companies			
International Nickel	38,910	45,000	$ 7.2
Consolidated Mining & Smelting		60,000	1.2
Noranda Mines	29,695		1.6
Ventures Ltd.		133,000	3.7
Aluminium Ltd.		75,000	2.4
			$16.1
Oil companies			
British American Oil	101,553		$ 4.1
Imperial Oil	83,293		3.6
Texaco of Canada	49,860		2.9
			$10.6

TABLE VII
(Text, page 91)

SELECTED CORPORATE SHAREHOLDERS OF INTERNATIONAL NICKEL CO. OF CANADA LTD.
(End, 1958)

Investors Group investment trusts:

Investors Mutual Inc.	37,500	
Investors Mutual Canada Ltd.	38,910	
Investors Group Canadian Fund	45,000	
Investors Variable Payment	10,100	
Investors Growth Fund of Canada Ltd.	2,000	
		133,510 shares

Massachusetts Investors Trust		116,800 shares

Calvin Bullock group:

Dividend Shares Inc.	30,000	
Bullock Fund	4,000	
Carriers & General Corp.	5,000	
Nationwide Securities Co. Inc.	2,000	
Canadian Fund Inc.	15,000	
Canadian Investment Fund	49,500	
		105,500 shares

duPont interests:

United Funds Inc.	48,500	
United Funds Canada Ltd.	10,000	
		58,500 shares

Miscellaneous U.S. groups in which some community of interest appears to exist:

Lehman Corp.	20,000	
One William St. Fund (Lehman Bros.)	50,000	
Lazard Fund Inc.	20,000	
Scudder Fund of Canada Ltd.	30,000	
American Mutual Fund Inc.	10,000	
Selected American Shares Inc.	15,000	
Loomis-Sayles Fund	5,500	
		150,000 shares

(Continued)

Patino of Canada Ltd.   14,100 shares

Groups in which Canadian or non-U.S.
capital predominates:
McIntyre Porcupine Mines Ltd.	156,500	
Power Corp. of Canada	4,400	
Canafund Co. Ltd.	6,000	
Commonwealth International Corp.	5,075	
Economic Investment Fund	3,000	
Dominion Equity Investments	2,000	
		176,975 shares

Holdings of ten Canadian life insurance
companies not including those of Metropolitan Life, Prudential Life,
Standard Life   61,175 shares
                                                      817,060 shares

Notes:

(1) Total number of shares outstanding in International Nickel: 14,500,000.

(2) Listings given above are compiled from published holdings of investment trusts, mainly those with Canadian connections, and of Canadian insurance companies. They are intended to illustrate the role of the investment trusts, and they do not show the main centre of control in the company.

TABLE VIII
(Text, page 177)

KEY ARGUS SHAREHOLDINGS
December 31, 1958 and August 31, 1961.

No. of shares	Company	Market Price (in millions)	% of outstanding common shares
	December 31, 1958		
400,000	B.C. Forest Products Ltd.	$ 5.0	11.6%
400,000	Canadian Breweries Ltd.	14.1	12.6
385,000	Dominion Stores Ltd.	30.0	23.9
900,000	Dominion Tar & Chemical Ltd.	12.9	18.0
1,500,000	Massey-Ferguson Ltd.	15.9	15.6
1,000,000	St. Lawrence Corp.	17.1	22.4
	Other securities	2.6	
		$ 98.8	
	Sundry investments at cost	1.9	
		$100.7	
	August 31, 1961		
400,000	B.C. Forest Products Ltd.	$ 5.6	11.6%
480,000	Canadian Breweries Ltd.	26.9	11.0
1,900,000	Dominion Stores Ltd.	30.9	23.6
2,475,000	Dominion Tar & Chemical Ltd.	46.4	17.4
426,150	Hollinger Consolidated Gold Mines	11.9	8.7
1,500,000	Massey-Ferguson Ltd.	18.2	12.3
107,499	Standard Radio Ltd.	2.1	49.9
	Other securities	1.9	
		$144.0	
	Cash and other assets	2.4	
		$146.4	

Notes:

(1) In comparing the figures for December, 1958 with those for August, 1961, it will be noted that in 1961 the Standard Radio holdings are shown separately. St. Lawrence Corporation and its subsidiaries have been taken over by Dominion Tar & Chemical. St. Lawrence owns 225,000 shares in Price Brothers & Co. Ltd.

(2) Scott Paper now has a much stronger position than Argus in B.C. Forest Products Ltd.

TABLE IX
(Text, page 178)

THE MAIN COMPANIES CONTROLLED
BY ARGUS
(Assets, end 1958)

Company	Total assets (in millions)
B.C. Forest Products Ltd. (control shared with Scott Paper)	$ 74.9
Canadian Breweries Ltd.	196.4
Dominion Stores Ltd.	74.2
Dominion Tar & Chemical Ltd. (including Howard Smith Paper)	172.5
Gypsum Lime & Alabastine Canada Ltd.	19.2
Massey-Ferguson Ltd.	312.3
St. Lawrence Corporation	102.6
Hinde & Dauch Paper Co. of Canada Ltd.	24.6
	$976.7

Note: The miscellaneous real estate ventures of Argus Corporation, operated by Canadian Equity & Development, are not included. (Don Mills, Erin Mills, Greater Hamilton). Canadian Foods Ltd. (formerly Canadian Food Products) is not included. It operates Childs of Canada, Hunts Restaurants, Honey Dew, Woman's Bakery, Industrial Food Services, etc. Argus Corp. also holds a controlling interest in Standard Radio Ltd. which controls CFRB, Toronto. Since 1958, the assets of St. Lawrence Corporation, Hinde & Dauch Paper Co. of Canada Ltd., Gypsum Lime & Alabastine Canada Ltd., have come under control of Dominion Tar & Chemical Ltd.

TABLE X
(Text, page 180)

THE DIRECTORS OF ARGUS CORPORATION AND THEIR PRINCIPAL OUTSIDE DIRECTORSHIPS *(1958)*

W. E. PHILLIPS *(chairman of Argus)*: Royal Bank of Canada, Crown Trust Co., Confederation Life Association, Duplate Canada Ltd. (P), Pittsburgh Plate Glass Co., Canadian Pittsburgh Industries Ltd. (CHM), Fibreglass Canada Ltd. (V-CHM), Brazilian Traction, Light & Power Co. Ltd., Canadair Ltd., Remington Rand Ltd., Stone & Webster Canada Ltd., Avco of Canada Ltd.

E. P. TAYLOR *(president of Argus)*: Royal Bank of Canada, National Trust Co. Ltd., Excelsior Life Insurance Co., Texaco Canada Ltd., Acadia-Atlantic Sugar Refineries Ltd., St. Lawrence Cement Co.

M. W. McCutcheon *(vice-president and managing director of Argus)*: Canadian Bank of Commerce, Montreal Trust Co., National Life Assurance Co. of Canada (CHM), London & Midland General Insurance Co., Avco of Canada Ltd.

D. G. BAIRD: *partner, Baird & Co., N.Y.*, Marine Midland Trust Co.

E. W. BICKLE: *partner, Wills, Bickle & Co.*, Canadian Bank of Commerce, Chartered Trust Co., The Manufacturers Life Insurance Co., Abitibi Power & Paper Co. Ltd., London & Midland General Insurance Co., Remington Rand Ltd., Trans-Canada Pipe Lines Ltd., Canada Steamship Lines, Canadian National Railways, Trans-Canada Air Lines.

G. M. BLACK, JR.: Imperial Bank of Canada, Confederation Life Association.

(Continued)

H. J. CARMICHAEL: Toronto-Dominion Bank (v-p), Conroy Manufacturing Co. (v-p), Canada Permanent Trust, Abitibi Power & Paper Co. Ltd., Hiram Walker-Gooderham & Worts Ltd., Ventures Ltd., Hayes Steel Products Ltd., Continental Can Co. of Canada Ltd.

P. M. FOX: Imperial Bank of Canada, Royal Trust Co., The Great Lakes Paper Co. Ltd. (chm), Montreal Locomotive Works Ltd., Claude Neon General Advertising Ltd.

J. W. HORSEY: Imperial Bank of Canada, Crown Trust Co., Northern Assurance Co., Salada-Shirriff-Horsey Ltd. (chm), Keystone Fund of Canada.

A. McCLASKEY: no directorships listed outside Argus group.

J. A. McDOUGALD: Canadian Bank of Commerce, Crown Trust Co. (chm & p), Avco Corporation of N.Y., Avco of Canada (chm), Hollinger Consolidated Gold Mines Ltd.

D. A. McINTOSH, Q.C. (*Fraser, Beatty & Co., lawyers*), Toronto General Trusts Corp., Confederation Life Association, Davis Leather Co. Ltd., Tiptop Tailors Ltd., Monarch Knitting Co.

H. R. MacMILLAN: Canadian Bank of Commerce, Canada Trust Co., Sun Insurance Office, International Nickel Co. of Canada Ltd., B.C. Packers Ltd., MacMillan & Bloedel Ltd.

K. S. MACLACHLAN: Rolland Paper Co. Ltd.

S. F. RAYMOND: Mutuelle Canadienne ltee. (p).

J. S. D. TORY, Q.C.: (*Tory, Arnold & Co., lawyers*). Royal Bank of Canada, Montreal Trust Co., Sun Life Assurance Co. of Canada, A. V. Roe Canada Ltd. (v-p), Algoma Steel Corp. Ltd., Ventures Ltd., McIntyre Porcupine Mines Ltd. (chm), Simpsons Ltd., Abitibi Power & Paper Co. Ltd., Moore Corp., Odeon Ltd., Slough Estates (Canada) Ltd., Thomson Newspapers Ltd.

TABLE XI
(Text, page 180)

LIFE INSURANCE AND TRUST COMPANY
DIRECTORSHIPS HELD BY ARGUS DIRECTORS
(Directory of Directors, 1959)

D. G. BAIRD	Marine Midland Trust Co. (*United States*)
E. W. BICKLE	Manufacturers Life, Chartered Trust
G. M. BLACK JR.	Confederation Life Association
H. J. CARMICHAEL	Canada Permanent Trust
P. M. FOX	Royal Trust Co.
J. W. HORSEY	Crown Trust, Northern Assurance Co.
M. W. McCUTCHEON	Montreal Trust, National Life Assurance Co. of Canada (CHM)
J. A. McDOUGALD	Crown Trust (CHM, P)
D. A. McINTOSH	Toronto General Trusts Corp., Confederation Life Association
H. R. MacMILLAN	Canada Trust Co.
W. E. PHILLIPS	Crown Trust Co., Confederation Life Association
E. P. TAYLOR	National Trust Co., Excelsior Life Insurance Co.
J. S. D. TORY	Montreal Trust, Sun Life Assurance Co. of Canada

INDEX OF COMPANIES

258 ANATOMY OF BIG BUSINESS

Canadian Westinghouse Co. Ltd. 33, 38, 41, 118, 146
Carling Breweries Ltd., The 174, 175, 176, 178
Carling Brewing Co. Inc. 130, 178
Carol Lake Road Co. 210
Celanese Corporation of America 103, 112
Cemp Investments Ltd. 63, 96
Central American Investment Trust 145
Century Shares Trust 89
Chartered Trust Co. 79
Chicago interests 32, 117
Child's of Canada Ltd. 178
Chrysler Corporation 32, 69
Chrysler Corporation of Canada Ltd. 42, 69, 76
Cleveland Cliffs Iron Ore Co. 198
Cleveland interests 32, 104
Collier, Norris & Quinlan 47
Columbia Cellulose Co. Ltd. 112
Confederation Life Association 128, 146, 181
Connemara Gold Mine 135
Consolidated Mining & Smelting Co. of Canada Ltd. 15, 40,
57, 91, 102, 105, 106
Consolidated Paper Corp. Ltd. 89, 90, 102, 105, 106, 113, 114,
172
Continental Can Co. of Canada Ltd. 181
Crosley Radio & Television 181
Crown Life Insurance Co., The 58, 60
Crown Trust Co. 146, 181
Crown Zellerbach Canada Ltd. 112, 115
Crown Zellerbach Corporation 103, 112, 115

Daily Mirror Newspapers Ltd. 114
Demerara Bauxite Co. Ltd. 132
Demerara Electric Co. 152
de Havilland Aircraft of Canada Ltd., The 96
Detroit Edison 147
Deutsche Bank 110
Distillers Corporation-Seagrams Ltd. 62, 63, 76, 129
Dividend Shares Inc. 90
Dominion Bank, The 49, 67, 72
Dominion Bridge Co. Ltd. 98, 102, 105, 172
Dominion Coal Co. Ltd. 137
Dominion Engineering Work Ltd. 47, 48, 105
Dominion Foundries and Steel Ltd. 93, 94, 119
Dominion Life Assurance Co. 84

INDEX OF PROPER NAMES
(Companies are listed separately)

Also from James Lewis & Samuel . . .

A History of Canadian Wealth

Gustavus Myers' classic of Canadian economic and
political history-writing, exposing our own home-grown
robber barons and con-men, the wheelers and dealers
in land and votes and lives.
Paper $2.95

Corporate Canada
14 probes into the workings of a branch plant economy

A down-to-earth book about Canadian business and
economic policy. It includes studies of Eaton's and the
CPR, practical aspects of the continuing absorption of
the Canadian economy by the U.S., and major government economic policies.
Written by contributors to the *Last Post Magazine* and
edited by Robert Chodos and Nick Auf der Maur.